D14928

Promoting Concordance in Mental Health

Note

Health and social care practice and knowledge are constantly changing and developing as new research and treatments, changes in procedures, drugs and equipment become available.

The authors, editor and publishers have, as far as is possible, taken care to confirm that the information complies with the latest standards of practice and legislation.

Promoting Concordance in Mental Health

edited by

Glenn Marland, Lisa McNay and Austyn Snowden

QUAY
BOOKS

A division of MA Healthcare Ltd

Quay Books Division, MA Healthcare Ltd, St Jude's Church, Dulwich Road, London SE24 0PB

British Library Cataloguing-in-Publication Data
A catalogue record is available for this book

ISBN-10: 1 85642 427 8
ISBN-13: 978 1 85642 427 1

Printed by Mimeo, Huntingdon, Cambridgeshire

Contents

Foreword

Promoting Concordance in Mental Health is an invaluable reference point for mental health practitioners involved in the prescription, administration and/or monitoring of psychiatric medication. As the authors so rightly point out, the ascendancy of person-centred care, recovery-focused approaches and psycho-social interventions, alongside ever more convincing critiques of biological explanations and pharmacological treatments, has diminished attention to 'good practice' in relation to medication. Indeed, an anti-medication movement is developing on the back of compelling texts asserting the long-term harm perpetrated by medication. Whilst these should not be ignored, it remains the case that for many, if not most, people who experience disabling mental health conditions, medication is prescribed. It is also true that such prescriptions are rarely administered in concordance with the person who will be taking the drug.

This book draws on the broader literature relating to person-centred care, rights, recovery and shared decision making to develop a model of concordance for mental health practitioners and the people with whom they work. This details the opportunities and challenges to respectful, constructive and collaborative partnerships; both are located in the attitudes, knowledge, understanding and social situation of both parties involved.

Although the text focuses largely on concordance in relation to medication, this is discussed in the context of therapeutic relationships as a whole. The qualities of a relationship based on shared expertise and experience, and the many and varied skills, interventions and approaches that might be helpful are described in detail: active listening and Socratic questioning, CBT and psychosocial interventions, together with a range of assessment skills and tools, and a problem-solving framework – to name but a few. In addition, the people involved are seen in the context of their whole lives and attention is given to the role that friends, family and informal carers can play and ways in which they can be assisted in this.

The beauty of this book lies in the use of credible case studies of three people in different situations, experiencing a range of challenges and receiving various treatments. These develop through the book to illustrate the model – from initial assessment to treatment following the ongoing developments in their complaints and the support provided. Thus, rather than providing an abstract set of prescribed techniques and interventions, the authors locate the developing model in day-to-day practice that all readers will recognise – demonstrating setbacks as well as successes and widening the focus of the practitioners beyond the questions that surround medication.

I wholeheartedly recommend this text to mental health practitioners, whether in basic training or working in advanced specialists roles. It provides a well-referenced, balanced and useful account of their role in relation to medication in the context of a supportive and collaborative relationship.

Julie Repper RGN, RMN, Ba(Hons), MPhil, PhD
Associate Professor – University of Nottingham
Recovery Lead – Nottinghamshire Healthcare Trust
Member of the Implementing Recovery – Organisational Change Project Team

Preface

This book is inspired by the need to place concordance at the heart of mental health practice. It is important to revisit medicine taking within the context of recovery-focused practice in mental health because practice based on compliance is unlikely to succeed and is not resonant with the principles of recovery. Concordance is a way of working together with people which extends beyond medicine taking. Mental wellbeing associated with recovery is promoted, however, when service users and mental health workers collaborate in a therapeutic alliance to reach concordance in medicine-taking. This is because the collaborative processes involve choice, self-determination and empowerment, which are features of mental wellbeing. The aim of the therapeutic alliance is to maintain an optimal therapeutic effect from medicine-taking, not to inculcate compliance. This book purports that practitioners should not aim towards compliance or adherence, but that, in collaboration with service users, should steer towards a therapeutic interaction with medicines, and working in concordance is the best way to achieve this. Although of relevance to all mental health workers, the book rests heavily on the nursing literature and this also reflects the normal situation in multidisciplinary team working of the nurse being the person best placed to have ongoing contact and to build a relationship to facilitate concordance. The very significant importance of other multidisciplinary team members in the promotion of concordance is, however, consistently reflected and acknowledged.

This book is a practical illustration of concordance working, utilising three scenarios which unfold throughout based on the experiences of Dougie, Murdo and Susan. Although it is intended that the reader will pick up useful pointers for recovery-based practice, it is recommended to read the book through from start to finish and not just to dip in to each chapter. Practice without theory is blind, and because key concepts in concordance working have become clichéd it is essential to begin with the sound conceptual understanding conveyed by Chapter 1. The book starts by clarifying the terms *compliance, adherence* and *concordance*. In Chapter 2 the dynamic biological interaction between medicines and the person taking them is outlined. Chapter 3 explores the importance of the therapeutic alliance in concordance. Chapter 4 illustrates how assessment can be conducted in a person-centred partnership and Chapter 5 gives some concordance-based interventions. Finally, Chapter 6 summarises all the key points made previously in ensuring that concordance is at the heart of mental health practice. Reflective exercises are included in each chapter and suggested responses are given at the end of the book.

The metaphor for concordance working shown on the book cover and referred to throughout is that of a dance. Concordance working is not simple, straightforward or continuously attainable. The mental health workers in the examples given sometimes find themselves out of step with the service users, but this is not fatal to the therapeutic alliance if it is recognised and worked through. It is important that, based on this awareness, attempts are made to get back in step using the premise of 'dancing not wrestling' (Miller and Rollnick, 2002).

The person being discussed is usually referred to as simply that: the 'person'. However, when it seemed clumsy or inelegant to use the term 'person', the alternative 'service user' has been adopted. Occasionally the term 'patient' is used for cogency and linguistic accuracy, because at these times the context is paternalistic and the person is cast in a passive role. No specific mental health service or legislative system is referred to or meant to be implied.

The benefits of written plans rather than just written notes are promoted throughout the book as a means of providing continuity and tangible links from one interaction to the next. These written plans evidence a scientific approach whereby learning and discovering is done together between service user and mental health worker.

Contributors

Gary W. Boyd
Gary is a graduate of Heriot-Watt University and the University of Surrey. After completion of his PhD research he completed postdoctoral research at Purdue University (Indiana, USA), the Imperial Cancer Research Fund and at the University of Dundee. In 2003 he took up a lectureship in Pharmacology at the University of the West of Scotland (Paisley campus) and teaches in the undergraduate and postgraduate courses in Biomedical Science, Forensics and Nursing. His research interests include studies of the regulation of ion-channel receptors in the CNS and the efficacy of exercise interventions in the prevention and treatment of CVS conditions.

Richard Clibbens
Richard is a registered mental nurse and general nurse, and has been a nurse consultant since 2000. He has a lead clinical role in the Wakefield Memory Service, where he undertakes diagnosis of dementia and is a qualified nurse prescriber. Richard completed a MMedSci in Clinical Nursing at the University of Sheffield in 1999 and is currently undertaking a PhD related to dementia in younger people at the University of Sheffield. He has published a number of articles and book chapters related to dementia, mood disorder and psychopharmacology of old age. Richard is a professional advisor to the Care Quality Commission and member of the Standards Development Group for the RcPsych Memory Services National Accreditation Programme.

Mick Fleming
Mick is a lecturer in mental health at University of the West of Scotland with a specific interest in, and extensive clinical and research experience of, the delivery of psychosocial interventions for people who experience serious mental health problems. He has a number of publications in the field of both psychosocial interventions and the nature of serious mental health problems, particularly schizophrenia.

Mervyn Granger

Mervyn Granger BSc (Hons) Health Studies, PGCert TLHE is Lecturer/Practice Educator, Specialist Practitioner-Community Mental Health Nursing, Nurse Independent/Supplementary Prescriber. Currently working as a Clinical Nurse Specialist within community mental health (older adults), he has specialised in the psychiatry of old age for 13 years. Within that time he has worked in a day hospital for older adults with mental health problems, piloted a nurse liaison post as a link between day hospital and community, and helped establish and worked in a specialist nurse-led dementia team, before developing his current role within a multi-professional frail, elderly and mental health community team.

Angela Kydd

Angela is a senior lecturer and researcher in gerontology at the University of the West of Scotland. She has designed and delivered workshops, degree modules and masters modules in dementia care and care of older people. In 1999–2002 she was programme lead for the BSc (Hons) Gerontological Nurse Specialist Course. In 2002 she was invited to write a gerontology programme for the World Health Organization, which was published in 2003. From 2003 to 2007 she was the Project Lead for the Erasmus Intensive Programme, which involved colleagues and students from Turku Polytechnic (Finland) and Linnaeus University (Sweden). She is currently running a masters module in frailty, which she teaches in Slovenia and will teach in Finland in 2012. She is director of studies for PhD students studying dementia care and ageing. She was lead editor and contributor to *The Care and Well-being of Older People*, a textbook for nurses published by Reflect Press in 2009.

Jeanette Laird-Measures

Jeanette is an RMN/RGN currently working as nurse team leader within an addictions team in Glasgow. She has extensive experience in working in mental health and addictions, and has been a Nurse Independent Prescriber since 2005. Jeanette recently published a case study on prescribing for depression, and has other publications to her name. She is currently carrying out an MRes degree, and is undertaking a mixed approach study into the nature of concordance in mental health nurse prescribing in Scotland.

Glenn Marland

Glenn is Senior Lecturer and Vice Chair of the Mental Health Subject Development Group, within the School of Health, Nursing and Midwifery, University of the

West of Scotland. He is a registered mental health nurse and has spent most of this career in nurse education. He is committed to team building, innovative curriculum development and effective liaison with stakeholders. His special interests are mental health promotion, research, writing for publication and leadership and management. Glenn's PhD study explored patterns of medicine-taking decision-making in people with a diagnosis of schizophrenia in comparison to those with asthma and epilepsy.

Billy Mathers

Billy Mathers is a lecturer in mental health nursing at the University of the West of Scotland. After qualifying as a mental health nurse he then trained in counselling. Thereafter he worked in forensic units for several years and later as a community psychiatric nurse (CPN) in east London. In his early research he studied the changing role of the CPN in newly formed community mental health teams and the views of service users and CPNs in regard to the value of intramuscular medicine and community depot clinics. This research has been presented at conferences in both national and international venues. He commenced working in higher education in 1995 and was for many years module leader for both pre-registration and post-registration mental health nursing programmes. Billy's doctorate in education study evaluated a training programme for acute mental health nurses and examined ways to increase their therapeutic clinical involvement. He is currently a campus module lead in the pre-registration mental health nursing programme and campus mental health lead in the mentorship programme.

Marie McCaig

Marie is a Mental Health Nursing Lecturer at University of the West of Scotland. She is a registered Mental Health Nurse who has experience in working in acute, rehabilitation, assertive outreach and condition management settings. She also has experience of working in a variety of jointly funded teams including local authority commissioning. In 2007 she graduated with a Masters in Advanced Health Studies, the final year of this involving a phenomenological study into the lived experience of assistive technology for individuals living in supported accommodation. She has been a lecturer at the university since 2008. During this time she has developed an interest in service user and carer participation, suicide prevention and men's health.

Lisa McNay

Lisa is a Lecturer in Mental Health Nursing at the University of the West of Scotland – a position she has held since 2006. She qualified as an RMN in 1989 and spent almost all of her clinical career working in the community – as a CPN, a research CPN and then as a Nurse Consultant working with people with long-term mental health difficulties. She has a particular interest in values-based practice.

Douglas Park
Douglas is Subject Librarian for the School of Health, Nursing and Midwifery on the Dumfries Campus. He has a keen interest in information literacy and provides assistance to locate and manage the plethora of electronic information available to both student and health professional.

Ange Pollard
In 2011 Ange graduated from the University of the West of Scotland (Dumfries Campus) with a BSc and is a registered Mental Health Nurse. Throughout her training she developed a keen interest in the recovery approach and older people's mental health, in particular dementia care.

Austyn Snowden
Austyn is a lecturer in mental health nursing and researcher in cancer distress at the University of the West of Scotland. He has designed and delivered workshops, degree modules and masters modules in research methods, medicine management and mental health. He is published in the field of mental health nurse prescribing, concordance, aetiology, distress management and the philosophy of research. He is the originator of concurrent analysis, a novel method of synthesising conceptually equivalent data, and is director of studies for postgraduate students studying topics such as concordance, palliative care in the private sector, and service user involvement in student assessment. He was lead editor of *Pioneering Theories in Nursing*, and author of *Prescribing and Mental Health Nursing*; both textbooks for nurses published by Quay Books.

Anna Waugh
Anna qualified as a Mental Health Nurse in 1993 and then graduated with BSc (Hons) from Nottingham University and MSc Health Professional Education from Huddersfield University. Clinically she has always worked in the field of older people's mental health, in day patient, inpatient, practice development and liaison services. Anna moved to full-time lecturing in 2004 and has special interests in people with dementia in general hospitals and suicide intervention and prevention.

Authorship

Editors

Glenn Marland RMN, RNT, B Ed, MN, Dip N, PGCRM, PhD
Senior Lecturer Mental Health Nursing
University Campus Dumfries
University of the West of Scotland
DG1 4ZN
glenn.marland@uws.ac.uk
01387 702110

Austyn Snowden RMN, RNT, BA(hons), BSc(hons), PGCRM, PhD
Lecturer Mental Health Nursing
University Campus Paisley
University of the West of Scotland
PA1 2BE
austyn.snowden@uws.ac.uk

Lisa McNay RMN, CPNDip, BA, PGDipCC, PGCE TLHE
Lecturer Mental Health Nursing
University Campus Dumfries
University of the West of Scotland
DG1 4ZN
lisa.mcnay@uws.ac.uk

Scenario writers
Susan MacPherson: Lisa McNay, Glenn Marland
Murdo McLeod: Jeanette Laird-Measures, Austyn Snowden
Dougie Collins: Anna Waugh, Angela Kydd, Mervyn Grainger

Key contributor
Gary Boyd: Life Science

Contributors
Mick Fleming and Billy Mathers: Psycho-social interventions
Marie McCaig: Physical and mental wellbeing
Ange Pollard: Therapeutic engagement

Clinical advisor older people
Richard Clibbens
Nurse Consultant for Older People's Mental Health
South West Yorkshire Partnership NHS Foundation Trust

Acknowledgement
Douglas Park
Subject Librarian, University Campus, Dumfries

Proofreading
Ange Pollard

CHAPTER I

Working towards recovery in mental health practice

Abstract

The terms *concordance, compliance* and *adherence* are used interchangeably, appearing in the literature for example as *adherence/concordance*. This leads to confusion and misunderstanding and in many cases inappropriate interventions. This chapter makes the case that conceptual clarity is needed to drive recovery-focused practice in relation to medicine-taking. A substantial portion of this chapter therefore defines the scope and practical function of concordance in relation to person-centred care. It introduces significant factors impacting on the complex relationship between the health professional and the person seeking help. In order to operationalise these issues in practice the book uses scenarios throughout that develop according to the theme of each chapter. This chapter finishes by introducing the three main service user scenarios which unfold throughout the book.

Key points

■ Concordance is not a synonym of compliance or adherence.

■ Recovery-focused practice is congruent with the concept of concordance.

■ Mental wellbeing is associated with concordance and recovery-focused practice rather than compliance and paternalistic practice.

■ Mental health workers should facilitate a therapeutic interaction with medicines rather than uncritical compliance with a prescription.

■ Conceptual clarity is needed to underpin recovery-focused practice which promotes mental wellbeing.

Key words

adherence, compliance, concordance, medicine-taking, mental wellbeing, recovery

Objectives

- Outline current practices in working towards recovery in mental health even when capacity to make decisions is compromised.
- Discuss professional attitudes and perspectives on concordance.
- Summarise ethics and obligations regarding concordance.
- Outline potential challenges to concordance considered a function of complex mental health problems.
- Introduce case studies.

Reflective exercise
Reflect on what concordance means to you and in your own words define concordance.

Introduction

Recovery is being able to live a meaningful and satisfying life, as defined by each person, in the presence or absence of symptoms. It is about having control over and input into your own life. (Scottish Recovery Network (SRN) 2006, p. 1)

Recovery is often depicted as a personally unique road or journey (Pelton, 2009; Raptopoulos, 2010), and it is more prevalent than some clinicians think. For example, longitudinal studies of people diagnosed with severe and enduring mental illness showed that half to two-thirds of the cohorts had positive outcomes exceeding the expectations of clinicians (Harding and Zahniser, 1994; Harrison *et al.*, 2001). These older studies have recent anecdotal support from more current narratives grounded in modern notions of recovery (SRN, 2006). Recovery is not just possible: it is likely.

Entering into, and ultimately leading, a treatment decision is part of the recovery journey. This process of engagement (Tait *et al.*, 2010) is characteristic of wellbeing. Traditionally, however, mental wellbeing and psychiatry have been uneasy bedfellows. Whilst mental wellbeing is associated with autonomy, self-determination, self-expression and self-responsibility (Evans, 1992; Clarke *et al.*, 2009), psychiatry has historically involved paternalism, compulsory powers and compliance (Breggin, 1993).

It is not the goal of this book to blithely oppose psychiatry, and it is acknowledged that the claim above is a radical over-simplification of a constantly evolving process. However, the dichotomy it represents is a useful starting point to understand the main theme of this book. Much of what opposes recovery is erroneously classed as treatment. This is often a matter of semantics and is therefore sometimes easy to spot and other times not. A significant project of this book is therefore to bring these issues out into the open and examine their impact where possible.

For example, although mental disorder can compromise people's capacity to decide for themselves, this is usually not permanent or all-encompassing (Patrick, 2006), and therefore does not justify paternalism as a default approach. Compliance, which stems from paternalism, implies an authoritarian relationship; the health professional decides and the patient is expected to comply. This evokes an image of the health worker as expert and places the patient in a dependent role. It is quite straightforward to understand dependence and autonomy as occupying different ends of a recovery spectrum. Recognising this is the first step to addressing it.

The process of regaining mental wellbeing is the essence of recovery, the most commonly agreed components of recovery (Repper and Perkins, 2003) being:

- Hope
- Meaning and purpose
- Control and choice
- Self-management
- Risk-taking
- Relationships
- Inclusion

The Scottish Recovery Network undertook a narrative research project to establish a Scottish evidence base of factors helping or hindering an individual's recovery. Emerging from this was the clear wish for mental health workers to reframe their role and become facilitative rather than directive and to be in tune with the service user's aspirations. They regarded demonstrations of empathy, trust, collaboration, shared power, respect, personal investment and kind gestures as most helpful in their treatment relationship with mental health professionals (Brown and Kandirikirira, 2007). Narrators felt specifically that wherever possible they should have a prime role in the decision-making, management and evaluation of their own medicine regime, not only to allow them to better manage the side-effects and establish responsive regimes, but also to address the issues of power relations, rights, self-determination and self-esteem.

This sounds intuitively moral. It is clearly the right thing to do. There is also significant evidence that it is the best thing to do. The purpose of this book is to show how this can be facilitated. It does this by operationalising theoretical discussions within clinical settings in order to bring these abstract issues to life.

This chapter begins by defining the terms *compliance*, *adherence* and *concordance* in order to illustrate the conceptual differences. It introduces recovery-oriented practice as a function of concordance, and shows how difficult concordance can be given the enduring conflation between concordance, compliance and (most recently) adherence. It then clarifies that medicines are useful, but that their utility depends upon a risk–benefit analysis. It shows that this can best be achieved by keeping the principle of concordance in mind, and introduces many evidence-based techniques to this end. The complexity of person-centred care in general is then briefly grounded in the ethical framework underpinning the concept. This is to illustrate the factors that everyone needs to keep in mind when coming to decisions in mental health care. The chapter finishes by introducing the scenarios that weave throughout the book.

Reflective exercise
Think about what you value most in life. Would it be possible without the freedoms implied by Repper and Perkin's components of recovery?

Compliance/adherence/concordance?
Table 1.1 summarises the definitions of compliance, adherence and concordance.

Table 1.1 Definitions of key concepts in medicine management (adapted from Treharne *et al.* (2006)).

Concept	Summary definition
Compliance	The paternalistic view that the person is a passive party who has his or her prescribed treatment enforced.
Adherence	The (still paternalistic) view that the informed (but still passive) person will stick (adhere) to taking the recommended treatment.
Concordance	The process of enlightened communication between the person and the healthcare professional leading to an agreed treatment and ongoing assessment of this as the optimal course.

Compliance

A widely accepted definition of compliance is that of Haynes (1979, p. 1).

The extent to which a person's behaviour (in terms of taking medications, following diets or executing other lifestyle changes) coincides with medical or health advice.

Compliance has proven to be difficult to measure. Direct measurement involves the detection of a chemical in a body fluid (Stockwell-Morris and Schulz, 1992) if the medicine is taken immediately before testing. However, even this measurement can be misleading. For example, frequency of use, metabolic rate, body mass, age and overall health can all influence outcome and therefore the results may be difficult to interpret. Indirect measures include therapeutic outcome, impression of the doctor, patient interview or pill counts. All these methods have clearer disadvantages. Health can change because of factors unrelated to medicines, doctors' impressions have long been shown to be unreliable (Mushlin and Appel, 1977), patient interview and pill counts are inconsistent with each other (Park and Lipman, 1964) and, of course, people can dispose of medicines without taking them. Patients who rate themselves as less than fully compliant are, however, sometimes thought by their doctors and case managers to be compliant (Trauer and Sacks, 1998). These problems all persist (Gadkari and McHorney, 2010).

In addition, the concept of compliance is irrelevant to enabling an understanding of the subjective experience of medicine-taking (Trostle, 1988), failing to reflect the conflicts that individuals face in managing their own wellbeing (Deegan and Drake, 2006). Interventions logically matched with the definition of compliance involve attempting to educate, convince or persuade the patient to follow advice. The patient's point of view may be driven 'underground' in response to persuasion to comply. The level of dose decided upon may be sub-therapeutic. The prescriber may then decide to raise the dosage, as the patient seems not to be responding. If the patient then resolves to follow the prescription an unnecessary burden of side-effects may occur, perhaps even resulting in toxicity and further disenchantment. This process also involves a waste of resources. The literature increasingly accepts the position that attempts to impose compliance are unlikely to succeed (Marland and Cash, 2005; Deegan and Drake, 2006). The terminology of 'compliance' was, therefore, modified to 'adherence', apparently denoting a greater emphasis on the patient's role as decision-maker (Myers and Midence, 1998).

Adherence

In 2009 the National Institute for Health and Clinical Excellence (NICE) produced their guideline *Medicines Adherence: Involving Patients in Decisions About Prescribed Medicines and Supporting Adherence* (Nunes *et al.*, 2009). On first review this seems a significant step forward. The title suggests that adherence relates to involvement in decision-making. However, this is not true according to the definition offered in Table 1.1. The definition of adherence relates to 'sticking' to recommended treatment. This remains implicit in the NICE guideline.

Adherence is defined as:

> the extent to which the patient's behaviour matches agreed recommendations from the prescriber (p. 1)

We would argue that this misses a crucial step. This definition is fine as long as it presupposes a concordant discussion. The guideline developers do make this absolutely clear:

> Addressing nonadherence is not about getting patients to take more medicines *per se*. It starts with an understanding of patients' perspectives of medicines and the reasons why they may not want or are unable to use them (p. 1)

However, without this precondition grounded in *concordance* we would argue that an uncritical acceptance of the concept of adherence will subsequently entrench *compliance*-directed interventions. On page 17 the guideline states that it was originally intended to entitle the guideline *Medicine Concordance*, but the developers thought this might be 'unhelpful to health care professionals' (p. 17). Whilst this is understandable because of the complexity of concordance, we suggest that changing it to adherence missed an opportunity to be more helpful to service users.

The theme is picked up in the latest NHS strategy document *Equity and Excellence: Liberating the NHS* (Department of Health, 2010). The founding principle of this document is

> We will put patients at the heart of the NHS, through an information revolution and greater choice and control:
>
> > Shared decision-making will become the norm: no decision about me without me. (p. 4)

This is concordance, not adherence.

Concordance

Concordance is essentially a process of collaboration. Concordance does not refer to a person's medicine-taking behaviour but rather to the nature of the relationship between the service user and mental health worker, which should be akin to a consultation between equals (Royal Pharmaceutical Society of Great Britain and Merck Sharpe and Dohme, 1996). The term *concordance* implies agreement on a contract (Treharne *et al.*, 2006; Snowden, 2008a). Concordance is based on shared decision-making, and for decisions to be shared mental health workers need to discuss options in a way that elicits and operationalises the person's point of view.

It is acknowledged that this method of working can be challenging. In some circumstances the person may not want to take medicines at all. Conversely, not all service users want to have a say in their medicine taking, and some would rather defer to the prescriber in all medicine-related decisions. Decision-making types have been delineated by Marland and Cash (2005), and this typology will be expanded upon in Chapter 6. In brief, the typology was developed to acknowledge that people have very different decision-making styles in relation to medicine taking, and it shows how individuals may change their decision-making type over time. Each type of decision-making presents its own challenges when working to promote concordance.

From compliance to recovery-orientated practice

The way that mental health workers have been socialised into thinking about medicine taking may be blocking the interventions most likely to succeed (Marland and Cash, 2001). This is because the value judgements inherent in the still pervasive label of 'non-compliance' serve to stifle creative attempts to enable service users to lead their own recovery journey (Deegan and Drake, 2006), and often these value judgements relate implicitly also to the term *adherence*. It is disappointing to see this error persist in the most recent guideline. For example, the term *adherence* has a long history as a 'problem'. An authoritative national report for the NHS identified non-adherence as a costly problem and went on to attribute the cause of this problem to patient behaviour:

> The challenges for research in medication adherence are similar to those for other health-related behaviours, such as smoking cessation, exercise and diet: how to influence and change behaviour (Horne *et al.*, 2005).

We will discuss the limits of such approaches in detail in Chapter 6. However, for now it is sufficient to note that following a review of the literature, Gray *et al.* (2002, p. 283) concluded:

> There is no evidence that telling patients to take medication works. Helping people make decisions that are right for them does. Mental health profession-als need to move from ensuring compliance to developing concordance.

Problems persist, however, for two enduring reasons:

1. Concordance is often used as a synonym for compliance. It should be becoming obvious this is wrong linguistically and philosophically. Concordance is not just a new and politically correct word for compliance.
2. Interventions in the field of medicine taking are based on the concept of compliance (for example Compliance Therapy – Kemp *et al.*, 1997) or adherence (Adherence Therapy – Gray *et al.*, 2006; see NICE guideline CG67).

Within the field of mental health both problems are compounded by the assumption that the 'mentally ill' are particularly non-compliant because of psychotic symptoms and lack of insight. However, this is not true. Non-compliance rates generally reported for schizophrenia are in the middle range of those reported for other medical conditions (Fenton *et al.*, 1997; Cramer and Rosenheck, 1998). In a systematic review of 103 studies of compliance with neuroleptics (Nose *et al.*, 2003), with an overall sample size of 23,796 people, a non-compliance rate of 25.78% was found, whereas around 50% of people with enduring health problems do not comply with medical regimes regardless of diagnosis (World Health Organization, 2003). This suggests that non-compliance is not solely accounted for by particular illness-related symptoms and that personal experience and individual ways of potentially incorporating medical treatment into an overall coping strategy merit careful assessment (Marland and Cash, 2005).

When the concept of compliance drives the relationship the service user learns either to acquiesce and not be responsible for their medicine-taking, or be blamed for a confrontational battle of wills with the prescriber and administering nurse. They may subsequently make unilateral medicine-taking decisions. The aim should therefore not be to inculcate compliance, but to facilitate a therapeutic interaction with medicines, representing an optimum balance between symptom control and side-effects (Repper and Perkins, 2003; Marland and Cash, 2005; Farmer, 2010). This dynamic equilibrium requires continual monitoring and adjustment of medicine regime or lifestyle, or both, and for some service users medicine taking is not part of their recovery journey. It is acknowledged that this is difficult, but this difficulty does not warrant the abandonment of the effort by supplanting more straightforward terminology. Table 1.2 contrasts the traditional paradigm of mental health services with the evolving model which is characteristic of recovery-focused practice.

Table 1.2 Past and future models of care (adapted from *Delivering for Mental Health* (Scottish Government, 2006)).

Past model	Evolving model
Most resources geared towards episodic treatment of acute episodes of ill health/distress	Geared towards supporting recovery from long-term problems
Hospital centred	Embedded in local communities, based on local community needs with increasing alternatives to hospital care and enhanced quality of inpatient care provision
Lack of choice in alternatives to pharmacological therapies; focused on illness and deficits, and risk averse	Enabling, person-centred recovery and strengths-based focus with a move towards positive management of individual risk. Maximising choice and access to evidence-based interventions
Disjointed care	Continuous whole-systems care
Reactive care	Preventive care and focus on early intervention
Service user as passive recipient	Service user as active partner and expert in his or her experience and recovery
Low emphasis on self care/management	Emphasis on facilitating self management and peer support
Carers undervalued	Carers supported as partners
Low-tech, with recognised problems with information systems	Improved technology with the potential for innovative use of technology

Why take medicines at all? From chemical substance to therapeutic agent

It is axiomatic that all medicines will exert toxic side-effects; these may range from relatively trivial to unpleasant and to life threatening. Why then do we use medicines that can cause serious side-effects? The answer of course is that they have also been demonstrated to have a desirable therapeutic effect. In these instances we carry out a risk vs. benefit analysis to decide whether or not to use a medicine. The risks of being exposed to the toxic side-effects are weighed against the expected benefit that the person will experience. So who makes this judgement? Who does this 'analysis'?

When a medicine undergoes pre-clinical and clinical testing, data are collected on both the beneficial therapeutic effect(s) of the medicine and its side-effects. In making their decision on whether the medicine is to be licensed, the authorities must decide whether or not the nature and seriousness of the side-effects is outweighed by the benefits that the person taking the medicine is expected to receive. This 'official' analysis does not of course end here. All medicines are also subject to post-marketing surveillance in order to detect any rarer side-effects which were not apparent at the clinical trial stages of development.

Once a medicine is licensed and in clinical use, the risk–benefit analysis continues – the clinician must form a judgement that the individual is likely to benefit sufficiently from taking the medicine to make the risk of 'suffering' any potential side-effects worthwhile. This particular analysis will also have to take into account the context in which the medicine is to be used. Does the person belong to a particular group more likely or less likely to suffer the most serious side-effects? Is the medicine contraindicated in the group to which the person belongs? If the dosing regime is complex or demanding, will the person be able to adhere to it? These and other contextual considerations may well alter the risk–benefit analysis in one direction or the other.

A risk–benefit analysis is of course also carried out by the person taking the medicine – are the therapeutic effects of the medicine sufficient to make them disregard the side-effects they may be experiencing? Is it worth it for them? When the clinician and the person being treated carry out this analysis concurrently in partnership and come to the same conclusion, we have concordance.

Aiming for a therapeutic interaction with medicines

To summarise our position so far, we suggest that the two main benefits to an open and honest therapeutic alliance with regard to medicine taking are:

1. It is more likely that a mutually acceptable use of medicines will be reached (Medicines Partnership, 2003; Weiss and Britten, 2003; Latter *et al.*, 2007) and;
2. The processes of engagement and collaboration intrinsically promote self-esteem, ownership and commitment (Marland and Cash, 2005; Deegan and Drake, 2006).

Sometimes, however, a service user does not follow a prescription even though it has evolved from a relationship based on concordance. Nevertheless it is illegitimate to say that this service user is non-concordant. Non-concordance implies a problematic *agreement*, not a problematic action. In other words, the initial agreement was wrong, or has changed, and therefore needs to be renegotiated. This does not require a value judgement regarding anyone's behaviour.

The other side of this coin is that without concordance it is possible to be fully compliant and relapse, or fully compliant and experience a high level of avoidable side-effects. People may be non-compliant and stay well. Compliance is therefore never an end point in itself. The aim should be to achieve a therapeutic interaction with medicines. Concordance working, akin to the principles of establishing on-going consent (Usher and Arthur, 1998), should be considered as a continually evolving picture and not as a snapshot. Pertinent questions to ask would be for example:

- Does this person have a therapeutic interaction with the medicine regime and if not why not?
- Is omitting a medicine a conscious decision or is it based on forgetfulness?

It is important to be aware of how the current attitude towards medicine-taking developed and how it continues to evolve, otherwise there is likely to be a mismatch between the service user's aspirations and those of the mental health worker (Marland and Cash, 2005). In other words, there is always room for manoeuvre. For example, there are clear alternatives to standard dosing with the existing medicine, such as:

- A change of medicine type.
- A targeted medicine regime in which dosages are increased or even initiated in response to warning sign detection and decreased or discontinued when clinical signs are stabilised (Carpenter and Heinrichs, 1983).
- A low-dose maintenance treatment using one-fifth or less of standard doses, with increases in response to warning signs (Herz *et al.*, 2000).

Without appropriate engagement working (Tait *et al.*, 2010) the service user may ignore or dismiss information, perhaps because it contradicts what he has learned from his own experience. The information may arrive at the wrong time or may not be understandable. It may be delivered in the wrong format, or simply be inaccurate. Useful strategies logically matched with the concept of concordance include:

- Use of timelines to understand relapse signature and the development of medicine-taking decision-making over time (Ford, 2000);
- Advance statements (Deegan and Drake, 2006);
- Differentiation of withdrawal effects and relapse signature (Otto *et al.*, 2010);

- Mutual sharing of knowledge of medicines between service user and mental health worker (Snowden, 2008a);
- Rating scales such as LUNSERS (Day *et al.*, 1995), including the subjective awareness of side-effects;
- If forgetfulness is a factor then behavioural prompting is indicated (Ryan-Woolley and Rees, 2005).

Many of these evidence-based interventions will be expanded upon throughout the text. However, an important general point is that there is evidence for the necessity for concordance beyond the field of mental health. For example, around 50% of people with enduring health problems have long been seen as not complying with medical regimes, regardless of their diagnosis (Ekerling and Kohrs, 1984). These rates have been consistently lower in acute illness (Cameron and Gregor, 1987). This trend towards non-compliance in advancing chronicity (Gadkari and McHorney, 2010) implies that chronic disease exerts consistent influence on people's willingness to comply.

In line with the earlier discussion on compliance prevalence across illness types, the consistency of this factor suggests that non-compliance cannot be solely accounted for by particular disease-related symptoms. Personal experiences of long-term illness and individual ways of incorporating medical treatment into an overall coping strategy merit careful assessment. Chronicity of illness often entails a close and insightful health worker and service user relationship. A deeper understanding of the service user's decision making processes may aid interventions to ensure harmony between their wishes and therapeutic effectiveness, regardless of disorder. This can be understood as person-centred care.

Person-centred care

Reflective exercise
Think back to your last contact with health services as a patient. Did you perceive care to be centred on your needs?

Person-centred shared care is now relatively well embedded as a normative aspect of contemporary heath care policy (Department of Health, 2010a; Scottish Government, 2010). However, the enactment of the concept remains problematic (Elwyn *et al.*, 2010). That is, clinicians consistently express a desire to share decision making with patients (Charles *et al.*, 2004) yet simultaneously express concerns that they do not have enough time for this type of consultation, or that it may not be appropriate for their particular patients (Legare *et al.*, 2008), given that they may not understand the decisions they may be asked to make.

This latter point is a rational concern, given that misunderstanding is known to undermine shared decision-making (West and Baile, 2010). The picture is not made clearer by considering patient expectations of consultation. We have already touched on different medicine-taking behaviour (Marland and Cash, 2005) and introduced the idea that there may be people who at certain times or events may want nothing to do with this type of decision. For example, in GP consultations there is evidence that people expect the consultation to entail examination, tests, diagnosis, treatment, prescriptions, medicine and a coherent outcome (Kenten *et al.*, 2010), but it is unclear that they want an equal part in these. In other words, there remains a considerable gap between the rhetoric of shared care and its enactment from both sides. Although the outlook of nurses may be different in this regard, the issues of different consultation expectations remain central to concordant decision-making.

We will return to this tension in some detail in Chapter 6. In particular, we shall consider the role of health beliefs, knowledge and their role in collaboration. We shall consider how individuals construct risk–benefit analyses as introduced above, and we will demonstrate the utility of maintaining an open mind. For now, we just need to clarify that the goal of concordance aligns with the ethics of the profession. We will therefore briefly consider the underpinning principles of mental health nursing and explain how these are articulated in practice.

Ethics

Ethics is the study of what is right and wrong. It is also called moral philosophy. It is enacted in practice by considering a balance of agreed values in any given situation. These values often (though not always) compete, which is the origin of most ethical dilemmas. The four principles we need to understand are autonomy, justice, beneficence and non-maleficence. These are defined in Table 1.3. As an introduction it is useful to consider the principles as interconnected and sometimes competing. An ideal interaction would therefore do good, do no harm, and respect an individual's autonomy within the spirit of agreed principles of social justice. However, this is rare. For example, we have already seen that all medicines have 'side-effects', which challenges the principle of non-maleficence given that some harm is only to be expected. A degree of compromise is therefore likely to be required.

Table 1.3 Ethical principles.

Term	Definition
Autonomy	The capacity of a rational individual to make an informed, un-coerced decision (one can immediately see that the concept of rationality can present problems in discussions in mental health).
Justice	A social construct also based on rationality, but which includes wider principles of fairness or equity, and describes what action a society will take under the breach of agreed rules.
Beneficence	Refers to actions that promote the wellbeing of others. In health, this means taking actions that serve the best interests of patients.
Non maleficence	Best summarised as 'first, do no harm'. It is considered more important not to harm somebody than to do them good, primarily because of the history of practitioners testing new and under-researched treatments on unsuspecting patients.

In order to articulate the language and scope of this compromise in mental health care these ethical principles are operationalised in law. For example, you will see from Table 1.4 that Millan (2001) uses the principles of justice, autonomy, beneficence and non-maleficence as a framework within which he introduces the principles of mental health care in Scotland.

In Millan's terms, any action should provide benefit ('Any intervention should produce a benefit that cannot reasonably be achieved without that intervention') without harm ('Care, treatment and support should be provided in the least invasive manner and environment compatible with the delivery of safe and effective care'). We need to understand the reasons *why* the person feels the way they do ('People should be fully involved in all aspects of their assessment, care, treatment and support. Past and present wishes should be taken into account'). That way their views can be respected ('Care, treatment and support delivered in a manner that affords respect for individual qualities') and acted upon ('Information needs to be understandable and in an appropriate format').

The reason for this brief diversion into mental health law is to show that the principles underpinning them are consistent. It is subsequently easier for us to decide how to act if we keep this ethical framework in mind. For example, these principles are translated into values such as those articulated in *Rights, Relationships and Recovery* (Scottish Government, 2010). The ten essential shared capabilities (Department of Health/Sainsbury Centre, 2004) taught to all UK-based undergraduate mental health nurses and designed to underpin the practice of all mental health practitioners are essentially expressions of how to act

Table 1.4 Core principles of the Mental Health Act (Millan, 2001, pp. 18–21).

Justice	*Non-discrimination* The same rights and entitlements as those with other health needs *Equality* No discrimination on grounds of physical disability, age, gender, sexual orientation, religion, racial origin, cultural or linguistic background or membership of ethnic group *Respect for diversity* Care, treatment and support delivered in a manner that affords respect for individual qualities, abilities and diverse backgrounds and takes into account, age, gender, sexual orientation, ethnic group and social, cultural and religious background *Reciprocity* Where compulsion is used there is an obligation on agencies to provide safe and appropriate services, including ongoing care following discharge from compulsion
Autonomy	*Informal care* Wherever possible, care, treatment and support should be provided without the use of compulsory powers *Participation* People should be fully involved in all aspects of their assessment, care, treatment and support. Past and present wishes should be taken into account. Information needs to be understandable and in an appropriate format *Respect for carers* Informal carers should be respected for their role and experience, receive appropriate information and advice and have their views and needs taken into account
Beneficence and non-maleficence	*Least restrictive alternative* Care, treatment and support should be provided in the least invasive manner and environment compatible with the delivery of safe and effective care *Benefit* Any intervention should produce a benefit that cannot reasonably be achieved without that intervention *Child welfare* The welfare of a child (under 18) should be paramount in any intervention imposed on the child *Age appropriate services* Agencies must minimise the effects of compulsion on the parent–child relationship and ensure contact between the child and those with parental responsibilities

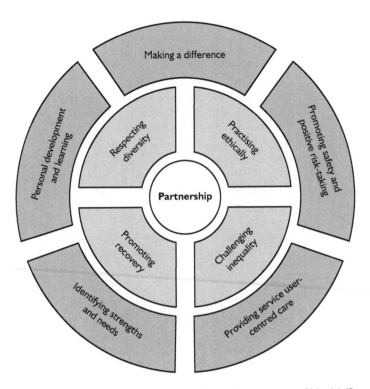

Figure 1.1 The ten essential shared capabilities (Department of Health/Sainsbury Centre, 2004).

within the ethical principles enshrined in current law (Figure 1.1). As you can see, partnership is at the heart of this agenda. Concordance is the goal of partnership.

Professional attitudes and perspectives
Concordance is ethically straightforward then. It is the right thing to do. However, this does not mean to say that it is always easy in the real world. In order to help professionals towards this goal, it is important to understand their attitudes and to provide them with knowledge on individual care-seeking behaviours. The suggestion that we, the professionals, may act as a barrier to concordance provides food for thought.

The mental health professional has to be aware that, in coming to seek help, the individual has usually followed a 'hierarchy of resort' which spans self-medication to consultation (Helman, 2007, p. 82). In 1980, seminal work by Kleiman demonstrated that healthcare covered three interconnected sectors: the popular sector (self-medication, advice from friends); the folk sector (non-medical therapists); and the professional sector. If one method fails, the individual will seek another. The concept of a hierarchy is a misnomer in Kleiman's model, as individuals who have sought help at two sectors and decided to pursue the third – medical help – can just as easily resort to the other sectors should the medical help prove, for whatever reasons, to fall short of that individual's expectations. However, as they are within the medical system, failure to follow medical advice then results in a label of 'failure to comply'.

In essence, to promote concordance between the health professional and the individual, the components of recovery detailed earlier in the chapter are a useful framework in which to examine one's attitude towards a service user's behaviour with his or her prescribed treatment(s). An individual needs hope, meaning and purpose, control and choice, self-management, risk-taking opportunities, a good relationship with his or her healthcare professionals and a feeling of inclusion in the process. As a framework, no single component is enough to create concordance. Healthcare professionals have to appreciate that individuals can change intrinsically (especially in recovery, which is often not a linear pathway from a state of vulnerability towards greater autonomy) and such changes are inextricably linked with extrinsic factors in the individual's life. For example, all the components above – as they relate to concordance – may be shattered by house repossession, death of a loved one, loss of a job, or even a change in a healthcare professional.

In order to normalise this point, it is interesting to examine health-seeking behaviours in 'well' individuals. Why does someone take vitamins and yet continue to smoke? Why do some people seek reiki therapy, go to pilates classes? or exercise furiously to the detriment of their joints? Individuals are unique, and some medicines, treatments or therapies appeal to them for reasons best known to them, while others do not. The reasons and the motivations behind care-seeking behaviours are complex and it is important to listen to the individual and try to understand his or her world experience. Helman (2007, pp. 196–223) provides a very detailed overview of the 'total medicine effect', which includes work on the therapeutic or damaging effect of the healthcare professional. Such works cite the placebo effect of the healthcare professional – if their ability to heal is validated by the individual then recovery is potentiated by the relationship alone. There is considerable evidence for this, and Benedetti's work in particular will be elaborated in Chapter 6, along with the importance of integrating and understanding the health beliefs of all involved.

Special challenges to promoting concordance in mental health and introduction to case study examples

As long ago as 1990, Corrigan *et al.* suggested strategies for overcoming barriers to active collaboration that may originate in the treatment, the service user, or the treatment delivery system. They presented a comprehensive picture of these potential barriers. Essentially these barriers often connect to the inequity in power between the mental health professional and the service user. They acknowledged that some of the barriers may arise from, for example, the clinician's aversive interpersonal style, and in this case any intervention aimed at improving collaboration would start with the clinician. A congruent issue appears related to assumptions clinicians make about capacity. If the notion of concordance is to be realised then service users must be presumed competent to make decisions regarding medicines unless proven otherwise. Special challenges associated with mental health problems may arise because of compromised capacity. It must not be assumed, however, that because someone is diagnosed with a mental disorder they lack capacity and cannot enter into decision-making, as most people do retain this capacity (Patrick, 2006).

By now we hope that you will agree that we have begun to develop a reasonably convincing justification for prioritising concordance. However, all of the writers in this book have been clinicians and some still are. We appreciate the need to maintain a sense of realism if concordance is to be taken as seriously as we believe it should. We have already seen how difficult this stance can be to maintain, with the abandonment of the term by the NICE working group. To this end we have therefore developed scenarios throughout the book that articulate these often complex theoretical constructs in practice.

For example, with respect to capacity Patrick (2006) outlines that to have capacity the person must have the ability to:

- Understand the treatment
- Remember their decisions
- Weigh up information
- Make a free choice
- Communicate their decision

The person needs to understand the treatment only in broad terms (Patrick, 2006), but we acknowledge that this may be difficult to operationalise. Remembering decisions is often problematic in dementia-type illness. The ability to weigh up information may be affected by a mental disorder which causes the person to distort information, such as in anorexia nervosa. This condition may also affect the ability to make a free choice, as may obsessive compulsive disorder or commanding auditory hallucinations. People with physical disorders, such as stroke or, for example, those with schizophrenia who become incoherent in expression, may have special challenges in communicating their treatment decisions. Many of these issues of capacity are apparent in the unfolding case scenarios.

These scenarios will unfold throughout the book to reveal the complexity of concordance in practice. We will see that concordance can wax and wane as described above. These developing scenarios are therefore useful for allowing analysis of these transitions. For example, the nurse may believe they are acting in the best interests of the person yet may inadvertently alienate them. By way of providing an overview of the status of particular therapeutic relationships in time, we will use small icons to illustrate the state of concordance of that particular relationship. This is intended to alert the reader that actions described within the text may not necessarily be having their intended impact, or that the relationship has otherwise broken down in some way. For example, the CPN in Scenario 3 is called Yvonne. The scenario is about Susan. Where concordance is being achieved the text will be accompanied by this icon:

Where concordance is compromised the text will be accompanied by this icon:

The same process will be used for Dougie, Murdo and their respective relationships. Here is an introduction to our scenarios.

Scenario 1: Dougie

Dougie Collins is a 71-year-old retired taxi driver. His wife, who was concerned by his worsening memory and word finding problems, had encouraged him to attend his GP surgery. He had also recently got lost when driving the car along a familiar route. He had dismissed these problems as nothing more than was to be expected for his age and was quite resistive to 'wasting the doctor's time.'

Scenario 2: Murdo

Murdo McLeod is a 62-year-old gardener who self-referred to his GP when his wife prompted him to take action. He had noticed a disturbance in his sleep pattern compared with the norm – he was waking up at 4:00 a.m. instead of 6:30 a.m. He had lost his appetite and noticed that his concentration was poor. He also said he felt 'flat' compared with normal. The GP felt he had mild to moderate depression and gave him some self-help leaflets and referred him to the Community Mental Health Team (CMHT).

Scenario 3: Susan

Susan MacPherson is a 20-year-old woman who is about to be discharged from a psychiatric hospital after a lengthy stay for her second admission. She has a diagnosis of schizophrenia which Susan herself does not agree with. She has previously been described by staff as 'resistive' and 'non-compliant' and has been referred to a CPN for follow-up.

Below are the people introduced throughout the book in relation to these scenarios.

Dougie Collins

Wife	Joyce Collins
Son	Paul
Daughter	Marie
Three grandchildren	Unnamed
Clinical Nurse Specialist	Chris McDonald
Community Mental Health Nurse	Shirley Menzies
GP	Unnamed
Nurse Consultant	James White
Consultant Psychiatrist	Dr Armstrong
Visiting Psychiatrist	Dr Jenkins
Consultant Physician	Unnamed

Murdo McLeod

Father	Frank
Mother	Jean
Oldest brother	Frankie
Two other brothers and two sisters	Unnamed
Wife	Mary
Son	Michael
Daughter	Francis
GP	Dr Robertson
CPN	Helen
Mental Health Support Worker	Catherine
Psychiatrist	Unnamed

Susan Macpherson

Parents	Unnamed
Two brothers	Unnamed
Uncle	Peter
Friend	Kate
Community Mental Health Nurse	Yvonne
Psychiatrist	Dr Jones
Practice Nurse	Beth
Clinical Supervisor	Jacqueline
Art Tutor	Mr Piper

Conclusion

Mental health workers need to be skilled in optimising service user participation, even when mental health problems undermine capacity. The ability to promote concordance and mental wellbeing in the face of these challenges is the hallmark of effective mental health working. The decision to take medicine or not, for the most part, rests ultimately with the service user. The process of reaching this decision may in itself promote mental health. The process of enforcing compliance to take medicine regardless of the service user's wishes militates against mental wellbeing and is justifiable rarely as an exception but never as the rule. A change towards working towards concordance rather than compliance will involve more than a change of nomenclature or changing the definition of compliance to make it more acceptable.

Note

A substantial part of this chapter has been based largely on work previously published as listed below:

Marland, G., McNay, L., McCaig, M. and Snowden, A. (2011) Medicine taking and recovery-focused mental health practice. *British Journal of Wellbeing*, **2**(2), 21–5.

Snowden, A., Fleming, M., Marland, G. and McNay, L. (2011) Towards concordance in schizophrenia: a case study. *Nurse Prescribing*, **9**(5), 234–42.

CHAPTER 2

Biology

Abstract

This chapter focuses on the biological impact of medicines on the body, and the impact of the body on medicines. It differs from the other chapters in that this discussion is largely factual in nature. It is acknowledged that the information presented here is only part of the impact and effectiveness of medicines in general, but it is an essential part. A discussion focused towards medicine concordance would be incomplete without a critical understanding of the concepts presented here.

The chapter begins with an introduction to the place of biology within a concordance framework. The principles of pharmacokinetics are then introduced. This section incorporates a breakdown of what the body does to process medicines. It can be summarised under the headings of absorption, distribution, metabolism and excretion. Each process is detailed using psychotropic medicines as examples where relevant in order to show how these issues are related to concepts such as dosing regimes. The section on pharmacodynamics then introduces evidence of how medicines exert their pharmacological effect. The links between these demonstrable effects and their capacity to impact on the person are discussed in some detail. This leads into the final section that puts these two fundamental processes together to explain medicine interactions. It uses clozapine, cigarette smoking (nicotine) and caffeine as examples, to show how these substances would be expected to interact, given our understanding of pharmacokinetics and pharmacodynamics, and what happens when we add another medicine into the mix. This chapter takes a 'value-free' approach. That is, all these factors can and perhaps should initially be understood without recourse to classification of mental illness.

Key points

- Concordance cannot be achieved without knowledge.
- The knowledge presented in this chapter is fundamental to achieving concordance.

- The notions of therapeutic effects and side-effects of psychotropic drugs are largely understood in relation to classification of mental illness.
- It is not necessary to understand psychiatric classification systems to understand the biological function of drugs, or the body's impact upon these drugs.
- Removing this distinction allows for a greater person-centred understanding of the risk–benefit analysis pertinent to therapeutic interaction with medicines.

Key words
Concordance, pharmacodynamics, pharmacokinetics, effects, side-effects

Objectives

At the end of this chapter the reader will have a critical understanding of

- Pharmacokinetics
- Pharmacodynamics
- A medicine-centred view of psychotropic medicines

Introduction

Figure 2.1 illustrates a model of shared decision-making. Many of the components of models such as these are discussed in detail throughout this book. Building a partnership, sharing consultation and negotiating an individually appropriate plan are requisite to concordance. However, it would be easy for the novice to miss the importance of fundamental biological knowledge within such frameworks. Whilst this is not Clyne *et al.*'s (2007) intention, competence in psychopharmacology is *assumed* within this model, buried within Section 4: having 'up-to-date knowledge of area of practice and wider health services'. It is important to reiterate that up-to-date knowledge requires the crucial component of biology. Ninety per cent of people with mental health problems take psychotropic medicines (Healthcare Commission, 2007). Anyone prescribing, administering or taking them, needs to be able to engage in a shared consultation with someone who knows *what the medicines are likely to do*.

This chapter focuses on this question by segregating the *intended* effect (e.g. 'antipsychotic') from the *actual* biological effect (e.g. lowering of blood pressure, sedation) in order to distinguish biology from aetiology. The purpose of this is to provide a value-free account of psychopharmacology as far as possible. The purpose of a value-free account is to focus on the biology as opposed to artificial constructs such as classification of mental illness (Kutchins and Kirk, 1997). For example, the main pharmacological effects of benzodiazepines involve the enhancement of the effects of GABA at the $GABA_A$ receptor (Riss *et al.*, 2008).

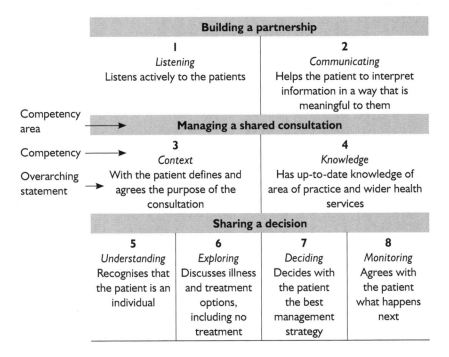

Figure 2.1 Competency framework for shared decision-making (Clyne *et al.*, 2007).

This activity increases the frequency of opening of the chloride ion channel of the GABA$_A$ receptors. Because the brain has spare benzodiazepine receptor capacity the magnitude and duration of these effects are dose-related in that larger doses have stronger and longer-lasting effects.

Benzodiazepines have anxiolytic, hypnotic, amnesic, sedative, muscle relaxant and anticonvulsant properties as a function of this neurological activity (Mandrioli *et al.*, 2008). Any of these properties may be desirable in a given instance, and all can be considered 'adverse effects' if undesired (Moncrieff, 2007). Sedation in particular is often described as an adverse event as well as a 'property', along with more commonly quoted adverse events such as ataxia and hypotension, confusion, cognitive deficits, dizziness, euphoria, weakness and unsteadiness. Many of these effects may be exacerbated in older adults and all are complicated further by polypharmacy.

So, taking a purely pharmacological perspective, is there any time during which the properties (including those commonly classified as 'adverse events') described above would be helpful for anybody? What would you expect to happen if you took one of these medicines? What would happen if you took this medicine at the same time as another medicine? Would you expect everybody to be affected in the same way? If not, why not? In order to understand these questions in more depth we need to understand some general principles regarding how medicines exert a clinical effect.

Therapeutics remains, as it has always been, the judicious use of poisons. We try to increase the judiciousness, and sometimes we succeed in this. (Stewart, 2009)

Pharmacokinetics

Pharmacokinetics is the study of what the body does to a medicine. It can be broken down into: absorption, distribution, metabolism and excretions. These will be discussed in turn.

Absorption

Absorption is the movement of a medicine into the circulation. The proportion of medicine dose that reaches the blood or plasma is called the bioavailability. The major effect of any medicine is usually produced by the amount of medicine that is free in plasma. The method of medicine administration can have a direct impact on bioavailability, as illustrated in Figure 2.2. The mechanism of bioavailability will be covered in more detail in the section on metabolism, as the issues are closely related. However, for now it is important to recognise that the liver inactivates many enteral medicine molecules before they can reach the circulation, thereby decreasing bioavailability. Some medicines may be *activated* by the liver, increasing bioavailability.

Some medicines are inactivated in the GI tract. For example insulin is broken down by stomach acids if given orally, which is why it is given subcutaneously. Other medicines may be given enteric coating so they can make it through the stomach into the gut where the active components can be absorbed. The permeability of the tissue to the medicine is also a factor, as is the pH, lipid solubility, transport mechanisms, blood supply and contact time. Lipid solubility affects absorption in that most absorption occurs via diffusion across the membranes, so the more lipid soluble the easier the diffusion. The pH of the site is important because most medicines are either weak acids or bases or both; the pH of the site will therefore determine the proportion of the medicine molecules which will exist in an ionised form, as only unionised molecules are able to diffuse across membranes. When

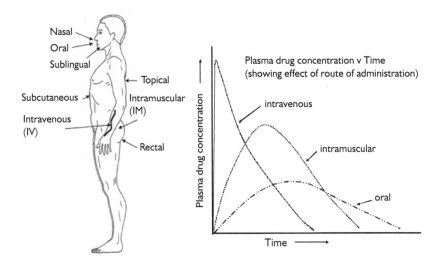

Figure 2.2 Routes of administration and their impact on medicine concentration over time.

medicine molecules diffuse across the gut lining they then have to diffuse into capillaries to complete the absorption process, the better the blood supply, the faster that diffusion can occur. In terms of contact time, this is again about the diffusion of medicine molecules across the gut lining – the longer the medicine is in contact with the gut lining the more medicine will diffuse. The amount of food in the stomach can significantly influence absorption rates, which is why some should be taken with food and others not.

Orally administered medicines are absorbed from the small intestine; the portal for absorption of nutrients into blood. The small intestine is surrounded by a very thin membrane with a large surface area and medicines enter the liver via the portal circulation. As discussed the liver may inactivate a medicine before it can enter systemic circulation and have its desired effect. If this happens to a medicine the dose may need to increase (if it is safe) to make sure enough survives to reach the systemic circulation or we may need to change the route of administration, e.g. intravenous (IV) injection (straight into systemic circulation) or into the peripheral circulation by intramuscular (IM), subcutaneous (SC) or rectal administration. Inhalation will also bypass the first-pass effects of the liver, but in this case the medicine must be volatile and lipid soluble – in other words it has to exist in vapour form or fine particulates. Glyceryl trinitrate for angina is given sublingually in order to avoid this first-pass metabolism.

Distribution

Distribution is the dispersal of the medicine around the body. It is important to understand this, as it impacts on how the medicine reaches its target. Once a medicine enters into systemic circulation by absorption (or direct administration) it is distributed into interstitial and intracellular fluids. Medicines which are not very lipid soluble cannot cross membranes easily, so they tend to stay in plasma or interstitial fluid. Very lipid-soluble medicines reach all parts but may accumulate in fat. The chemical nature of the medicine (for example pKa) determines how easily a medicine can access a part of the body. Medicines which bind to plasma proteins are trapped in the blood, and very large molecules tend to stay in the plasma. Tissue proteins, cardiac output, regional blood flow and capillary permeability all impact on how the medicine is distributed through tissues. Medicines are more easily distributed in highly perfused organs like liver, heart and kidney, and less so in low perfused organs like muscle, fat and peripheral organs.

Disease and the presence of other medicines can impact on distribution. For example, any disease affecting the circulation is bound to have an impact – see Figure 2.3. Hydrostatic pressure pushes water out of the capillaries and osmotic

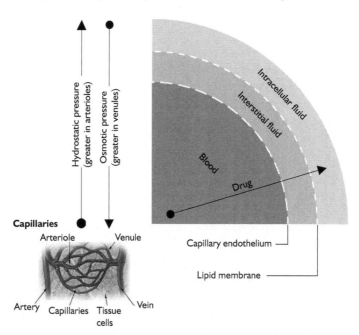

Figure 2.3 Hydrostatic pressure in arteriole favours water-soluble medicines crossing into surrounding tissues.

pressure drives water back. Because the blood in the capillaries is constantly flowing, equilibrium is always reached, but the balance differs at different points, favouring hydrostatic pressure at the arterial end and osmotic pressure at the venous end, where solutes are passed back into the bloodstream.

Metabolism

Most medicines are metabolised in the liver, although other tissues are also involved. Metabolism is a bio-transformative process, directed towards elimination of toxins. It impacts on exogenous substances (medicines) in two main ways:

- to inactivate the medicine for future excretion or elimination
- to activate the medicine for the desired effect (e.g. promedicine)

In most cases the metabolites are inactive. Sometimes the metabolite is also active; for example, amitriptyline is metabolised to nortriptyline, which is also a tricyclic antidepressant; codeine is metabolised to morphine, which is a more powerful opiate. Occasionally the metabolite may be the preferred compound.

Medicine metabolism is usually separated into two phases. Phase 1 reactions involve oxidation, reduction or hydrolysis, which introduce a new chemical group to the medicine molecule and generate metabolites which are more or less chemically active. For example, oxidation is mainly carried out by the cytochrome P-450 enzymes in the liver, and we shall return to these in more detail later. Knowledge of the enzyme systems and the effect that medicines have on them and *vice versa* makes adverse event prediction meaningful and clinically important. However, for now it is enough to know that the purpose of all these processes is to make the chemical water-soluble. In the case of oxidation it does this by adding oxygen or removing hydrogen from the chemical. Sometimes this reaction produces metabolites that are sufficiently water soluble to be eliminated immediately. Water is a *polar* molecule (the two O–H bonds are polarised, leaving the O slightly negative and the hydrogens slightly positive). In general terms 'like dissolves like', so if the medicine metabolites are more polar they will dissolve more readily in water.

Many metabolites undergo further reactions to finish this process. These are Phase 2 reactions. The purpose of the whole process is ultimately to rid the body of the medicine, and it does this by inactivating the chemical and making it more water-soluble. Different medicines may be metabolised by different enzyme systems. The liver has high concentrations of most medicine-metabolizing enzyme systems and is the first organ perfused by chemicals absorbed from the gut. As discussed above in the section on absorption, medicines taken into the GI tract will be partially metabolised by the liver enzymes before they enter the general circulation. In some medicines this 'first-pass' metabolism is so extensive that very little survives to reach the systemic circulation.

Excretion

Excretion refers to the elimination of waste products from the system. Medicines can be eliminated by renal excretion or by metabolism or both. The function of this process is important as it relates directly to dosing intervals. Most medicines are eliminated by a first-order process. With first-order elimination, the amount of medicine eliminated is directly proportional to the serum drug concentration (SDC). The purpose of therapy is to ensure the amount of medicine administered during a dosing interval exactly replaces the amount of medicine excreted. When this equilibrium occurs (rate in = rate out), steady state is reached.

Hepatic metabolism often makes medicines more polar and thus more water soluble. The resulting metabolites are then more readily excreted by the kidneys. The biliary system also contributes to excretion by ensuring that the medicine is not reabsorbed from the GI tract. Generally, the contribution of other systems such as the intestine, saliva, sweat, breast milk, and lungs to excretion is small, except for exhalation of volatile anaesthetics. Excretion via breast milk may be significant for a breastfeeding infant, however.

Nearly all water and most electrolytes are both passively and actively reabsorbed from the renal tubules back into the circulation. All of the water is reabsorbed because water moves freely across biological membranes, so it simply diffuses back across the tubule membranes. The electrolytes being charged cannot simply diffuse back as the tubules are festooned with transport proteins designed to return them to the plasma to maintain the tissue's electrolyte balance.

Polar medicine molecules similarly cannot simply diffuse back and there are no transport proteins to actively reabsorb them, so they stay in the urine. However, polar compounds, which include most medicine metabolites, are unable to diffuse back into the circulation and are excreted unless a specific transport mechanism exists for their reabsorption (as for glucose, ascorbic acid and B vitamins). As with other aspects of pharmacokinetics, changes in the system are related to ageing, such that renal medicine excretion at age 80 is typically reduced to 50% of what it was at age 30, meaning that more of the active medicine products will remain in the system. Caution should therefore precede prescribing of any medicine to older people, particularly those with kidney disease, given that this clearly has a marked impact on excretion.

The process of pharmacokinetics as a whole is summarised in Figure 2.4.

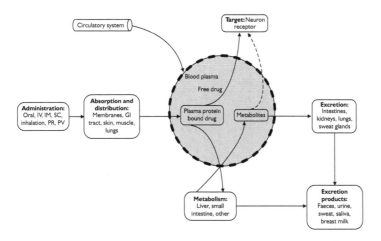

Figure 2.4 The process of pharmacokinetics.

Pharmacodynamics

Pharmacodynamics refer to what the medicine does to the body. This process relates to the 'target' in Figure 2.4. It is important to understand the role of neurotransmitters in this regard. Neurotransmitters are chemicals which mediate messages between neurons. They exert their effect both pre- and post-synaptically. Each synapse within the central nervous system is made up of two nerve cells separated by the synaptic cleft, and neurotransmitters are released into the cleft following activation (action potential) of the first neuron. The neurotransmitter then diffuses across the synaptic cleft where it binds (or not) to receptors on the post-synaptic neuron. These receptors (protein molecules) are specifically activated by a particular neurotransmitter. The neurotransmitter either fits or does not fit. The next nerve is either more likely, as likely or less likely to fire as a result of this neurotransmitter binding. Activated neurons can then send signals to the next neuron, which modulates the possibility of it firing as a consequence. There are around 100 billion neurons in the brain, each with a number of synaptic connections. Brain activity is the sum of these trillions of signals.

Medicines exert their effect by impacting on this process. In other words neurotransmitter receptor proteins are the target for many medicines. Medicine molecules have a shape that allows them to 'fit' into the receptor protein and this process causes or blocks any further action by the receptor. The medicine molecule can be an agonist (Figure 2.5, top left) or an antagonist (Figure 2.5, top right). An agonist refers to a molecule that has the ability to activate a particular receptor(s),

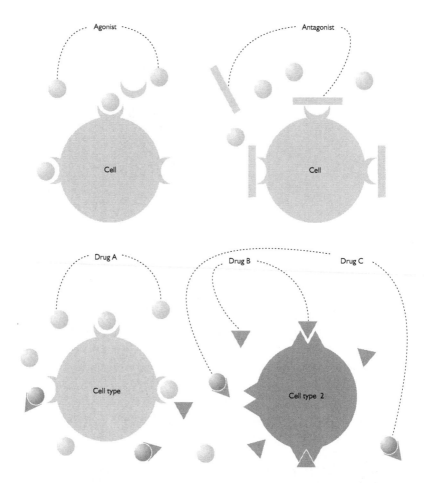

Figure 2.5 Medicines and their receptor actions.

and as depicted in Figure 2.5. the agonist produces a subsequent action within the cell. This often takes the form of a cascade of cellular reactions that alter its function in some way. An antagonist binds to the receptor in question but does not activate it. Such binding of an antagonist to a receptor prevents its activation and so prevents an action in the cell. In Figure 2.5 the antagonist can be seen to prevent anything else from facilitating an action at this point. So where underactivity within a particular system is thought to be a problem, an agonist would be considered useful. Where overactivity is problematic an antagonist may help.

Although the holy grail of medicine therapy is to target only the desired receptor in the desired area, in practice this never happens. For example the bottom part of Figure 2.5 shows a mixture of different medicines' effects. Medicines A and B can be seen to fit specific receptors. Medicine C on the other hand fits either receptor. This is likely to mean that medicine C will have a broader impact. Also, even where medicines like A or B are developed it is difficult to restrict their activity to a particular region. For example, amisulpiride was developed to only have affinity for D2 and D3 dopamine receptors (these receptors will be discussed very shortly). Putting aside the issue that a particular trait can be attributed to a particular deficiency within a particular brain region, D2 and D3 receptors are widespread throughout the system and therefore the desired effect is not the only effect established.

A related complication is that overlaying these primary actions are many feedback mechanisms that also alter the structure and function of the initial targets for these medicines. For example serotonin pathways in the brain are closely linked and interact with dopamine pathways in the brain. Feedback mechanisms inside the cell are thought to be responsible for the therapeutic lag seen with many psychiatric medicines. Nevertheless, it is useful at this point to examine the dopamine hypothesis of schizophrenia for illustrative purposes. The dopamine hypothesis suggests that psychotic symptoms may be a function of dopamine over activity within a particular area of the brain. This is a highly contentious theory, but we do not have to discuss this at this point. It is known, however, that there are dopamine pathways in the brain. The dopamine hypothesis predicts that if a medicine could reduce overactivity in the appropriate area then it may have a therapeutic effect.

In more detail, the dopamine pathways originate in the substantia nigra, ventral tegmental area (VTA) and hypothalamus. These project axons to eight areas of the brain which are typically divided into four major pathways:

- The **mesocortical pathway** connects the VTA to the frontal lobe. It is thought to have a role in emotion and motivation. This is one of the pathways thought to be responsible for the 'positive' symptoms of schizophrenia. It is also closely associated with the mesolimbic pathway.
- The **mesolimbic pathway** carries dopamine from the VTA to the nucleus accumbens via the amygdala and hippocampus. It has been shown to be related to mechanisms of reward and desire, and is implicated in neurobiological theories of addiction, psychoses and depression.
- The **tuberoinfundibular pathway** runs from the hypothalamus to the pituitary gland. It regulates the secretion of prolactin from the anterior pituitary gland.

This is why dopamine blockading medicines cause increased lactation (including men), menstruation irregularities and sexual dysfunction.

■ The **nigrostriatal pathway** runs from the substantia nigra to the neostriatum. The pathway is involved in the basal ganglia motor loop, which means it is involved in voluntary movement. Loss of dopamine in this pathway is associated with Parkinson's disease. This is why dopamine antagonists aimed at addressing the pathway imbalances in the mesolimbic and mesocortical pathways above create Parkinson's-like effects.

It is currently beyond our ability to target a medicine at one area without impacting on all the pathways. So, for any desired effect (reduction of 'positive symptoms') there is a trade-off: a long list of potentially life threatening neurophysical changes. These translate in clinical practice to a description of a particular medicine's 'side-effect' profile, although it will now be obvious that referring to these effects as side-effects is disingenuous. The wider action of any dopamine antagonist is reasonably predictable given our knowledge of these pathways. It may be more instructive to consider all of these actions as 'effects' of the medicine. That some of the effects are undesired is not a property of the medicine, and 'side-effects' are rather a function of perspective. Consider the vasodilator Viagra, for example. This was originally developed as a vasodilator to treat angina. Its side-effect is now its marketable function, and ironically it is not recommended for people with cardiac issues.

The picture is therefore more complex than the simplistic but enduring 'magic bullet' ideal portrayed by the media and encouraged by pharmaceutical companies. For example dopamine reacts with at least five types of dopamine receptor. Amisulpiride was developed to target specific types of these receptors (Figure 2.6) as the mesocortical and mesolimbic pathways are thought to have more of these particular receptors, and these are thought to be the more relevant dopamine pathways in terms of schizophrenia.

Now, it is important to remember that these systems do not act in isolation. For example, serotonin pathways are closely linked to these dopamine pathways. Nevertheless, each specific dopamine receptor (referred to as D1, D2, D3 etc.) has different properties when activated. The same is true of most neurotransmitter systems – in particular serotonin, which has seven major receptor classes and further subtypes within these major classes. Serotonin is also referred to as 5-hydroxytryptamine (5HT). From a pharmacological perspective then, it would seem we need to also include some recognition of the interaction occurring between and within these systems. So, whilst taking a very minimalist approach to receptor activation may seem sensible, so may a 'catch-all' approach. For

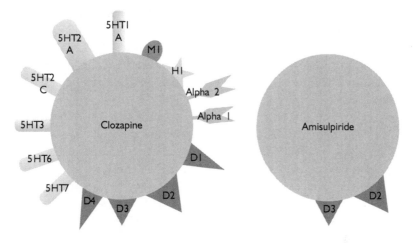

Figure 2.5 Medicines and their receptor actions.

illustrative purposes we will use clozapine as an example of what this means. Figure 2.6 shows the clozapine molecule next to an amisulpiride molecule in a format that shows the receptors they are known to interact with.

It should be immediately clear that clozapine has the potential to bind with various subtypes of dopamine, serotonin, muscarinic acetylcholine, histamine and alpha adrenergic receptors. That it has a consistent clinical function at all is difficult to explain from a biological perspective. On the other hand, many of its effects are easy to predict. It causes drowsiness (histaminergic), hypersalivation (muscarinic), tachycardia (alpha adrenergic), constipation (serotonergic and muscarinic) as well as inducing many cognitive effects (dopaminergic and serotonergic).

Effects and interactions

Putting these last two sections together we can now extend the discussion to explain how medicines may act and interact depending on the nature of individual pharmacodynamics and pharmacokinetics. We have seen that older people can be considered at greater risk of medicine toxicity due to the ageing process impacting on pharmacokinetics. We have also seen that any medicine is likely to trigger a range of effects due to its initial impact on various neurotransmitters. The picture becomes even more complex when we add another medicine into the mix, but it is still understandable within the concepts introduced here. For example, many medicine–medicine interactions happen because one medicine interferes with the metabolism of another, causing higher or lower plasma concentration of each than would otherwise be the case. The clinical impact of this may vary from person to person, but the issues are reasonably predictable. Given that in the UK 92% of people with mental health problems in inpatient psychiatry take two or more psychotropic medicines (Healthcare Commission, 2007) it is important to understand how these pharmacological reactions occur and predict their clinical outcomes.

A quick search of PubMed for 'medicine interactions' in November 2010 revealed 188,760 articles. This literature is of course impossible to keep up with. There are many sources of support and information, but there is great diversity in the range, quality and consistency of this information (Abarca *et al.*, 2006a). It is consequently important to understand a few basic principles and have a clear idea of what to look for in ascertaining the clinical impact of medicine interactions.

We have already discussed pharmacodynamics and pharmacokinetics. These both play their parts in medicine interactions:

- *Pharmacokinetics*: a change in medicine effect occurs because of a change in its concentration, due to the impact of another substance. A memorable example is the effect that grapefruit juice has on felodipine concentration (see Figure 2.7). Felodipine is an antihypertensive. Blood pressure is reduced more when felodipine is taken with grapefruit juice than when it is taken with water. The clinical impact of this increase in bioavailability is an increase in the likelihood of adverse vasodilatory effects such as headache (Wilkinson, 2005).

- *Pharmacodynamics*: a change in the medicine effect occurs without a change in medicine concentration. A good example is the increased efficacy in terms of pain relief when paracetamol is combined with codeine. The sum is greater than the parts in terms of clinical impact on pain.

Pharmacokinetic effects are broadly related to physical changes in the body and the interactions mentioned above. These may be a function of disease or age; for example Parkinson's disease decreases dopamine receptor sensitivity. This is why it is treated with L-DOPA in order to increase the amount of dopamine to offset this. Ageing affects pharmacodynamic responses through changes in receptor binding or in postreceptor response. A corollary is that older adults are particularly sensitive to anticholinergic medicine effects, for example. This is important because many psychotropic medicines (e.g. antipsychotics, tricyclic antidepressants, some antihistamines, many over-the-counter hypnotics and cold preparations) have this property. Anticholinergic effects include constipation, urinary retention (especially in elderly men with benign prostatic hyperplasia), blurred vision, orthostatic hypotension and dry mouth. In order to understand these effects clearly we need to return to the principles of metabolism introduced above in a bit more detail.

Cytochrome P450

You will recall from the discussion of medicine metabolism and excretion that the liver (and other tissues) produces enzymes that facilitate Phase 1 reactions, and that these reactions help to eliminate medicines from the body. The function of these reactions is to render lipid-soluble medicines more water soluble so that they can be excreted via the kidneys.

Cytochrome P-450 (CYP) is the most important super-family of medicine-metabolising enzymes. They are present all over the body but predominantly in the liver. Not all of the CYP enzymes act on all medicines, but each acts on many. At least 17 mammalian CYP gene families have been defined, and they are categorised in the format *number, letter, number*, which correspond to family, subfamily and gene product. So for example CYP1A2 and CYP2C19 are common, and act on many psychiatric medicines. This is clinically important because when one enzyme is acting on two or more medicines it becomes more likely that a medicine interaction will occur. For example, the enzyme CYP2C19 is inhibited by the presence of fluoxetine and induced by the presence of phenytoin. A medicine interaction may follow.

The diversity of the CYP super-family allows the liver to perform oxidation on a huge variety of chemicals. Table 2.1 shows examples of common medicines seen in psychiatry, the enzyme predominantly involved in their metabolism, and medicines that induce or inhibit the particular enzyme. A substrate here refers to a molecule that is acted upon by an enzyme.

Before we go on to discuss a clinical example of these interactions, there is a final complication to incorporate. Each of the CYP proteins is unique and not everyone has the same amount of each. This is why individuals may be described as poor metabolisers (PMs) or extensive metabolisers (EMs) of certain medicines (Prior and Baker, 2003). For example, according to (Matchar *et al.*, 2007) roughly 7% of Caucasians are CYP2D6 PMs, whereas only 1–2% of Asians and 2–4% of African-Americans are CYP2D6 PMs. By comparison 10% of southern Europeans have a duplication of the CYP2D6 gene, which is associated with EM.

There is a large genetic component to this, and there is increasing interest in genetic testing to ascertain people's capacity to metabolise different medicines. Some authors are hopeful this may lead to better individual care. Evidence remains unclear at the time of writing as to the clinical utility of such tests (Fleeman *et al.*,

Table 2.1 P450 Medicine interaction table: selected examples of medicines often seen in psychiatry

Substrates

CYP1A2	CYP2C9	CYP2C19	CYP2D6	CYP3A4,5 and 6
clozapine	diclofenac	lansoprazole	amitriptyline	clarithromycin
duloxetine	ibuprofen	omeprazole	clomipramine	erythromycin
fluvoxamine	piroxicam	diazepam	murdoipramine	alprazolam
haloperidol	naproxen	phenytoin	imipramine	diazepam
imipramine	phenytoin	phenobarbitone	paroxetine	midazolam
naproxen	warfarin	amitriptyline	haloperidol	triazolam
olanzapine		clomipramine	risperidone	chlorpheniramine
theophylline		clopidogrel	thioridazine	aripiprazole
		cyclophosphamide	aripiprazole	buspirone
		progesterone	codeine	haloperidol
			dextromethorphan	methadone
			duloxetine	pimozide
			tamoxifen	quinine
			tramadol	sildenafil
			venlafaxine	tamoxifen
				trazodone

Inhibitors

cimetidine	fluconazole	fluoxetine	bupropion	clarithromycin
fluoroquinolones	amiodarone	fluvoxamine	fluoxetine	itraconazole
fluvoxamine	isoniazid	ketoconazole	paroxetine	ketoconazole
ticlopidine		lansoprazole	duloxetine	nefazodone
		omeprazole	cimetidine	erythromycin
			chlorpheniramine	grapefruit juice
			clomipramine	verapamil
			doxepin	diltiazem
			haloperidol	cimetidine
			methadone	amiodarone
				fluvoxamine

Inducers

tobacco	rifampin			carbamazepine
	secobarbital			phenobarbital
				phenytoin
				St John's wort

2010). Nevertheless it is clear that different enzyme expression accounts to some extent for the variation in medicine metabolism between individuals.

The grapefruit juice example
CYP3A4 is a useful example of what this means, given that it is involved in 60% of all medicine metabolism. For example, you will recall that these enzymes occur all over the body. The small intestine has many CYP enzymes, and in particular

CYP3A4. There is therefore the theoretical possibility that if CYP3A4 could be blocked in the intestine then that action could increase the bioavailability of any medicine that is normally oxidised by CYP3A4 in the 'first-pass' effect. This is how grapefruit juice increases the plasma concentration of felodipine. Felodipine is used to treat hypertension and angina: a function of the heart muscles not receiving enough oxygen. Its therapeutic dose is calculated the same way as any other medicine: by estimating its bioavailability, which is usually about 15% of the ingested dose. This percentage is arrived at because 85% is normally metabolised through the first-pass effect. Taking grapefruit juice at the same time as felodipine can increase its bioavailability considerably.

In detail, at the top of Figure 2.7 felodipine is ingested in tablet form and taken into the gut. There is potentially 100% of the tablet available at this stage. In circle A, at the bottom left, the gut starts to metabolise the felodipine with CYP3A4. However, some of this action is blocked because of the presence of grapefruit juice. As a consequence the felodipine entering the portal vein is not as metabolised as would normally be the case. On entering the liver the felodipine

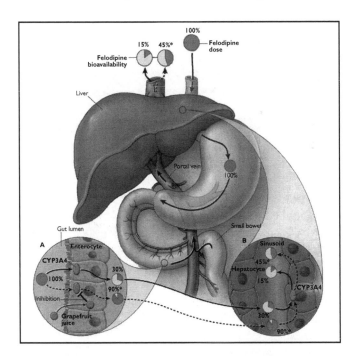

Figure 2.7 First-pass metabolism after oral administration of a medicine, as exemplified by felodipine and its interaction with grapefruit juice.

is further metabolised through the first-pass effect. However, because more of the original medicine remains than there would have been had the CYP3A4 not been inhibited by the grapefruit juice (circle B, bottom right), the resulting bioavailability is higher than usual. This has the clinical impact of reducing blood pressure beyond clinical intention and increasing heart rate as a function of vasodilation. The dotted lines represent the grapefruit situation, whereas the full lines are the 'usual' metabolism of the medicine.

This type of biological reaction is common. CYP3A4 plays a role in the metabolism of many medicines used in psychiatry, so these types of interactions are important to know. For example, clozapine is metabolised by it, along with CYP2C19 and CYP2D6. Clozapine is principally metabolised by CYP1A2 however. This is clinically important for similar reasons discussed in the grapefruit juice example in that several other medicines are also metabolised principally by this method.

For example, if the SSRI fluvoxamine is given at the same time as clozapine this has the consequence of increasing serum clozapine levels. This is because Fluvoxamine inhibits CYP1A2, which subsequently diminishes its capacity to metabolise clozapine. A dose of 50 mg fluvoxamine per day has been shown to increase clozapine concentrations three-fold and has been shown to increase nine-fold in some people with doses of 100 mg to 200 mg per day (Wetzel *et al.*, 1998). Given that clozapine toxicity can cause delirium, seizures and coma it should be clear that these types of interaction can be very dangerous.

It is interesting to note that smoking and caffeine *induce* CYP1A2 activity, which means that stopping smoking and the intake of caffeine can be dangerous in some individuals, given that serum levels of clozapine may rise as a consequence of the removal of this process. Seizures have been reported in smokers taking clozapine who have then stopped smoking. This is important in light of current smoking cessation targets and the high prevalence of smoking within the group of people who are prescribed clozapine (Brownlowe and Sola, 2008).

As a further complication, medicine-related metabolism issues are not limited to competition for a specific CYP. Table 2.1 showed medicines that may be a substrate for, and an inhibitor or inducer of, the same CYP. However, it is also known that a medicine or its metabolites may alter the activity of a specific CYP without being a substrate. Thus co-prescribed medicines may affect the serum levels of substrates of those CYPs. These mechanisms are more complex than this brief overview can illustrate (see Prior and Baker, 2003). Nevertheless it is important to understand the principles of these interactions and their potential clinical consequences, as it should be clear now that there are many factors likely to underpin medicine interactions, and that many of these may be clinically significant.

In principle it should be straightforward to predict the groups of substances that may cause problems. That this is not always the case is in part down to the fact that medicines are metabolised by many of these enzymes, offering plenty of alternative methods of metabolism. Nevertheless, the older or less healthy the body, the more likely these reserves are to be stretched to capacity. Likewise, if someone does not express as much of the particular enzyme due to genetic issues these secondary systems are likewise stretched. It is at these points that clinical issues may be noted, as expected levels of metabolism are not achieved in practice. From a clinical perspective these risk factors should always generate caution in practice.

Below are the major medicines featured throughout the unfolding scenarios. Throughout the book the clinicians and recipients will be considering the therapeutic effects of these medicines in their individual contexts. The boxes below summarise their mechanism of action and their main effects and side-effects. For full details of the side-effects, cautions and contraindications associated with these medicines see the latest edition of the *British National Formulary* (*BNF*).

Scenario 1: Dougie

Box 2.1 Mechanism of action and clinical efficacy of sodium valproate

Mechanism of action of sodium valproate

Sodium valproate was first used in the management of epilepsy. Like semi-sodium valproate (Depakote) it breaks down to valproic acid, which is the therapeutic agent. It is marketed as a mood-stabiliser, although it is unclear what this term means or how this function occurs (Healy, 2008). The main hypothesis suggests that it prevents 'kindling'. Kindling entails the theory that extreme physiological reactions are more likely if they have happened before. This is true in anticonvulsant therapy. Its generalisation to mood is unproven.

Valproate is believed to increase levels of the neurotransmitter GABA within the CNS. GABA has an inhibitory function. However, valproate also has many other effects/side-effects because:

- the receptors it impacts upon have multiple functions within the brain and the rest of the body.
- its wider mechanism of action is unknown.

Platelet counts should be taken every six months as valproic acid can increase bleeding time, especially in older adults (Haddad *et al.*, 2004). Lowering the dose may restore platelet count. Always investigate bruising.

Some of the effects and side-effects of valproate to be considered by Dougie and Chris (Healy, 2008).

Main beneficial effects	Main side-effects
Anti-manic activity, possibly due to its initial sedative effects	Fatigue, lethargy Weight gain, GI disturbance Blood dyscrasias Jaundice, hair thinning

Box 2.2 Mechanism of action and clinical efficacy of donepezil

Mechanism of action of donepezil

Alzheimer-type dementias involve the death of cholinergic neurons throughout the cerebral cortex. The resulting fall in acetylcholine levels is believed to underpin the cognitive decline. Donepezil is an acetylcholinesterase inhibitor; it therefore prevents the breakdown of the acetylcholine which is still being released by the surviving cholinergic neurons. Donepezil and medicines like it effectively increase the acetylcholine levels in the cortex and so may delay further cognitive decline. However, acetylcholinesterase inhibitors occur naturally as toxins in venom and have been used as nerve agents, inducing non-stop muscle contractions and paralysis through irreversible inhibition of acetylcholinesterase (Sanson *et al.*, 2009).

Donepezil selectively inhibits brain acetylcholinesterase, and because of its long half-life it can be taken once a day. However, it also exerts its effects outside the brain and therefore has many other effects/side-effects because:

■ the receptors it impacts upon have multiple functions within the brain and the rest of the body
■ its wider mechanism of action is unknown

Some of the effects and side-effects of donepezil to be considered by Dougie and Chris (based on information from Grainger and Keegan (2011))

Main beneficial effects	Main side-effects
Delays further cognitive decline in AD	Nausea, vomiting, anorexia, fatigue, hallucinations, muscle cramps

Box 2.3 Mechanism of action and clinical efficacy of zolpidem

Mechanism of action of zolpidem

Benzodiazepines exert their effect by interacting with $GABA_a$ receptors. All benzodiazepines have anxiolytic, hypnotic, sedative, amnesic, muscle relaxant and anticonvulsant properties, but different medicines have different relative proportions of these effects. Zolpidem is not strictly classified as a benzodiazepine although it exerts its effect at the same receptor binding site. It binds predominantly to $GABA_a$ $\alpha1$ receptor subunits and this appears to be associated with sedation. It has less affinity for other receptor subunits. It has a short half-life (2–3 hours) and works quickly, aiding sleep but not maintaining it. Because of its short half-life it may be safer for older adults as it would be less likely to accumulate than a medicine with a longer half-life

However, it also exerts its effects outside the brain and therefore has many other effects/side-effects because:

■ the receptors it impacts upon have multiple functions within the brain and the rest of the body.

Some of the effects and side-effects of Donepezil to be considered by Dougie and Chris (based on information from Healy (2009)

Main beneficial effects	Main side-effects
Effective in short term	More side-effects than benzodiazepines Dangerous interaction with alcohol
Short half-life so relatively free of hangover	Tolerance

Box 2.4 Mechanism of action and clinical efficacy of perindopril

Mechanism of action of perindopril

Perindopril is an angiotensin converting enzyme (ACE) inhibitor. ACE is the enzyme responsible for converting angiotensin I to angiotensin II. Inhibiting the enzyme therefore lowers tissue concentrations of angiotensin II. Angiotensin II is part of the rennin–angiotensin system, which is involved in maintaining blood pressure. Angiotensin II is a vasoconstrictor and it also stimulates (directly and indirectly) reabsorption of Na^+. Decreasing the level of angiotensin II therefore has an anti-hypertensive effect. The anti-hypertensive effect of ACE inhibitors may also be partly due to their ability to inhibit the degradation of bradykinin, a known vasodilator.

Some of the beneficial effects of ACE inhibitors, e.g. in the treatment of heart failure, diabetic nephropathy and in the prophylaxis of adverse CVS effects, appear to be independent of their blood pressure-lowering effects. It has been suggested that these may be due to the effects of the medicines on the autonomic nervous system.

Some of the effects and side-effects of perindopril to be considered by Dougie and Chris

Main beneficial effects	Main side-effects
Anti-hypertensive	Hypotension (especially first dose), cough, hyperakalaemia, headache, dizzyness, fatigue, nausea, renal impairment
Increase natriuresis	May worsen inflammatory pain
'Improved' cardiac function	
Prophylaxis of adverse cardiovascular events	

Box 2.5 Mechanism of action and clinical efficacy of ibuprofen

Mechanism of action of ibuprofen

Ibuprofen is a non-steroidal anti-inflammatory drug (NSAID). NSAIDs work by inhibiting the enzyme cyclo-oxygenase and thereby decreasing levels of prostaglandins in the tissues. These prostaglandins have pro-inflammatory, pyretic and hyperalgesic properties, so decreased levels of these substances account for the beneficial effects of the NSAIDs.

Some of the effects and side-effects of ibuprofen to be considered by Dougie and Chris

Main beneficial effects	Main side-effects
Relief of pain	GI upset, nausea, diarrhoea, GI bleeding/ulceration
Anti-inflammatory	
Anti-pyretic	

Box 2.6 Mechanism of action and clinical efficacy of bendroflumethiazide

Mechanism of action of bendroflumethiazide

Bendroflumethiazide is a thiazide diuretic. It works by inhibiting the reuptake of sodium by the kidneys. The increased level of Na^+ in the renal filtrate exerts an osmotic pressure which draws/retains water into/in the filtrate, hence the increased diuresis.

Some of the effects and side-effects of bendroflumethiazide to be considered by Dougie and Chris

Main beneficial effects	Main side-effects
Increased diuresis	GI disturbances, postural hypotension, electrolyte imbalances, altered blood-lipid levels
Anti-hypertensive effect	

Scenario 2: Murdo

Box 2.7 Mechanism of action and clinical efficacy of fluoxetine

Mechanism of action of fluoxetine

Fluoxetine is a selective serotonin reuptake inhibitor (SSRI) anti-depressant. As the name suggests, these medicines block the reuptake of serotonin by the neurons which released it and so increase the effective concentration of serotonin in the synapses. This increased concentration of serotonin is believed to mediate the anti-depressant effect of the medicine.

Some of the effects and side-effects of fluoxetine to be considered by Murdo and Helen

Main beneficial effects	Main side-effects
Anti-depressant effect	Gastro-intestinal disturbances, appetite changes, hypersensitivity reactions, vasodilatation, postural hypotension

Box 2.8 Mechanism of action and clinical efficacy of amisulpiride

Mechanism of action of amisulpiride

Amisulpiride is an antipsychotic medicine. It was designed with the 'dopamine' theory of schizophrenia in mind. It is an antagonist of the type 2 and 3 dopamine receptors (D2, D3), the idea being that this would decrease the presumed overactive dopamine-mediated signalling in the mesocorticolimbic system(s) of the brain.

Some of the effects and side-effects of amisulpiride to be considered by Murdo and Helen

Main beneficial effects	Main side-effects
Relief/prophylaxis of 'positive' psychotic symptoms	Insomnia, agitation, anxiety, drowsiness, gastro-intestinal disturbances

Box 2.9 Mechanism of action and clinical efficacy of mirtazapine

Mechanism of action of mirtazapine

Mirtazapine is unlike any of the other anti-depressants in terms of its mechanism of action. The others tend to work by influencing the handling of noradrenaline and/or serotonin in the synapse (see fluoxetine above), whereas mirtazapine affects the amount of these neurotransmitters being released by neurons. Mirtazapine is an antagonist of α_2-adrenoreceptors which are designed to limit the amount of serotonin/noradrenaline that a neuron releases into the synapse. Antagonising these receptors therefore increases the amount of these neurotransmitters released into the synapse.

Some of the effects and side-effects of mirtazapine to be considered by Murdo and Helen

Main beneficial effects	Main side-effects
Anti-depressant	Sedation when treatment is initiated
	Increased appetite, postural hypotension, dry mouth, peripheral oedema, fatigue, confusion, insomnia. Suicidal thoughts/behaviour

Scenario 3: Susan

Box 2.10 Mechanism of action and clinical efficacy of olanzapine

Mechanism of action of olanzapine

Like most antipsychotics, olanzapine acts primarily as an antagonist of D2 receptors. This can create a feeling of indifference. Olanzapine also acts on the serotonin system by blocking $5HT_2$ receptors. Blocking $5HT_2$ reverses hallucinations caused by LSD. Blocking $5HT_2$ has also been shown to be sleep-enhancing and anxiolytic. However, it also has many other effects because these receptors have wider functions than enhancing sleep or creating indifference, and:

- olanzapine acts on other receptors as well
- olanzapine produces more weight gain than any other antipsychotic. It raises blood lipid and sugar levels, increasing the risk of diabetes and metabolic syndrome. The biological mechanism of these effects is unclear, but one theory is that they may be related to the blockade of $5HT_2$ receptors. There seems to be some stimulation of appetite and a reduction in metabolic rate particular to olanzapine and clozapine in this regard, possibly related to further action on the histamine system (Healy, 2008). There is also an increase in thirst, often sated with sugary drinks, further exacerbating the problem.

Clinical efficacy: pros and cons of olanzapine as experienced by Susan (based on information from BMJ Group and Pharmaceutical Press, 2010).

Main beneficial effects	Main side-effects
Reduction in feelings of agitation and associated voice hearing experiences	Rapid weight gain
	Increased appetite
	Drowsiness
	Fatigue

Box 2.11 Mechanism of action and clinical efficacy of aripiprazole

Mechanism of action of aripiprazole

Unlike most antipsychotics, aripiprazole acts primarily as a partial agonist at multiple receptors; mainly dopaminergic, but also serotonergic, histaminergic, adrenergic and cholinergic. It does not completely activate most receptors that it acts upon. It also antagonises some receptors whilst acting as an agonist at others. It is its action as a partial agonist of $5HT_{2C}$ receptors that is thought to explain its lower relative risk of weight gain compared to other antipsychotics. However, aripiprazole also has many other effects/side-effects because:

- the receptors it impacts upon have multiple functions within the brain and the rest of the body
- it acts on multiple receptors

Aripiprazole is a 'high potency' antipsychotic, meaning that it is particularly likely to cause akathisia (Healy, 2008). This means that caution should be exercised, particularly in elderly patients

Some of the effects and side-effects of aripiprazole to be considered by Susan and Yvonne

Main beneficial effects

Reduction in feelings of agitation and associated voice hearing experiences

Main side-effects

Fatigue

Gastro-intestinal disturbances

Headache

Conclusion

If you are trying to facilitate concordance you will need to understand from a biological perspective the impact the medicine will likely have on the person, and the impact the person will likely have on the medicine. We have discussed these pharmacokinetic and pharmacodynamic issues in detail. We have not had to discuss a disease-centred model of mental illness in order to do this. In brief, people's age, health status, culture and concomitant treatment will likely play a role in the outcome of any pharmacological intervention. The effects of any medicine and medicine interactions are largely predictable, and this information should be understood and shared in order to approach concordance. The finer points of these discussions, such as when and how to share this information, including instances where it may be appropriate not to do so, are discussed in detail in the rest of this book. Nevertheless, none of these discussions is complete without a thorough understanding of the details presented in this chapter.

Reflective exercise

Choosing a particular medicine to prescribe involves careful consideration of the biological effects of the medicine and the context in which it will be taken. Such considerations must include the pharmacokinetics and pharmacodynamics of the medicine as well as the effects the medicine is expected to produce. The *BNF* is an essential starting point for gathering the information needed to make these choices.

Consider the following possible substitutions of some of the medicines being prescribed for the service users in this book.

Dougie
Temazepam instead of zolpidem

Murdo
Trazodone instead of fluoxetine

Susan
Haloperidol instead of aripiprazole

CHAPTER 3

Recovery and the therapeutic alliance

Abstract

In this chapter the stories of Dougie, Murdo and Susan unfold, giving insights into the possible causes of and the background to the mental health problems they begin to experience. They come into contact with mental health workers who try to engage with them and develop an effective working relationship. Various barriers and promoters to the establishment of a therapeutic alliance, which is foundational to concordance, are illustrated.

Key points

- Mental health workers who promote dignity and respect and are sensitive to service users' need to have hope for their future are well placed to establish effective engagement.
- Hope-inspiring relationships are associated with essential features.
- The involvement of significant others with service user consent is foundational in the establishment of concordance.
- The therapeutic relationship starts with the first point of contact.

Key words

Engagement, therapeutic alliance, recovery

Objectives

- Become familiar with the backgrounds of Dougie, Murdo and Susan
- Illustrate the need to establish engagement in working towards concordance
- Outline the skills required of the mental health worker in the establishment of therapeutic engagement
- Illustrate some barriers and pitfalls, as well as some of the promoters in the establishment of engagement

Introduction

Complaints and recovery stories from people labelled 'mentally ill' (Fisher, 2008) were the catalyst of the recovery movement that globally evolved from the USA (Fisher, 2008; NHS Education for Scotland and Scottish Recovery Network, 2008). Expert experiences and values of service users, their families and carers (Repper and Perkins, 2009) fundamentally underpin recovery-focused approaches in mental health practices. However, as described in the scenario of Susan, it is evident that service providers do not always acknowledge and afford service users such rights, and despite the constructive approach of Yvonne, her community mental health nurse, this can lead to inherent distrust of all service providers and so detrimentally impact upon opportunities to positively promote recovery.

Unlike the aftermath of a road traffic collision and the subsequent customary telecommunications to arrange recovery of the damaged motor vehicles, inspiring recovery in mental health is not so prescriptive. To reignite an individual's belief of 'hope' (Brown and Kandirikirira, 2007), the primary catalyst for volition of internal changes towards recovery (Deegan, 1988; Repper and Perkins, 2003; Scottish Recovery Network, 2006), service providers need the intrinsic and pivotal component of 'understanding self' to structure sure foundations for all therapeutic relationships (Stickley and Freshwater, 2008). Known also as self-concept, self-consciousness and self-awareness (Tait, 2007), 'self' is built upon a lifetime of personal and unique values (NES, 2011), experiences and characteristics (Sharples, 2007) and encompasses everything known or believed about one's self (Hayes and Orrell, 1998).

The narrative of one service user illustrates this point.

> Drawn from the associated personal experiences of severe mental ill-ness, such self-awareness has been intensely deepened. Sleep deprived and traumatised after compulsory admission to an acute ward, I struggled to acknowledge surrounding events and could not recall the name of the admission nurse and on making this enquiry their chilling response informed me that I had not forgotten their name because actually they had never told me. A simple yet passing opportunity that could so easily have promoted a sense of common humanity, but only caused personal worthlessness and hopelessness to plummet even lower and so triggered heightened and consuming desires to plan and execute a suicide attempt.
> (Ange Pollard – personal communication)

Although an extreme example, this encapsulates the potential impact that service providers' actions or inactions (Sharples, 2007) can potentially have on the wellbeing of vulnerable individuals and, as highlighted in the scenario of Dougie and Joyce, irrespective of the means or settings, therapeutic relationships commence on first contact.

Certainly in nursing, Hildegard Peplau is recognised as the pioneer of interpersonal relationships (Stickley, 2002; Reynolds, 2009), the concept that requires contribution and participation of service providers and service users (Peplau, 1952, cited in Stickley (2002); Hewitt *et al.* (2009); and Reynolds (2009)), to form the notable therapeutic cornerstone of mental health nursing (Stickley, 2002; Reynolds, 2009). However, establishing and maintaining such therapeutic engagement requires service providers to ensure that the core elements trust, empathy and unconditional positive regard are ever present (Sharples, 2007; Nelson-Jones, 2008; Stickley and Freshwater, 2008) and likewise, cognisance and profound understanding of the following essentials for hope-inspiring relationships:

- Valuing service users as human beings
- Accepting the experiences of service users as being very real for them and understanding what those personal experiences mean
- Believing in service users' abilities and potential
- Attending to the present priorities and interests of the individual
- Capacity to convey to service users that failures and setbacks are part of the recovery process
- Highlight that all futures are uncertain and applies equally to service user recovery
- For service providers, discovering ways of sustaining personal hope and guarding against despair and burnout
- Acknowledging that as service providers, accepting lifelong learning is paramount for personal development and growth; (Repper and Perkins, 2003), which understandably necessitates acute self-awareness and active listening skills (Rogers and Pilgrim, 1994, cited in Repper and Perkins, 2003; Maidement, 2004; Gamble, 2006; NHS Education for Scotland and Scottish Recovery Network, 2008; Sharples, 2007; Reynolds, 2009) to facilitate instillation of hope of recovery (Varcarolis, 2006).

Scenario 1: Dougie

Dougie Collins was born one of two boys into a working class family in Glasgow. Early in his life he spent much of his time on his uncle's farm outside Glasgow, helping out when he could or playing with his cousins across the ranging country side. He left school to work full time on his uncle's farm age 15 and found great satisfaction in driving or working the farm equipment. He was at his happiest when driving the newly bought tractor in any weather. Rather than stay on the farm, as conscription age approached he decided to join the army, the King's Own Scottish Borderers, as a boy soldier aged 16. He was part of the counter-insurgency in the jungle in Malaya and although he returned well, he rarely speaks of his experiences during this time. He did suffer from terrible nightmares, decreasing in frequency over the years. In the past six months he has had disturbed nights and occasionally sleepwalks – although he never says what his nightmares or troubled nights consist of. Joyce, his wife, does not ask him. She has learned to respect that he has never wanted to talk about his time in Malaya, but she knows from what he says in his sleep that he is still fighting his own war with his memories.

When he demobbed, Dougie became a taxi driver in Glasgow. He was late to romance and at the age of 30 he met and married Joyce, who had been working in a ticket office on the railways in Glasgow. Dougie and Joyce had two children, Paul and Marie. Dougie worked hard and eventually started his own taxi business. Joyce stayed at home to look after the children, taking some evening cleaning work. Dougie's children excelled at school: Marie went on to become a doctor and Paul became a designer. They both moved to Edinburgh, where their respective jobs were. Paul and Marie both went on to have three children, who visit their grandparents regularly.

We meet Dougie aged 71. He is fit and well, apart from his arthritis, for which he has been prescribed ibuprofen 400 mg three times a day. Now retired, Dougie sold his business at 65, as he found the job to be difficult and stressful. He bought a caravan in Ayr and Joyce and Dougie have been enjoying time at their caravan. They love social nights at the pub, where Dougie regularly gets up to sing. They enjoy seeing their grandchildren, particularly the 'wee one' called Shania, who at four keeps them all busy and entertained. Dougie is a friendly, amiable Scotsman. His early life experiences in the army taught him that life was far too short to worry about anything too long. He defers to his wife to make the important decisions and he trusts her implicitly. However, he has recently had doubts about the fact that his memory was not what it was and that he seems to get into a muddle quite a lot of the time. He wonders if all Joyce's worrying and fussing is making him make mistakes and he has recently become angry at several of her concerns over him. He feels it was rather extreme that she made him go and see their GP.

Dougie is ambivalent towards engaging with services and is currently doing this to make his wife happy. He may be at the 'suffering in silence' phase, where the person is experiencing some element of memory loss and disorientation but feels unable to discuss it openly with anyone around them and working apart from people they are close to (NHS Education for Scotland, 2009). Dougie will have been suspecting a number of things are wrong with him and his overriding emotional reactions may be fear and denial (NHS Education for Scotland, 2009).

Dougie's medical history

Dougie has been a smoker all his life. He thinks he started smoking when he joined the army. He admits to smoking 30 a day, but Joyce says it is more than this. Both Dougie and Joyce enjoy a drink, but have never felt that drinking dominates their lives. Dougie had no health problems until the age of 66, when he developed arthritis. He experiences pain mostly in his hands, but sometimes it flares up in his knee joints. He has also developed borderline hypertension and is on peridopril 4 mg daily. In tandem with the hypotensive medicine, Dougie takes bendroflurozide 5 mg daily. The only exercise Dougie takes is some walking and a lot of gardening. He loves his garden and spends a few hours a day outside in the garden when not at the caravan. When he is at his caravan, Joyce and he take local walks around the area.

Initial contact from mental health services

Clinical Nurse Specialist Chris McDonald (who is a Supplementary and Independent Nurse Prescriber) made arrangements to visit Dougie at his home in two days' time. He spoke with Joyce, explaining that he would be attending with a colleague, Shirley Menzies, Community Mental Health Nurse. This was routine practice and allowed one nurse to assess the person and the other to interview the carer or relative. This not only gives a better overall picture but helps to overcome any discomfiture that carers can experience when speaking about the person in their presence.

What Joyce understood

Joyce received a telephone call two days after her visit to the GP with Dougie. The caller was a very polite nurse called Chris MacDonald. He spoke slowly and quite loudly, which annoyed Joyce because she was well aware that this is the common way to speak to older people. He was asking if he and a colleague, Shirley, could visit the Collins' house this afternoon. They wanted to come and do an initial assessment of Dougie and interview Joyce. Joyce was eager for Dougie to be seen so she agreed, although she had no idea what 'an initial assessment' was and she was unsure as to why she was being 'interviewed'. Joyce had no idea that she was an integral part of the therapeutic relationship. For health service professionals this relationship is key, because if she does not agree with Dougie's treatment there will not be a concordant relationship between the practitioner, the individual and their significant other. However, this does need to be made clear in order that the 'significant other' does not feel under scrutiny as Joyce clearly did.

Joyce really wanted to ask what time these nurses would come, as she had arranged to meet her daughter Marie at 4:00 p.m. in Glasgow. She desperately needed to talk to Marie, but this visit would have to come first and she would cancel Marie. Anyway, by the time she got the house cleaned and made cakes and biscuits for the nurses she would be too tired to travel into Glasgow. If the nurses saw that the house was a little dusty they might think she was unable to take care of herself, let alone her husband. She didn't know whether to tell Dougie now or later. He was happy in the garden – if she told him now she would upset him. Yet if she sprang the visit on him he might fly into a rage and then these polite nurses would think he truly was crazy. What should she do?

She phoned Marie and cried as she explained she could not meet her today and that the nurses were coming sometime this afternoon to do an 'initiation'. Marie tried to reassure her – she told her to tell Dougie now and let him get himself prepared. Marie, as a doctor, understood that this 'initiation' probably meant an initial assessment and she told her mum this just meant 'first meeting'. Yet as a daughter Marie was scared. If her dad had dementia and her mum could not cope, what would their future hold? What could she do? She had a busy job and was a mum herself. She lived 60 miles away.

What Dougie understood

Joyce came to see him in the garden. She looked a little anxious and she told Dougie that two nurses were coming to see them that afternoon. She said that one would assess Dougie and the other one wanted to interview her. Dougie remembered the GP saying that he would be seen at a memory clinic; he had no idea that people were coming to his house. Did they think he was worse than they had first thought? He chose not to drive, but they were still able to get buses. What were they going to ask him? He knew he was a bit muddled at times, but interviewing Joyce as well? Why? Had she said something? Was she telling them things that made him look bad? What happened if he failed the assessment? Would they take him away and put him in a home? He would have to get cleaned up and look the part if he had to convince them he was alright. His morning in the garden was clearly over and he resented the fact that people were coming to see how he lived. This was Joyce's doing – it had to be. Dougie's gender, background and culture meant that it was difficult for him to discuss his feelings openly. Men 'sorted themselves out'. This type of personality can possibly lead people to delay accessing services and provoke a hostile reaction to diagnosis, meaning that engagement and partnership in subsequent treatment and nursing care plans can be problematic (World Health Organization, 2002).

Joyce's history

Joyce is 69. She is slightly overweight and has had Type 2 diabetes from the age of 55, which is well controlled on medicine. She has suffered from recurrent leg ulcers in the past and she thinks each time she gets one they take longer to heal. Joyce is a worrier, by her own definition. She has looked after Dougie all her married life and does all the cooking, cleaning and social arrangements. Joyce looks after Dougie's tablets: she puts his tablets out every meal time, orders repeat prescriptions when necessary and arranges when Dougie needs to see the GP for a check-up. Joyce has always dealt with the family and business finances and made all the important decisions in the lives of her children during their childhood and early adulthood. She has longed for Dougie to give up his taxi business for many years, their children had done well and were now independent and she wanted to start enjoying life. She was delighted when Dougie did retire and was excited about their new 'free' life when they bought the caravan in Ayr. Recently Dougie had been acting strangely. He seemed worried and had bad nightmares, sometimes getting up and walking about. She had slept in the spare room for the last few weeks. She missed him. She also worried about his actions: just a few days ago he had gone to the local shops and came back in a panic that he got lost. He now had stopped driving. He had told her he 'wasn't feeling up to it'. How would they be able to check on the caravan? She could not drive.

Dougie's recent behaviour has scared her. She had an uncle who had dementia and she was terrified that this is the way Dougie was going. She felt sad, angry and most of all she felt robbed. Sad that a fine man such as Dougie, without an enemy to his name, should be doing things that were so embarrassing and childish, angry that Dougie did not seem to be taking her concerns seriously and that she might be robbed of the man she married and of the dreams they had had for a long and happy old age together. Dougie and she used to talk a lot about their retirement plans and the hopes and dreams they had for their old age and their grandchildren. Now all they seemed to be doing was fighting – she wanted him to see that he was not himself at the moment. It might be nothing, but if he did not get help how would he know, and of course – how would she know what she was up against?

Joyce will see her once active and happy social life slipping away. She too is approaching her seventies and she could easily be looking into a future of caring for a demanding partner, whose behaviour is beginning to make her feel alienated and alone. As a woman and a wife it is more likely that she will be the principle caregiver and may also have less social support to perform this function, leading to a negative impact on her mental wellbeing (World Health Organization, 2002).

The therapeutic alliance

At this stage, without knowing, the CNS Chris had caused much anxiety in the Collins' house. If he had asked to speak to Dougie after telling Joyce that he was visiting he would have saved Dougie the feeling that his wife was 'joining forces' with the health professionals. He could also have tried to give some idea of the time he would be visiting. The therapeutic relationship starts before the first meeting; it starts at the first point of contact. Chris could also have reassured Joyce that this was just an informal visit and that they would come after lunch (so they would not be hungry). He could also have put her mind at rest and said that some people found meetings in the home stressful and that she was not to worry. Dougie and Joyce have been married for 41 years and whilst treating the individual is at the heart of person-centred care, the context, coping strategies, significant people and support systems of every individual have to be taken into account. People do feel judged when a stranger enters their home. This is a heightened feeling when that stranger happens to be assessing one family member's cognitive abilities. Accepting help at such a difficult time makes one feel vulnerable; therefore to cope with this an individual wants to put on a good front.

The National Audit Office (2008) highlighted that fear of dementia was the most significant barrier to gaining diagnosis. Dougie had already asked the GP if he was 'losing his marbles', which showed his fear of a diagnosis of dementia. For some people the direct confirmation of a diagnosis of dementia makes it real, whereas they may believe that if it is not diagnosed then they do not have it. For many people a diagnosis of dementia conjures up awful images of highly dependent people who have lost all their dignity, worth and humanity. Hope is not often a word used in conjunction with dementia in the media; more often than not they discuss dementia as a debilitating, dreadful disease in which there is no hope. There are few images of people living well with dementia in the public domain. It is therefore not surprising that people who suspect they have dementia go through a number of experiences before they move towards a diagnosis. Dougie may have passed through the initial awareness stage several months ago and is now between the suspecting and covering-up phases (Keady and Gilliard, 2001). As a nurse working with Dougie, Chris's aims should be concerned with helping Dougie towards the revealing phase in a manner which is supportive, amplifies Dougie and Joyce's strengths and holds on to hope for their future when the couple may believe there is none.

In addition, neither Dougie nor Joyce knows why Chris is coming to the house. The word 'assessment' has made Joyce concerned and she is already changing her behaviour in light of her belief that she will be scrutinised and found wanting. Informed consent to the visit has also not been achieved, again due to the lack of information provided both at the GP surgery and by Chris. Cheston and Bender (2003) assert that the initial contact and the assessment process should be the first step in a long-term collaborative relationship and that due to the nature of cognitive testing and baseline assessment the therapeutic relationship is threatened by an ongoing and repeated exposure and confirmation of the person's cognitive deficits. The first contact by a community mental health nurse is characterised by information gathering and cognitive testing, when it could be argued that Chris's first visit should be concerned with establishing a trusting relationship, answering the questions of the person and their carer and gaining an understanding of what the person wants from engagement with services.

Reflective exercise

(a) Consider how you make first contact with people from your service.
(b) Are there any barriers or challenges service users may face by your approach?
(c) Are you confident that you lay positive foundations for the therapeutic alliance through that first contact?
(d) What would you have done differently for Dougie and Joyce?

Scenario 2: Murdo

Murdo McLeod was born in Glasgow in 1950, the youngest son of Frank and Jean. He had three brothers and two sisters. A third sister had died in early childhood. The family were very close and as he grew up he was particularly proud of his oldest brother Frankie, who was a talented sportsman and musician. Murdo had always been more reserved than the rest of the family, but like the rest of the family Frankie always looked out for their youngest member and ensured he was included in everything.

Murdo was a thoughtful boy who often appeared lost in his own world. He got on reasonably well at school because he always applied himself as needed. On his 13th birthday he got a bike from his parents, and spent much of his late childhood spare time cycling and exploring the local hills, and was often teased by his brothers and sisters for disappearing off on his bike from dawn to dusk. Often he would be gone for hours, happy with his own company and the mountains.

At 15 Murdo left school. He had done reasonably well and could have continued his education, but preferred to leave and earn his independence. He went to work for the local council and stayed with them all his working life, finding his niche in the parks and gardens department. He was a loyal and trustworthy employee, always punctual, and over the years became increasingly valued locally as he took great pride in his work, making a notable job of floral displays and park maintenance. Where others would rush jobs to finish early, Murdo would ensure plants were tended properly, grass cut neatly, and any preparation work was taken care of. He was popular with his workmates, although they teased him for his dependability and some of them took advantage of his nature by leaving their own work undone, knowing that Murdo would feel obliged to do it.

Murdo met Mary in 1974 at a local gig. His brother Frankie's band was supporting the headline act and he had got free tickets for Murdo and a friend. Mary was very impressed that Murdo knew the band, especially as he seemed such a quiet soul. She was even more impressed that he was not drunk like everyone else, and did not seem to be anything other than what he said he was. She thought he was incredibly shy, but then so was she. They married a year later.

Life was good for the McLeods. They had a nice council house close to Murdo's work and had two healthy children soon after they were married, a boy (Michael) and a girl (Frances). Mary did most of the parenting as Murdo worked extra hours to pay for everything, but he loved his children and they loved him. He was a strict parent, as his parents had been, but the children were largely well behaved, so there was rarely any cause to exercise any discipline. They did well at school and the family was happy.

In 1990 Murdo's father was diagnosed with lung cancer. Despite being hounded by Jean to go and get his worsening cough looked at, Frank had left it a long time before contacting the GP, and so by the time he came to the attention of the specialist the cancer had spread out of control. Murdo took this news very badly. He and his father had always been close, but never demonstrative, so Murdo never felt that he knew what to say.

Reflective exercise

Can you think of any reasons why Murdo may find it particularly difficult to grieve the death of his father?

Frank died surrounded by family, and Murdo subsequently became very withdrawn. He found it difficult to concentrate, and became unusually irritable with Mary when she asked him to tend to jobs around the house that he normally did as a matter of routine.

After about six months things gradually returned to normal. Over the next few years the children did very well at school and Michael became a lawyer in a local firm. Frances later finished her MBA and went to work for a university in America. After the children became independent Murdo took redundancy from his council job at the earliest opportunity. Local cuts to budgets made the work increasingly difficult to do properly. He and Mary moved up to the Highlands as they had always promised themselves, and enjoyed a peaceful couple of years. He joined a local golf club and began to enjoy a slower pace of life.

Murdo became bored with the endless recreation, and with a like-minded colleague from golf used the remainder of his redundancy money to set up in business as a landscape gardener. There was plenty of work and the business flourished. Mary meanwhile had been working towards her Open University degree in history. She now has a part time job at the local library and is something of an expert at tracing family trees. Her maiden name was Campbell, and between her ancestors and that of the McLeods she has turned up some fascinating leads. She carries out similar searches for friends and is something of a local celebrity in this regard.

Unfortunately, Murdo's mother died a year ago. His reaction was very similar to when his dad died, but this time he does not seem able to get back to normal despite the passage of time. Murdo said to Mary one night that he was not 'able to get back to living at all'.

Reflective exercise

Why is it significant that Murdo does not seem to be getting back to normal one year after his mother's death?

Although he continues to work his concentration remains poor, his temper is unusually frayed and he has not slept properly in over a year. Recently things have deteriorated further. His appetite seems to have gone and his workmates have noticed a marked deterioration in his work. Usually a source of pride, the work seems tiresome and a chore. He turns down work he would normally have enjoyed. He shows no interest in his younger colleagues, who he has normally kept a close eye on in order to pass on hints and tips where appropriate. The business is now being carried heavily by his partner and standards are dropping. Mary and the children eventually persuade him to see his GP.

Dr Robertson saw Murdo at the surgery the following week. They did not know each other, as Murdo had not been to the GP since his move. He never smoked and rarely drank alcohol. The last time he had seen a GP was when Frances had appendicitis nine years ago. Within the visit Murdo was polite and answered the questions asked of him, but Mary embellished the answers where appropriate, as Murdo's minimalist answers did not appear to be conveying the whole picture as she saw it. Dr Robertson checked his recent medical history, ordered some blood tests and asked whether Murdo got any pleasure out of anything anymore. Murdo responded that he did not, and could not remember when he last had.

Dr Robertson said he suspected that Murdo might be depressed, but he would like to wait for the return of the physical tests. However, given his excellent general health he thought these would be within the normal range and so asked Murdo and Mary if they would be willing to see one of the other specialists in the clinic. Her name is Helen, a community mental health nurse with prescribing authority. Dr Robertson said that if it was okay with them he would go ahead and arrange an appointment for them. If the results turned up anything untoward then he would see them again; otherwise Helen would be the primary contact for now. Murdo and Mary agreed, apparently pleased to be physically OK and to have a plan of action. As predicted, routine blood results were within the normal range, so they attended the clinic the following week to meet Helen. Helen is a CPN working in a community mental health team (CMHT). She has prescribing authority, having been a nurse independent and supplementary prescriber for some years and offers the people who are referred to her appointments in the GP surgery, in addition to home visits. Although the CMHT is small, each member has different areas of responsibility, and Helen, who works both with adult acute presentations and severe and enduring problems, works closely with Catherine, a mental health support worker, and a visiting psychiatrist who visits twice a month.

Although they may work together for some time, Helen recognised that for Murdo and Mary to get the most of the contact with the service and for them to work together in a recovery-focused way it was essential to form a therapeutic alliance. This was based on her experience with similar service users and also Helen's familiarity with the notion of nursing being a process in which human beings are free and are expected to be involved in their own care and in decisions involving them (Paterson and Zderad, 1988). Helen appreciated that the first assessment appointment would be characterised by a formal assessment which would feed into ongoing assessment, and that it was a necessary step towards helping Murdo and Mary engage with the service. Likewise, Helen was also aware that for recovery-orientated practice to take place in her sessions with Murdo and Mary she needed to offer different elements to reduce symptoms and not rely on medication alone (Fisher, 2003).

Scenario 3: Susan

Susan MacPherson was born in Dumfries into a middle class family, the third of three children. Her mother is a vet and her father is a land-owning farmer. She was not particularly close to her two brothers whilst growing up: as well as being a few years older than her they liked nothing better than getting involved in work around the farm, which was not really of interest to Susan. Susan was a rather solitary child, who liked nothing better than immersing herself in her own world, which involved mainly drawing and painting, as well as reading. Susan enjoyed school and did make a couple of friends, but contact out of school was rather difficult given the rural nature of the farm. Susan was very able academically, but art remained her passion. Her parents were supportive of her art as a hobby, but were very clear that this was not a reasonable choice to make in terms of a career as 'there is no money in art and it will not be likely to lead to a job'. Susan tried to make them see that her art could be more than just a hobby. After quite some time her father suggested that she spend some time shadowing her Uncle Peter, who was a noted architect in the area, because architecture involves drawing but is also a 'real job'. She complained to her mother that she did not like this time spent with her uncle, but her mother suggests she should not become manipulative about this as everyone was trying to help.

Reflective exercise
Consider why Susan's mum might describe her as being manipulative.

Susan succeeded in achieving the grades at school to gain access to university to study architecture in Edinburgh and her family were very proud of her. Initially she was happy to be away from home for the first time, living in student accommodation with a group of people her own age, and she felt free. However, she very quickly realised that studying architecture was the wrong choice for her and that art was where her heart lay. But how could she tell her parents when she knew what their reaction would be? Susan became increasingly unhappy and decided that she had to tell them, which she did during the Easter break. They were appalled. They told her that she must continue with her course or they would not support her financially.

Towards the end of first year at university her attendance at classes became erratic, and when she did turn up she appeared unkempt and somewhat rambling in her conversation. She isolated herself from her friends and when she did meet up with them they found her conversation to be 'strange.' She did not turn up for her first exam and her friend Kate looked for her and found her hiding under her bed. Susan told Kate that she was scared she would come to harm. Kate alerted Student Services and they arranged for her to be assessed by mental health services. It was recommended that she be admitted to the local psychiatric hospital for further assessment – Susan was not agreeable to this and therefore she was compulsorily detained. During her stay in hospital she was found to be hearing voices and to be suspicious, particularly of male staff and male patients. She was prescribed olanzapine to which she responded well and was discharged. She felt very embarrassed by this experience and just wanted to put it behind her, as did her parents. She resumed studying architecture – she felt she had no choice. She experienced stigma issues from her fellow students who were fully aware of her history. This led her to become socially isolated from her peers, although Kate persevered in her attempts to maintain their friendship. In addition, she had considerable weight gain and felt that she had let herself go. She stopped taking the olanzapine. She was in despair and eventually stopped attending classes altogether.

She was compulsorily admitted to hospital for a second time with a similar presentation to the first occasion. She was again treated with olanzapine and had a good response. Susan, as well as feeling embarrassed by this second episode and admission to hospital, was also feeling really upset that she had been given a diagnosis of schizophrenia.

Reflective exercise

(a) Consider why Susan might be feeling embarrassed being admitted to hospital again.

(b) Consider why Susan might be feeling upset that she has been given a diagnosis of schizophrenia.

In preparing for discharge the staff felt that it was really important that she continue to comply with taking olanzapine – after all, it was clearly working for her – and had suggested that if she had remained compliant that maybe this second episode could have been avoided, a view shared by her parents. The ward staff have referred Susan to Yvonne, a community mental health nurse, advising Yvonne of her history, her excellent response to olanzapine in that she is now symptom-free, has been non-compliant in the past and does not accept her diagnosis of schizophrenia.

Yvonne arranges to meet Susan on the ward – hoping to start trying to engage with Susan prior to discharge. Susan is initially very quiet and appears reluctant to spend time with Yvonne. Susan says that no-one has listened to her so far, so she does not expect Yvonne to be any different. Yvonne acknowledges Susan's lack of faith in mental health services and asks Susan to give her the opportunity to listen and try and make a difference. Yvonne understands that engagement has to be actively worked at to achieve and can take some time and therefore she does not take this personally. Rather, she explains that she would like to be able to spend some time with Susan to help them get to know each other and that she is very open to how that contact should be. After a tentative start they discover that they share a real interest in reading, and although Yvonne is not artistically talented she also enjoys art. Yvonne is aware that this focus on engagement is really necessary to help in the achievement of a strong therapeutic alliance, upon which their work together will be built. Susan picks up on Yvonne's genuine interest in her and her obvious enjoyment and commitment to her role as a nurse. This really helps Susan 'warm' to Yvonne and she starts to look forward to their contact. Susan is discharged from hospital and is happy to agree to ongoing contact with Yvonne.

CHAPTER 4

Assessment through partnership

Abstract

The therapeutic alliance acknowledges the scientific and clinical expertise of the mental health worker and the service user's knowledge of their subjective experiences. In facilitating decision-making the practitioner should promote open discussion to enhance understanding of attitudes and values. Useful techniques to promote collaboration and assessment through partnership are illustrated in relation to the unfolding scenarios. The recovery journey can include periods of relapse and it is important that as much learning as possible is derived from these experiences.

Key points

■ The process of collaboration in an active therapeutic alliance helps to promote mental wellbeing.

■ Although each person's decision making with regard to medicines is individual, decision-making patterns tend to fall into particular types.

■ Assessment tools and forms used by mental health workers as useful aids can be misinterpreted by service users and need to be implemented with awareness and sensitivity.

■ Concordance working relies on the service user and mental health worker keeping in step and keeping pace with each other.

■ Assessment is ongoing.

Key words

Assessment, partnership, strengths-based approaches, stress vulnerability model

Objectives

■ Outline how the stress vulnerability model can be applied to gain an understanding of the recovery journey.

- Develop awareness of typical forms of medicine-taking decision making.
- Illustrate the use of some useful assessment tools and frameworks.

Introduction

The stress vulnerability model (Zubin and Spring, 1977), which is increasingly influencing practice, contends that, although underlying genetic, biological or biochemical and psychological factors produce varying degrees of vulnerability, episodes of illness are triggered when stressors overwhelm people's coping. This therefore acknowledges that aetiology is multi-factorial and that interventions should have several facets. There are a number of functions of the assessment process, including: to facilitate a diagnosis; to establish a baseline of abilities and needs from which care can be planned; to educate the person and their carers about treatments and services available; and to inform the potential multi-agency team of the person's needs (Craddock *et al.*, 2008). It is vital to understand the situation from the service user's and carer's point of view. Working collaboratively can evoke anxiety in service users and anxiety may also be evoked in the mental health worker who may prefer not to risk stirring up strong emotions. Avoidance, stemming ultimately from a desire to protect by the mental health worker, may masquerade as protection of the service user.

A variety of techniques to probe and reframe events significant to the person can be used. Paul and Elder (2006) explain the use of Socratic questioning as a key tactic in the area of critical thinking. Brown *et al.* (2009), speaking from an occupational therapy perspective, see Socratic questioning as a method of asking objective, critical questions to effectively enlarge the boundaries of knowledge. These authors point out that the probing and open-ended nature of this form of questioning helps to lead their profession into the postmodernist era, and it is in this paradigm that concordance, with its person-centred focus, is positioned. The open-ended nature of Socratic questioning is also an area which Clarke (2011) feels is important since it often leads to 'unpredictable and/or surprising conclusions' (p. 275). Clarke maintains that Socrates was less concerned with definitive answers than the process of discovery. This fits comfortably with the concept of concordance, which reacts against the paternalistic and directive nature of the biomedical model by seeking to place the person at the heart of their own medicine/treatment decision-making.

Where decisional conflict exists, an aid such as the Ottawa Personal Decision Guide (O'Connor *et al.*, 2010) or Common Ground (Deegan *et al.*, 2008) is useful. Competencies (Schinkel and Dorrer, 2006) such as active listening, a belief in and encouragement of change, a clear focus on the individual (not their illness), empathy and understanding should be demonstrated. This collaboration will provide enhanced clarity with respect to the meaning which medicine-taking/ treatment holds for the individual, and an understanding of how this in turn relates to the person's identity.

Collaborative decision making is linked to a reduction in symptoms, and when implemented well demonstrates and upholds choice, self-determination and empowerment (Clarke *et al.*, 2009) and a reduction in perceived stressors (Jackson, 1983). Collaboration encourages self-awareness, allowing the individual the opportunity to act more consciously: choosing to act, rather than feeling 'acted upon' (Burnard, 2002). Increased self-awareness is also linked to an enhanced ability to cope, with improved awareness of limitations (Jack and Smith, 2007).

The skilled art of allowing the individual the opportunity to talk through their experience without judging, interrupting or making assumptions also requires that the practitioner demonstrate self-awareness (of their role and code of practice). This will be discussed in detail in Chapter 6, as there is evidence that nurses are not as good at this as they think they are (Latter *et al.*, 2010). However, even allowing for this, there is benefit to using reflection during discussions, as this can validate what the person is saying giving the sense that their feelings have been recognised and they are valued (Starwards, 2010). Feeling valued has been claimed to reduce relapse risk (Hickie, 2002).

A strengths-based approach assists practitioners in facilitating concordance through discussion of the service user's skills and capabilities. Some strengths are common to the majority of people: for example, the ability to determine aspirations (Weick and Pope, 1988), or the fact that we are experts by experience (Faulkner, 1988). This helps move beyond viewing people as a collection of symptoms and deficits (Repper and Perkins, 2003). Empowering processes increase self-esteem and self-awareness which are core to recovery (Repper and Perkins, 2003) and central in developing resilience (Kuyken *et al.*, 2009). It is therefore useful for both the service user and mental health worker in collaboration to explore patterns of coping and vulnerability to stressors (Ford, 2000). This exploration relies on the mental health worker having a gentle, sensitive outlook and willingness to patiently keep step with the service user and not insensitively force the pace. This is particularly important when the service user uses denial as a conscious or unconscious coping mechanism (Marland and Cash, 2005). It is useful to consider the type of medicine-taking decision making which the service user tends to rely on (Figure 4.1). They describe three different types, with the third consisting of two further subtypes:

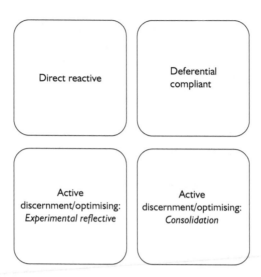

Figure 4.1 Medicine-taking typology (Marland and Cash, 2005).

1. *Deferential compliant type*: in which the service user leaves all medicine-taking decisions to the prescriber and complies even in the absence of insight. This type of decision making leaves the person particularly at risk of side-effects as they defer all medicine-taking decisions and continue to take medicines even when they experience side-effects. This illustrates the point that compliance itself does not represent an ideal end point. When working towards concordance the mental health worker needs to be particularly vigilant and diligent in side-effect monitoring. It is also significant that some service users will comply with their medicine regime even when in the absence of insight they do not believe themselves to be ill.

2. *Direct reactive type*: in which the service user denies the need for medicines and ceases to take medicine when well to assert wellness, or in reaction to side-effects or stigma.

3. *Active discernment and optimising type* (ADOT) in which the service user develops an ability to reflect on past experiences and discern a relapse signature. This type is divided into two stages:

   (i) *Experimental-reflective* stage: perhaps most readily identified with concordance working, as the service user deliberately and actively experiments to achieve the optimum medicine regime. This can be carried out unilaterally or in concordance with the prescriber. It may involve 'shaping', which is reducing the medicine taken to see if beneficial effects can be maintained and side-effects reduced, and 'recovery testing', which is ceasing to take medicines to prove or disprove their need.

(ii) *Consolidation* stage: the service user has found an effective way of using medicines and is reluctant to consider any changes.

The important point is that people have different behaviour and attitudes to medicine taking. As a consequence, there is unlikely to be any generalisable intervention that would improve medicine management. This could go some way to explaining the failure of global strategies tailored to this end (Snowden, 2008a).

We will now further explore the unfolding scenarios keeping in mind all the principles we have discussed so far. In short, we need to integrate the knowledge we have discussed in Chapter 2 in relation to the individuals we got to know in Chapter 3. We need to organise this information to the end of developing a therapeutic relationship as discussed in this chapter. This is the first stage of a concordant assessment process.

Scenario 1: Dougie

In early dementia the assessment priority may be to assess suitability for and commence memory-enhancing medicine. It is to be remembered, however, that the assessment stage is a key milestone, not only for the therapeutic alliance but for Dougie starting to work through the psychological tasks around his experience of dementia (Weaks *et al.*, 2009). Mountain (2008) asserts that once the purpose of the assessment has been agreed, a structured format or framework should be followed to ensure the completeness of the process. Part of gaining the agreement is to elicit the person's understanding of the need for the assessment and how it has come about and then agreeing how the assessment should progress.

The therapeutic alliance

A therapeutic working relationship between a practitioner and a service user involves not only knowing the history of the individual presenting, but knowing something of the significant person in their lives. A couple like Dougie and Joyce have been together for 41 years and they have unspoken agreements (and disagreements) about how they live and how they operate. Dougie's memory problem will have a significant impact on Joyce's life. In fact it already has had an impact on Joyce's life. She was the one who had to fight to get him to go to the GP and the one who had told the GP 'something had to be done', which was a clear indication that she was struggling to cope.

Taking the meaning of concordance from Chapter 1 as a way of *working together with people which extends beyond medicine taking*, this case illustrates the need to form a therapeutic alliance with this couple. Illness can alienate people from one another and the unhappiness this causes can be blamed upon the illness interfering in a close relationship, whereas it is sometimes also the treatment of the illness that may exclude a significant other from a patient/professional relationship.

Assessment of Dougie

Prior to arriving at Dougie and Joyce's house, Chris visited the GP surgery and checked Dougie's notes for a medical history and to check his most recent blood results. He was looking for possible indicators of treatable causes of impaired cognitive functioning, e.g. anaemia, poorly controlled diabetes and reduced thyroxine levels. He also wanted to check whether Dougie had any known allergic reactions noted.

Chris arrived at 2:30 p.m. accompanied by his colleague Shirley. They introduced themselves and described how they planned to proceed. Chris settled down to assess Dougie in the living room and Shirley went through to the kitchen with Dougie's wife. The two nurses planned to base their assessment on subjective and objective information gathered. Chris saw that Dougie was anxious and started by asking Dougie what he enjoyed doing. At first Dougie was quite resistive to questions, but Chris did put him at ease and they talked about Dougie's garden for a while. Chris then said that he wanted to ask Dougie some questions to check his memory and he carried out the objective testing of Dougie's cognitive functioning using the DemTect (Kalbe *et al.*, 2004; see Table 4.1) and the Mini Mental State Examination (MMSE) (Folstein *et al.*, 1975; see Table 4.1).

The results obtained were indicative of a dementia: the DemTect result was 6/18 and the MMSE 24/30. Structured initial assessment by nurses and Allied Health Professionals in a memory assessment service has been shown to be as accurate in determining a diagnosis as formal consultant-led diagnosis (Page *et al.*, 2011). There was no evidence that Dougie was depressed – he was engaging and seemed to respond well to Chris. Depression can cause cognitive impairment and therefore be mistaken for dementia; either subjectively (see Table 4.1) or objectively e.g. Patient Health Questionnaire (PHQ-9) (Kroenke *et al.*, 2001). Depression for someone with dementia can cause a significant negative impact on quality of life for the person with dementia and family carers (Appleby, 2007). Also, there is some evidence to suggest that depression can present as an early indicator of the onset of a dementia and even predispose to its onset (Even and Weintraub, 2010; Rapp *et al.*, 2010); see Table 4.1.

Table 4.1 Depression and dementia onset signs and symptoms.

Some signs of depression	Some signs of dementia (onset)
Loss of/reduced pleasure in activities	Difficulty retaining and recalling new
Problems with retaining and recalling new	information
information	Reduced concentration
Reduced concentration	Disturbance of mood – depression,
Reduced self-care	euphoria, emotional lability
Loss of interest in maintaining standard of	Anxiety
cleanliness and order around the home	Irritability
Altered appetite, e.g. reduced or	Fatigue
increased	Loss of spontaneity
Forgetting anniversaries and birthdays	Becoming socially withdrawn
Changes in consumption of alcohol or	Loss of functional abilities, e.g. cleaning,
cigarettes	cooking, shopping, self-care becoming
Forgetting to take medicine	difficult
Lability of mood	Altered appetite
Irritability	Changes in consumption of alcohol or
Anxiety	cigarettes
Fatigue/moving more slowly	Disorientation in time, place and/or
Sleep disturbance	person
Becoming socially withdrawn	Loss of confidence/indecisive
Wishing they were dead	Missing appointments
Significant change in routine	Forgetting to take medicine
	Forgetting anniversaries and birthdays

Chris | Dougie

Chris observed that Dougie looked pale. Dougie stated that he was tired and had had enough. As Shirley and Joyce were still in the kitchen, he decided to just chat to Dougie. He soon discovered that Dougie loved cars, so Chris asked Dougie his thoughts on what constituted a 'good car'. Chris was aware to give something of himself to Dougie and told him of a problem he had recently had with his car. During this conversation he found out that Dougie missed driving. He had decided not to drive at the moment. Even if he did drive, Joyce refused to be a passenger. Such informal chats can frequently highlight what an illness means to a person and although Chris wanted to ask more, he knew it was time to stop asking questions.

Assessment of Joyce

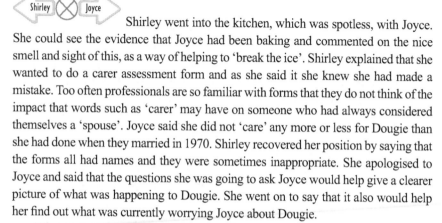

Shirley went into the kitchen, which was spotless, with Joyce. She could see the evidence that Joyce had been baking and commented on the nice smell and sight of this, as a way of helping to 'break the ice'. Shirley explained that she wanted to do a carer assessment form and as she said it she knew she had made a mistake. Too often professionals are so familiar with forms that they do not think of the impact that words such as 'carer' may have on someone who had always considered themselves a 'spouse'. Joyce said she did not 'care' any more or less for Dougie than she had done when they married in 1970. Shirley recovered her position by saying that the forms all had names and they were sometimes inappropriate. She apologised to Joyce and said that the questions she was going to ask Joyce would help give a clearer picture of what was happening to Dougie. She went on to say that it also would help her find out what was currently worrying Joyce about Dougie.

When Joyce had finished answering the questions, she burst into tears. The questions that stuck out in her mind were whether Dougie 'recognised his partner' and all the bits about guardianship and risks and benefits. She and Dougie had been such a good team. Is this what they had to face now? Shirley tried to reassure her by saying that the form helped her to get a better picture, but Joyce felt angry – what picture did this woman want? Could she not see that there were problems? Of course there were, but she and Dougie weren't at that stage yet. It was the 'yet' that she found so upsetting. Shirley again tried to recover her position by remarking on the lovely smell of baking. Joyce too recovered her position and started to put a tea tray together, asking Shirley if they could join Chris and Dougie. Joyce was pleased to see Dougie chatting to Chris about cars and initially she felt better, until she realised that he was tired and doing his best to put on a good show.

Chris took the lead in the conversation that followed. The assessments completed, Chris explained the results and their possible indications. He also described the options available for referral to a consultant psychiatrist and, following further assessment, possible diagnosis. It was explained that this may result in his being considered for treatment with a 'cognitive enhancer'. What these are and how they work was explained at a level they found understandable. It was emphasised that they were not a cure, they were not suitable for everyone, they did not work for everyone and that the prescription was determined by the cause of the memory problems and the degree of impairment. Dougie was also advised of additional tests that would be carried out prior to his attending the consultant, i.e. the screening of bloods and a CT (computerised tomography) scan (Scottish Intercollegiate Guideline Network, 2006).

For Dougie and Joyce there were still a number of unanswered concerns. Dougie is not sure whether he wants to know that he definitely has dementia or Alzheimer's disease; what is the difference anyway? Chris asked about his driving but did not say whether he should or should not be driving. Dougie would love to be able to nip up to the caravan and get some jobs done. He is also not sure about Chris and had wanted to ask him questions, but as Chris had asked him so many Dougie had felt too tired to ask his own questions.

Dougie felt down and lost both with the uncertainty of the situation and his unanswered questions, and Chris had then gone on to talk about more assessment and medicine, which he had felt too exhausted to listen to. He had had enough – he was overwhelmed by what he thought was going to be his life and how it felt like it was all happening to him, not with him.

Chris had a difficult job to do that day. He knew that commencement on cognitive enhancers might significantly improve or maintain Dougie and Joyce's current life and that was his priority. As he and Shirley left the house they both had the feeling that they had become out of step with Dougie and Joyce. Chris was concerned particularly that he had left Dougie more upset than he had found him. He wondered if he could have focused upon the strengths that the couple had and discussed how these could be strengthened and utilised to help them through this diagnosis stage of their journey. Chris realised that he had not explored Dougie's wish to drive in enough detail and understood that for Dougie this issue was as much about his identity as it was about his practical needs. He had felt he had tried to give too much information and had maybe not given them the information they wanted. He felt he knew that the couple had not heard him when he was talking about cognitive enhancers and seeing the psychiatrist. When he heard Shirley's account of her assessment of Joyce, he realised that the two of them had actually put a strain on the already anxious couple.

Chris had been concerned for a while about the impact of dual first visits and the precedence that cognitive testing had taken when he felt the needs of the service users were not fully addressed. Chris decided to take these issues to supervision with the nurse consultant, James White.

Reflective exercise

(a) What does your assessment process look like?
(b) Do you ask for and get feedback on your assessment process to inform development of your practice?
(c) How 'strengths based' is your assessment?

Chris is right to be concerned: working with older people adds complexity to concordance in medicine-taking and the therapeutic relationship, which for many older people can be the difference between life and death.

Older people are seen as 'at risk' where medicine taking is concerned due to factors which go beyond concordance. Their physical health status can change rapidly, leading to changes in how the body processes medicines, they are more susceptible to adverse medicine reactions, and they may have multiple and complex long-term health conditions for which treatments may increase the risk of medicine interactions. In addition, the older person may deteriorate more rapidly due to ageing when long-term physical health conditions are not treated with appropriate medicine regimes and they may have an increased rate of unplanned hospital admissions due to adverse medicine reactions, including the development of delirium states (Banning, 2007). Due to these risks, the need for Dougie and Joyce to have someone they feel they can and should 'pick the phone up to' is essential on a minimum of two levels. When Dougie feels able to talk openly about his fear regarding the changes in his memory and thinking ability, it may be a small window of opportunity to support Dougie to reveal his problems and move towards taking on his diagnosis, working beyond and making the best of it (NHS Education for Scotland, 2009).

The therapeutic alliance may be the deciding element as to how Dougie is able to move on as Chris responds to Dougie's individual requests for support and information. In addition to this, Dougie will be more susceptible to iatrogenic complications from his medicines regime, which could be subtle in nature earlier on, but develop to life-threatening conditions quickly if not identified early. The ability of Dougie and Joyce to gain access to appropriate information from Chris, in the presence of trying to describe subtle changes, can only be stimulated by a health professional who has come to know the couple and understand their needs and aspirations, and whom they trust to help when they need it.

When Chris met James for his clinical supervision he outlined his concern about the initial assessment processes. The priority to gain a diagnosis and, when appropriate, commence 'cognitive enhancers', seemed at times to put Chris out of step with the needs of service users. Chris used Dougie as an example of this and discussed with James the need to gain balance and become focused upon the pace of the service user.

James reminded Chris of the need for a framework to guide both the assessment process and the ongoing therapeutic relationship, which would be openly shared and discussed with Dougie and Joyce. Such a framework is encompassed by stages and tasks which, following diagnosis, have been suggested by Weaks *et al.* (2009) as the person with dementia's journey:

- Exploring the possibility of life as normal
- Evaluating the usefulness of different sources of information
- Understanding changing roles and relationships
- Understanding emotional processes
- Addressing deep psychological questions around personal identity
- Facing up to and challenging stigma
- Creating a modified personal and social identity
- Telling and retelling their story
- Finding a way through the health system

This is a significant amount of psychological work and Chris, using the therapeutic alliance and counselling approach, is key to supporting Dougie through this. Weaks *et al.* (2009) assert that central to this work is the opportunity to express emotions about the diagnosis and to maintain or regain a sense of control. Chris decided that he would reframe his approach with the key tasks as a basis for his interventions.

In their study focusing upon the skills of mental health nurses working effectively within a counselling approach that incorporates psychosocial issues in early dementia, Weaks *et al.* (2009) suggest that the following emerged as essential skills for nursing when working with someone in Dougie's situation:

- Self-awareness/reflexivity
- Emotional sensitivity
- Sensitivity to relationships
- A facilitative/enabling way of working with clients
- A framework for practice
- Organisational change skills

It could be argued that the skills outlined are essential for all therapeutic alliance building. These skills however, were seen as additional or developing to staff already working at an experienced/specialised level. What is apparent is that the skills to support someone through the diagnosis and early stage of dementia are similar to those required to foster recovery, and they support the development of a positive relationships based on the process of concordance.

Chris rang and asked Dougie if he could visit again to answer any questions he had not given Dougie the opportunity to ask. Dougie readily agreed, surprised and encouraged that Chris had been honest about needing to give Dougie and Joyce more time.

Chris started his second visit with the question: 'Can you tell me what you would like me to help you with?'.

Reflective exercise

(a) What other questions can you list which set a collaborative tone to your discussion?

(b) What would you ask if a client was unable to articulate their needs or was not clear on what they wanted?

(c) How do you support elements of the psychological tasks and stages in your practice?

The next stage

Chris discussed the assessment process, explaining the possible reasons for people experiencing difficulties with their memory, thinking and ability to function as they were used to. Chris also explained what options there were to address some of the issues, including referral to Dr Armstrong and consideration for treatment with medicine designed to regain and maintain (for a time) cognitive function, i.e. cognitive enhancers. Both Joyce and Dougie were so relieved to hear that there was some kind of treatment for people with dementia. Joyce's recollection of her uncle's experience of having dementia was the grief of the family that 'nothing could be done'.

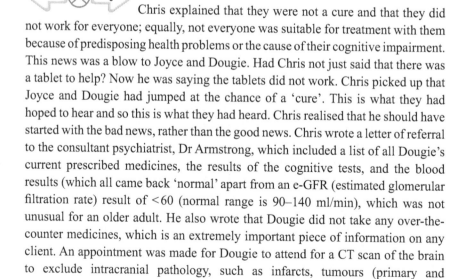

Chris explained that they were not a cure and that they did not work for everyone; equally, not everyone was suitable for treatment with them because of predisposing health problems or the cause of their cognitive impairment. This news was a blow to Joyce and Dougie. Had Chris not just said that there was a tablet to help? Now he was saying the tablets did not work. Chris picked up that Joyce and Dougie had jumped at the chance of a 'cure'. This is what they had hoped to hear and so this is what they had heard. Chris realised that he should have started with the bad news, rather than the good news. Chris wrote a letter of referral to the consultant psychiatrist, Dr Armstrong, which included a list of all Dougie's current prescribed medicines, the results of the cognitive tests, and the blood results (which all came back 'normal' apart from an e-GFR (estimated glomerular filtration rate) result of <60 (normal range is 90–140 ml/min), which was not unusual for an older adult. He also wrote that Dougie did not take any over-the-counter medicines, which is an extremely important piece of information on any client. An appointment was made for Dougie to attend for a CT scan of the brain to exclude intracranial pathology, such as infarcts, tumours (primary and secondary) and establish a more definitive diagnosis. The scan was performed two weeks later and revealed evidence of generalised atrophy and cerebral vascular disease (consistent with a 'mixed dementia'). These results were also sent to Dr Armstrong.

Assessment by the Consultant Psychiatrist

Dougie and Joyce attended Dr Armstrong's clinic approximately eight weeks after Chris and Shirley's assessment. She had seen Chris's assessment and wanted to assess Dougie for herself. Dr Armstrong used the Addenbrooke's Cognitive Examination – Revised (ACE-R) (Mioshi *et al.*, 2005). The score was 80/100 and was indicative of a dementia. This, coupled with the results of the interviews with both Dougie and his wife, the scan and some recent episodes of acute confusion, suggested a gradual onset of dementia over the past few years (although Dougie did not agree). Dr Armstrong, hearing Dougie's disagreement at his suggestion of a two-year onset, summarised the results of the tests and Joyce and Dougie's self reporting, emphasising Dougie's retained strengths and abilities. It was not essential that Dougie was 'made' to understand – such understanding might come over time. At this time, the National Institute for Health and Clinical Excellence (NICE) had not influenced the restriction of the initial prescribing of the 'cognitive enhancers' to someone scoring ≤ 20 on the MMSE, NICE Technology Appraisal Guidance TA217 (2011).

Treatment

Dr Armstrong told Dougie and Joyce of Dougie's diagnosis. They sat quietly, both taking in the enormous implications this had for them. Their future had been shattered. No, they had no questions just yet. No they did not want to go over medicine options at this point; please prescribe what you recommend and we will discuss it with Chris. Dr Armstrong prescribed donepezil 5 mg following a check of Dougie's cardiac function with an electrocardiogram (ECG); acetylcholinesterase inhibitors carry a caution for use when the person has cardiac conduction abnormalities, unstable angina and congestive heart failure (galantamine only lists the last two). It was the local protocol that only a consultant psychiatrist could initiate treatment of acetylcholinesterase inhibitors: they would prescribe for the first 12 weeks, at which point, if all was well, the ongoing prescribing would be undertaken by the GP. Any subsequent reduction could be carried out by the GP or independent nurse prescriber.

Dougie phoned Chris upon their return home. Now he was clear about what he wanted and felt that he and Chris had bonded both as a nurse and as a service user, and also as men, with common interests and other things to talk about when talking about dementia was too much. Chris returned to see Dougie and listened as Dougie raged about the unfairness of it all and his overwhelming sense of loss. Listening was Chris's key response whilst assessing for an indication that the losses were too great and he should ask Dougie about thoughts of suicide. A deeper understanding grew between the men of what the evolving needs for Dougie were and how Chris could respond.

Chris knew he had to be careful. Dougie and Joyce had recently received Dougie's diagnosis. Both Dougie and Joyce were in shock and Chris knew that in order to help, he had to work with the many strengths that this long-married couple already had. To 'take over' would be damaging to the therapeutic relationship he was intent on building. Chris took into account the subjective reporting of Dougie and his wife, who provided a history of the changes that Dougie had and was experiencing and the impact they had had on both of their lives. One example was that Joyce got frustrated when she asked Dougie to do things and he forgot. Chris suggested using sticky notes on the fridge door. Dougie could take note and do the job, so that only the notes left on the fridge door were the jobs still to be done. Chris also emphasised the benefit of putting things (such as keys, and appointments) in one place. Developing practised routines saved much effort in always trying to remember where things were. A further strategy to help Dougie would be for him to have an appointments diary or calendar (Dougie preferred the calendar). They could record who had visited and who they were expecting to visit/hospital appointments/dental appointments/social functions and so on. This would give Dougie a clear idea of what was happening and when.

After four weeks, during which time Chris monitored Dougie for any adverse effects, Dr Armstrong reviewed Dougie (subjective reporting indicated improvement and no adverse effects) and the decision was made to increase the donepezil to 10 mg, the recommended therapeutic dose.

Scenario 2: Murdo
Assessment
When Murdo arrived for his first appointment, Helen, the community mental health nurse, could tell from his demeanour in the waiting area that he was struggling. He did not initially respond when he was called to the consultation room; he was staring at the floor and made no eye contact. Although accompanied by Mary, he was not engaging in conversation with her and appeared oblivious to his surroundings.

Helen had always followed a humanistic approach in her interactions with service users, carers and colleagues. Some of the origins of this philosophy stem from the work of Paterson and Zderad (1988) who describe nursing as involving two human beings (nurse and patient) who are willing to enter into an existential relationship with each other. As Murdo was accompanied through to the consultation area with his wife, Helen began to suspect that there might be some initial challenges to developing the partnership necessary to complete a comprehensive assessment of his health and wellbeing due to the apparent lack of verbal response.

Helen helped Murdo and Mary feel as comfortable as possible to allay any fears and concerns they may have had. She outlined how the first session was going to progress: in other words, she was going to begin the process of assessment in discussion with both Murdo and Mary, and then she would make some decisions with Murdo about how he wanted to proceed. She ascertained that Murdo wanted his wife present and participating; Murdo was very keen for her to be as involved as possible and said he had nothing to hide. In March 2011 (Moore, 2011), the Chief Nursing Officer for Scotland asserted that service users should be at the heart of service delivery. To that effect, Helen made no assumptions about what she thought Murdo's experience had been. Instead, she encouraged him to tell his story and helped him construct a timeline (Ford, 2000). These can span a short term or a long term, and help the person focus on events that may be part of their recovery journey. Table 4.2 shows what Murdo was able to construct with the help of Helen.

Many timelines are more inclusive than this, and would cover more details of the recent history, for instance. However, Murdo had great difficulty with the session and found it challenging talking about his history. Helen thanked him for participating in the exercise and said that they would refer to the contents in subsequent sessions when they would be exploring issues that would be helpful to his recovery.

Through discussion during the hour they were together, Helen was able to gather a detailed picture of Murdo's current situation, and with the help of his wife she was able to fill in the gaps that Murdo left out. It seemed that Mary had first noticed about six weeks previously that Murdo was not eating his meals. He appeared to have lost his appetite. At night, he would fall asleep at the usual time (between 11:30 p.m. and midnight), but he would be wide awake before 3:00 a.m. He started to pace the floor, and eventually spent the remaining night-time

81

Table 4.2 Murdo's timeline.

Year	External events	Changes to thoughts, feeling and behaviours
1950	Born in a busy city, big family. I enjoyed school and my home life was good	I guess I was a confident lad, but wasn't the star pupil, if you know what I mean. I don't understand this – I don't know and can't remember my thoughts and feelings then, it was a long time ago.
1966	Left school and started work	Well, everyone worked then didn't they? It was expected. I just fell into the habit of working hard all week and playing hard at the weekend. I guess people at work liked me, I steadily got promotion and I worked with the same company all my working life.
1974	Met Mary, my wife; married, two children	Well, I don't know. I guess I had to think about more than just me. It was good having the children; I looked on life very differently. People said I was a good father then.
1990	My father died of lung cancer	I took this really hard as dad and I had always been so close. My life just did not seem complete without him.
1996	The children left home to go and study	It didn't really affect me much, I mean, I was always at work, and they had such busy social lives at the weekend that I barely saw them. I think my wife felt it more than me.
2004	Retired from the company. We moved north to live the peaceful life	Everything slowed down; I built up friendships at the golf club, and my wife and I spent more time together. I enjoyed getting the garden sorted, but found myself easily bored.
2009	Working as a landscape gardener; I started two years ago. My mother died	It was good to feel useful again. Mary thought I would be bored being at home and she was right. I had enthusiasm for my work and was playing golf most weekends. Then mum died and everything changed for me.
2010	Working as a gardener – one year on (when going off sick a few weeks ago)	I feel I am not coping. I feel stupid, as if everything I do is wrong. I think that I have no purpose and that people would be better off without me. I can't even decide whether to dig, plant or weed, it's all too much to think about. I can't even think about the golf club, they must all hate me. This just happened, I don't know why. My mum died last year, I just haven't got going since then somehow.

hours in the sitting room so that he did not disturb his wife. He stopped reading his newspapers and did not have the volition to go to the golf club. Murdo then started expressing ideas of worthlessness, and Mary found that reassurance did not help him. This behaviour prompted him to go to his GP at her insistence, who then referred him to the service.

Helen asked Murdo how he felt about what was happening to him, and what he understood of his experience both from reflection and from discussion with Mary and the GP. Murdo was very clear that he felt perplexed. Until he actually saw his GP he had not realised that he was unwell, and that his loss of appetite for instance was a symptom of 'something'. He just thought it was part of being middle-aged. Mary said that she knew straight away he was ill as she had seen this with her brother, who had had a similar episode some years ago. However, she felt that Murdo was not accepting he was ill – she even said 'Murdo has never done the whole illness bit, it isn't in his nature; it must be quite a shock for him'.

Helen recognised that Murdo appeared to be suffering from a depressive episode (Box 4.1) as classified by the DSM-IV criteria (American Psychiatric Association, 2000).

Box 4.1 Major depressive episode (American Psychiatric Association, 2000)

A. Five (or more) of the following symptoms have been present during the same two-week period and represent a change from previous functioning; at least one of the symptoms is either (1) depressed mood or (2) loss of interest or pleasure:

(1) depressed mood most of the day, nearly every day, as indicated by either subjective report (e.g. feels sad or empty) or observation made by others (e.g. appears tearful)
(2) markedly diminished interest or pleasure in all, or almost all, activities most of the day, nearly every day (as indicated by either subjective account or observation made by others)
(3) significant weight loss when not dieting or weight gain (e.g. a change of more than 5% of body weight in a month), or decrease or increase in appetite nearly every day
(4) insomnia or hyper-somnia nearly every day
(5) psychomotor agitation or retardation nearly every day (observable by others, not merely subjective feelings of restlessness or being slowed down)

(6) fatigue or loss of energy nearly every day
(7) feelings of worthlessness or excessive or inappropriate guilt (which may be delusional) nearly every day (not merely self-reproach or guilt about being sick)
(8) diminished ability to think or concentrate, or indecisiveness, nearly every day (either by subjective account or as observed by others)
(9) recurrent thoughts of death (not just fear of dying), recurrent suicidal ideation without a specific plan, or a suicide attempt or a specific plan for committing suicide

Helen was able to gather from the discussion that Murdo had no physiological problems at present that could have been causing this. His mother had died a year ago and in Murdo's words he hadn't quite 'picked up' since then, but this episode reflected ongoing depression rather than an acute bereavement reaction. Murdo was certainly experiencing clinically significant distress and impairment in social and occupational functioning. He did not, however, disclose suicidal ideation, and felt he had protective factors in his life (his wife and friends).

For the last part of the assessment on their first meeting, Helen needed to determine the clinical severity of Murdo's depression, so that she could help Murdo to decide a course of action. She asked Murdo to complete a PHQ-9 (Pfizer Inc., 1999), which is a depression inventory scale. The reason this particular scale was chosen was because of its common usage within the shared care and extended service. There would be continuity if, for example, the GP wanted to measure progress at a later stage. Table 4.3 shows that Murdo scored 22, which suggested a severe episode.

Recommendations

Helen discussed with Murdo and Mary the initial assessment findings. She explained that although Murdo's behaviours met the diagnostic criteria for clinical depression, it was highly likely to respond to a combination of medicine, social and psychosocial interventions as suggested in the NICE guidance 90 (NICE, 2010). When Helen was talking, she got the feeling that both Murdo and Mary were overwhelmed by what she was saying, so she asked them directly if they had anything to add or if they had any questions. Murdo said nothing, but Mary said she thought it was related to the bereavement last year. She also asked what Helen had in mind when she said 'different approaches'. Helen said she would explain.

Table 4.3 Patient Health Questionnaire (PHQ-9), with scoring instructions. Murdo's score is in bold.

NAME: __Murdo__ DATE: today

Over the *last 2 weeks*, how often have you been bothered by any of the following problems?

	Not at all	Several days	+half the days	Nearly every day
1. Little interest or pleasure in doing things	0	1	**2**	3
2. Feeling down, depressed, or hopeless	0	1	2	**3**
3. Trouble falling or staying asleep, or sleeping too much	0	1	2	**3**
4. Feeling tired or having little energy	0	1	2	**3**
5. Poor appetite or overeating	0	1	2	**3**
6. Feeling bad about yourself – or that you are a failure or have let yourself or your family down	0	1	**2**	3
7. Trouble concentrating on things, such as reading the newspaper or watching television	0	1	2	**3**
8. Moving or speaking so slowly that other people could have noticed. Or the opposite – being so fidgety or restless that you have been moving around a lot more than usual	0	1	2	**3**
9. Thoughts that you would be better off dead, or of hurting yourself in some way	**0**	1	2	3

TOTAL: 22

10. If you checked off *any* problems, how *difficult* have these problems made it for you to do your work, take care of things at home, or get along with other people?

Not difficult at all ___ Somewhat difficult ___ Very difficult ___ Extremely difficult _✓_

Table 4.3 (continued)

INSTRUCTIONS FOR USE

PHQ-9 QUICK DEPRESSION ASSESSMENT SCORING TOOL AND INTERPRETATION

For initial diagnosis:

1. Patient completes PHQ-9 Quick Depression Assessment.
2. If there are at least four 3s in the [grey] highlighted section (including Questions #1 and #2), consider a depressive disorder. Add score to determine severity.
3. Consider Major Depressive Disorder – if there are at least five 3s in the [grey] highlighted section (one of which corresponds to Question #1 or #2)

Consider Other Depressive Disorder

– if there are two to four 3s in the [grey] highlighted section (one of which corresponds to Question #1 or #2)

Note: Since the questionnaire relies on patient self-report, all responses should be verified by the clinician and a definitive diagnosis made on clinical grounds, taking into account how well the patient understood the questionnaire, as well as other relevant information from the patient. Diagnoses of Major Depressive Disorder or Other Depressive Disorder also require impairment of social, occupational, or other important areas of functioning (Question #10) and ruling out normal bereavement, a history of a Manic Episode (Bipolar Disorder), and a physical disorder, medicine, or other medicine as the biological cause of the depressive symptoms.

To monitor severity over time for newly diagnosed patients or patients in current treatment for depression:

1. Patients may complete questionnaires at baseline and at regular intervals (e.g. every two weeks) at home and bring them in at their next appointment for scoring or they may complete the questionnaire during each scheduled appointment.
2. Add up ✓s by column. For every ✓: Several days = 1; More than half the days = 2; Nearly every day = 3
3. Add together column scores to get a TOTAL score.
4. Refer to the accompanying PHQ-9 Scoring Card to interpret the TOTAL score.
5. Results may be included in patients' files to assist you in setting up a treatment goal, determining degree of response, as well as guiding treatment intervention.

PHQ-9 SCORING CARD FOR SEVERITY DETERMINATION

Scoring – add up all checked boxes on PHQ-9. For every ✓: Not at all = 0; Several days = 1; More than half the days = 2; Nearly every day = 3

Interpretation of Total Score: Total Score Depression Severity: 1–4 Minimal depression, 5–9 Mild depression, 10–14 Moderate depression, 15–19 Moderately severe depression, 20–27 Severe depression.

They discussed the possibility of antidepressant medicine and as Murdo and Mary had faith in medicines generally Helen suggested that a course of fluoxetine, starting with a 20 mg tablet dose once daily (in the morning), be commenced. This medicine was suggested by Helen for several reasons. Firstly, the local GPs in the area were running an enhanced service for depression. As part of that service, a local care pathway had been developed which was based on the NICE guideline 90 for depression. The NICE guidance recommends alternatives to tricyclic antidepressants because of strong evidence which suggests that there is a reduced likelihood of leaving treatment due to intolerable side-effects. The local pathway recommends fluoxetine or citalopram as first-line medicines of choice for moderate to severe depression. Helen had prescribed both to previous patients, and had found citalopram particularly useful when panic disorder was also present. As Murdo did not appear to have such symptoms, she recommended fluoxetine instead. She explained to Murdo that fluoxetine had fewer side-effects than other medicines, but that it sometimes caused nausea in the first few days.

Murdo initially said he was not sure that tablets were necessary. He went on to explain that when Mary's brother had depression several years ago, he was a 'changed man' when he was put on strong tablets. Helen was able to help Murdo explore his concerns by encouraging reflection and giving honest information. She explained that the SSRI medicines were much newer, had some side-effects, but did not over-sedate like the ones that his brother-in-law had taken years ago. She also helped Murdo and Mary to talk about their fears, and explained that medicine was only one part of the treatment. Over the coming weeks psychosocial interventions would be introduced along with self-help materials.

Helen ⊗ Murdo

As part of the discussion, Helen gave Murdo a patient information leaflet about the medicine. It covered all areas, including when to take it and how long it took to take effect. She also gave two booklets to Murdo and his wife, encouraging them to read them together. One was a handbook on sleep hygiene and one was a simple booklet about depression. Helen acknowledged with them that Murdo was unlikely to have the concentration for a while to read the books in great detail, but she reassured them that things would improve.

At this stage in the session, which was coming to a close, Helen noticed that Murdo had become much quieter and appeared distracted, not concentrating on what was being said. Helen decided to end the session there, and they set a mutually convenient date and time for an appointment the following week.

Reflective exercise

(a) Why do you think Murdo became so distracted at the end of this session?

(b) Do you think the questioning and assessment process in general had anything to do with it?

Assessment – second appointment

Since the previous session, Helen had been in supervision with her mentor. During that session she had reflected that Murdo and Mary had probably been overwhelmed the previous week. He was unwell, with moderate to severe clinical depression, and could easily have felt bombarded by Helen's questions. Helen had decided to start the second session with an opportunity for Murdo and Helen to reflect on the previous week, and on how things had been for them since, so that they had a chance to share with Helen any thoughts or concerns they had about the assessment process, Murdo's condition, and his ongoing treatment.

However, when Murdo and Mary arrived, Helen could see a marked change in Murdo's presentation. He was pacing the floor in the waiting area, appeared restless and agitated, and was unkempt. They went into the room, and Murdo reported that he had not slept all week. He seemed guarded and was reluctant to answer some of Helen's questions. His wife reported that he was questioning her whenever she was on the phone, and seemed to be frightened of going outside. He again denied suicidal ideation.

However, Murdo's condition concerned Helen. She decided to acknowledge that the previous week had been very difficult for both Murdo and Mary and said to them that she was aware it had been a challenge. Mary was able to say that they left that first session feeling drained and overwhelmed. Neither had spoken very much on the short drive home, but as the evening wore on they had started to talk together about what had been discussed. Helen noticed that when Mary was speaking, Murdo was attentive and questioned her a few times in a suspicious manner.

Helen then intervened, using gentle questioning to get a fuller understanding of what Murdo was now experiencing, as it was a marked change from the previous week. She explained to Murdo and Mary that she wanted to ask some of the questions from the team's mental health assessment (discussed in more detail in Chapter 5) to help her make sense of the changes and help the decision-making. The tool had questions such as: was he having difficulty understanding other people's motives and intentions? Was he suspicious?

As a result of Murdo's responses and Mary's input, such as validating Murdo's responses and giving examples of his changed behaviour, Helen began to suspect that he was experiencing some psychotic symptoms – he certainly appeared suspicious. She asked him directly if he was hearing voices; Murdo became agitated and said he was not prepared to answer 'those sorts of questions'. Mary was shocked at this question and asked Helen quite openly what was going on. Helen explained very carefully that some people with depression experience symptoms such as paranoia and auditory hallucinations. She told Mary and Murdo that she believed he was having some uncomfortable feelings, and that in her experience a second medicine introduced at this stage would help him feel more comfortable. Neither Murdo nor Mary seemed to understand what was happening, but they were willing to try anything to take away Murdo's distress.

Recommendations

Helen was aware of research which suggested that full remission of depression is an attainable goal, even with psychotic features, but for some patients, combination and augmentation strategies using atypical antipsychotic medicine early in treatment may increase the likelihood of this remission taking place (Kennedy and Lam, 2003). Because Murdo had only been taking the fluoxetine for one week, it would not have started to have an antidepressant effect, so Helen would not expect at this stage to see his mood begin to improve. However, fluoxetine does not have antipsychotic properties *per se*, so she felt his symptoms of suspiciousness warranted early intervention. Kennedy and Lam (2003) suggest that this combination and augmentation strategy enhances the process and is a more useful approach than waiting for the depression to lift with anti-depressants alone.

Helen therefore discussed the introduction of amisulpride 200 mg bd as a starting dose with Murdo and his wife, outlining side-effects and expected effects with them. Amisulpride is an atypical antipsychotic (see Chapter 2) and in Helen's prescribing experience is generally well tolerated, hence her preferred choice. Murdo seemed relieved when Helen was explaining things, and shared with her and Helen that he thought he was 'going mad'. He had not appreciated that depression could affect him this way. Murdo was very happy to try this medication, as he recognised that things had changed.

Helen ⊗ Murdo
Helen also decided to arrange for a support worker, Catherine, to be involved in his care package; Catherine is part of the mental health team and works alongside the CPNs delivering care planned in conjunction with service users and their CPN. Helen explained to Murdo and Mary that she would speak to her in the allocations meeting on Wednesday and arrange for her to visit Murdo at home weekly, and begin a programme of support which would eventually include going outside.

Helen realised straight away by Murdo's reaction that she had become paternalistic in her approach, not only deciding on bringing another person into the mix but also determining the direction in which care was to proceed. Murdo said that he was uncomfortable having a stranger come to his house. Helen recognised that the introduction of a new person into the care team might arouse suspicion in someone with possible paranoid ideation. She then remembered that Catherine was in the surgery at the time, so Helen asked Murdo and Mary if they would like to meet her and then decide if they wanted her involved in Murdo's care. She also said that if they did want her involved, they would decide together on an agenda.

At this stage, Helen was keen to foster a relationship with Murdo and his wife which would enhance the likelihood of achieving concordance. She did not want him to feel bulldozed into agreeing with things that appeared to be directed by her as that was anathema to the whole nature of a concordant approach. However, Murdo agreed to meet with Catherine at the end of the session, and he said he would phone during the week if he felt it was necessary for Catherine to be involved.

Reflective exercise

(a) What do you think of Helen's initial approach here – i.e. going ahead and saying she would arrange for Catherine's involvement without prior discussion with Mary and Murdo?

(b) Where does that sit with fostering concordance?

Towards the end of the second session, Helen tentatively introduced the idea that Murdo might at some stage benefit from a short inpatient stay. Her reasoning was based on previous experience, as when a person becomes severely depressed to the extent that they develop a sense of alienation and they develop concurrent thoughts of suicide, an inpatient stay is a means of managing risk as well as offering respite. Although Murdo was not expressing suicidal thoughts, his depression was so severe that Helen felt it was entirely possible they might develop. She wanted Murdo to know what his choices were. However, both Murdo and his wife were reluctant to consider this and expressed a strong desire to receive all care and support in the community. Because Helen felt that Murdo was experiencing some psychotic symptoms, as evidenced by his suspiciousness in particular and his guarded demeanour, she discussed with Murdo and his wife that she wanted to discuss the possibility of the visiting psychiatrist, Dr Jenkins, assessing Murdo in the next clinic; they agreed but did express some concern about the involvement of a new psychiatrist, and an appointment was made for the following week.

Reflection

Butler *et al.* (2007) suggest that care pathways improve the effectiveness of treatment for depression. Murdo's assessment was carried out by the GP initially, then Helen the CPN, and subsequently by the psychiatrist. They all followed the same consistent approach as outlined in the local care pathway; by including Murdo and his wife throughout, assessment was achieved through partnership.

For example, Helen used the PHQ-9 assessment tool to determine the severity of Murdo's depression; this same tool is used by both the GP and the psychiatrist. Murdo participated in the process, and Helen's explanation of what the questionnaire was and of its purpose helped Murdo's decision to participate. He said later when discussing his experience that he felt 'informed and included'. Another example is related to Helen discussing prescribing with Murdo and Mary. By using reflective techniques, Murdo was able to think out loud about all the issues surrounding the decision to try medicine and come to a conclusion, which in this case was to try fluoxetine, and subsequently amisulpride.

There were times on reflection where Helen recognised that concordance was threatened, in part by the interventions she offered. In particular, she identified through supervision using reflective practice that Murdo and Mary may well have felt overwhelmed by their experience in the early sessions, as coming to terms with a diagnosis of depression is not easy. She recognised that she asked a lot of questions that at times may have left Murdo exhausted. Indeed, he lost concentration and became distracted at one point; also she had decided on introducing a support worker with little consultation, based purely on the knowledge that it had helped others, so it would probably help Murdo and Mary. This exemplifies that clinical supervision and reflective practice are crucial to the development of practitioners and ultimately to improved practice.

Scenario 3: Susan

Assessment

Yvonne is committed to working within a recovery approach as advocated by *The National Review of Mental Health Nursing in Scotland: Rights, Relationships and Recovery* (Scottish Executive, 2006). She is keen to continue working in a way with Susan that will promote the development and maintenance of a sound therapeutic alliance.

Yvonne has arranged to visit Susan at home following her discharge from hospital. She has ensured that she and Susan have agreed a suitable day and time. Susan is welcoming and they sit together with a cup of tea. Susan says that she feels that she is settling into her flat well, enjoying her own company and is enjoying the freedom of not being restricted to a ward routine. Yvonne reinforces that she sees her role as a supportive one and that she is keen to hear her story, but at her pace. She explains the aim of this will be to understand what is important from Susan's perspective, what her priorities are and how might they work together to achieve these. Susan says that she would be happy telling her story through time and that it is important for her not to feel pressurised to do this too quickly. Yvonne stresses again that she will not force the pace. They agree that Yvonne has no need at this stage to ask her lots of questions which will have already been asked and documented in hospital. With this Susan feels that her early impressions of Yvonne are likely to be right – that she will really listen. However, time will tell. Susan says that her current main concern is that she is really unhappy with her medicine.

Susan is prescribed olanzapine 10 mg daily. Olanzapine is an atypical antipsychotic medicine. The mechanism of action is discussed in Chapter 2. As with the discussion on donepezil above, if you are going to prescribe/administer/discuss a medicine you need to understand it. Refer back to pp. 47–8 in Chapter 2 for an outline of olanzapine.

Yvonne asks Susan what her current key concern is. Susan feels a bit embarrassed and reluctantly discusses her weight gain. Yvonne asks what her weight was before starting olanzapine and what it is now. This shows a weight gain of 4 stones and Susan goes on to recount how this is affecting her life. She feels very sluggish and feels really self-conscious about her appearance. Yvonne discusses with Susan that olanzapine is known to have the propensity to lead to a significant weight gain (BMJ Group and Pharmaceutical Press, 2011a). Susan says that she raised her concerns with the hospital staff, but she got the impression from them that they thought it 'better to be fat than psychotic'. Although she does not want to have difficulties and end up back in hospital, neither does she really want to remain on this medicine when it is affecting her weight so significantly. Are there no other options she asks? Yvonne explains that most atypical antipsychotics have the propensity to increase weight, although not usually as significantly as olanzapine, and also that there is another medicine which is sometimes referred to as being 'weight neutral', as it has a lower relative risk of weight gain compared to other antipsychotics. Susan asks why this is. Yvonne explains that antipsychotics act on multiple receptors and it would appear that it is likely to be its action on a particular serotonin receptor which accounts for this. Susan asks if she might be considered for a change of medicine. Yvonne says that there is a lot to be considered regarding different medicines and usually involves the weighing up between desired effects and side-effects. She said that she could understand Susan's concerns and wishes and she commits to discussing this issue with the psychiatrist Dr Jones, who will be taking over Susan's care now that she has been discharged from hospital.

Yvonne discusses with the multidisciplinary team Susan's concerns regarding her unhappiness with her medicine due to significant weight gain. She goes on to discuss the impact that this is currently having on Susan in terms of her self-esteem, as she is very conscious of her appearance, and the likely impact on Susan's confidence in getting on with her life, e.g. in relation to study/ employment, socialising and relationships. She also raises her concerns about the possible implications for Susan's physical health. The team are at first not keen to consider alternatives because olanzapine has been successful in symptom management and she has just been discharged from hospital. Yvonne says that she understands this; however, they are all aware about the link between service users being unhappy with medicines and their likelihood to keep taking them (Deegan and Drake, 2006). Susan has stopped her medicine before, and therefore Yvonne feels that not exploring a possible change would be an unsatisfactory option and that Susan has to have meaningful involvement in order to make an informed choice. On balance they agree that a change of medicine could be considered and so Yvonne suggests aripiprazole as a possibility because it is weight neutral (BMJ and Pharmaceutical Group, 2011b). Yvonne advocates for involving Susan fully in making this decision and proposes to do this on her next visit.

On the next home visit Yvonne explores with Susan the discussion she has had with the team, that aripiprazole could be considered. Susan is pleased that Yvonne has acted on her key concern. Yvonne says that this is the medicine which she had mentioned (although not by name) at their last appointment which is considered to

Table 4.4 Problem solving grid.

Key problem: I have gained 4 stones since starting on olanzapine and this is stopping me from having the confidence to mix socially with old acquaintances, or even thinking about applying for a job, or going back to studying.

Option 1 To continue taking olanzapine at the present dosage.	Option 2 To continue taking olanzapine at a reduced dosage	Option 3 To not take medicine	Option 4 To change the medicine to one with a different side-effect profile – aripiprazole
Advantages I have felt less edgy and suspicious and no longer hear voices	**Advantages** It may be that the weight gain would be less and I would continue to feel less edgy suspicious and not hear voices	**Advantages** I could find out if I need to take medicine at all and would not have any side-effects	**Advantages** Maybe I could lose weight and still feel less edgy suspicious and not hear voices
Disadvantages I have no life carrying on like this. I have had really rapid weight gain and eat too much	**Disadvantages** The voices might return and I don't want to end up back in hospital	**Disadvantages** The voices might return and I don't want to end up back in hospital	**Disadvantages** This would be a leap into the unknown for me

Decision I think I would like to try the new medicine but would like to find out more about it and also look at a plan to minimise the risk of ending up back in hospital.

be weight neutral. To help with decision-making Yvonne suggests using a simple problem solving framework (Table 4.4) together to consider the options (Baker and Fletcher, 2009). Susan finds herself agreeing to this. Yvonne explains the process, which involves outlining the problem in Susan's words and then going on to explore the range of options now open to her by looking at the advantages and disadvantages of each option.

Yvonne explains that the evidence suggests that aripiprazole is as effective as other antipsychotics, but that it also has side-effects including fatigue, gastrointestinal disturbance and headache (*BNF* – see Chapter 2, p. 29). She has brought along written information about aripiprazole and gives this to Susan to read over before their next appointment. The effects and side-effect profile of aripiprazole (summarised in Box 4.2 and detailed in Chapter 2) were further discussed between Susan and Yvonne with reference to the written information at their next appointment. On balance, Susan decides that she wants to switch to aripiprazole with the proviso that she is supported during the changeover period to reduce the possibility of experiencing difficulties that might mean her needing to be admitted to hospital. Although she still disputes the diagnosis of schizophrenia she does realise that she has not had good mental health. Yvonne briefly outlines the idea of relapse signature (Herz and Melville, 1980) and asks if Susan would be interested in this approach. Susan likes this idea. Yvonne and Susan discuss her weight gain further and decide that it would be useful if she was to make an appointment to see the practice nurse so that her physical health could be assessed more generally and to explore possible options regarding weight loss.

Box 4.2 Some of the effects and side-effects of aripiprazole to be considered by Susan and Yvonne (based on information from BMJ Group and Pharmaceutical Press, 2011b)

Main effects	Main side-effects
Reduction in feelings of agitation and associated voice hearing experiences	Fatigue Gastro-intestinal disturbances Headache

---

Physical health assessment

Susan attends for an appointment for a physical health assessment with the practice nurse, Beth. This assessment provides the opportunity to discuss past, current and future physical health concerns. Beth explains to Susan that if possible she should have a physical health assessment at least once every 15 months (Scottish Executive, 2006). A paper copy of the Physical Health Check (PHC; Rethink, 2008) is then used to support and structure the appointment. Susan finds some elements of the PHC more daunting than others and is worried that Beth might think that she has gained weight because she is lazy or stupid. Susan is also unsure what information Beth has in relation to her; every so often Beth looks at the computer. Susan thinks she would feel better if she could read what Beth was reading, but feels it might seem rude to ask.

Reflective exercise
(a) Have you been in a similar situation recently and if so how did this make you feel?
(b) What concerns did you have?
(c) What could Beth have done or said to improve the situation?

Beth initially ascertains fixed risk factors, asking questions relating to Susan's family history and personal history. This may highlight any illnesses that Susan may be predisposed to, such as heart disease, thyroid conditions, cancer or diabetes. Dynamic risk factors are then assessed. This involves a discussion of Susan's current lifestyle preferences (e.g. smoking, diet, sexual health and physical activity levels). Beth asks Susan to describe 'a typical day' to encourage conversation and clarify patterns, behaviours and preferences.

Beth explains that the physical health assessment may be carried out over a succession of appointments. This enhances the experience for all concerned; allowing Beth and Susan the opportunity to process and reflect on the questions asked, enabling Beth the opportunity to build a relationship before asking more sensitive questions, and allowing Susan to feel valued, particularly where issues relating to volition, concentration or recall may impact on the physical health assessment.

Baseline measurements are an essential part of the assessment. These are carried out with kindness, consent and consideration (Nursing and Midwifery Council, 2008). It has been some time since Susan has had these measurements taken and Beth offers a clear explanation as to why the measurements are being taken. Choice and control are encouraged throughout (Repper and Perkins, 2003):

I need to measure your blood pressure, weight and waist circumference today. What order would you like us to start?

Have you had your blood pressure taken before? What do you remember about that experience?

Do you have any anxieties about your blood results?

Previous research in relation to carrying out physical health checks in individuals with schizophrenia highlights the effectiveness of the check in uncovering physical illness in individuals who may not report physical health concerns freely (Jeste *et al.*, 1996). Susan is relieved to find that her blood pressure, respiration and temperature are within normal limits. However, her Body Mass

Index is 32, which is in the 'obese' range, and puts her at risk of developing heart disease, Type 2 diabetes or some cancers (NICE, 2006).

Beth and Susan continue through the PHC and reach the 'Action Plan' stage (p. 10). Beth asks Susan 'What if you were to make a change... what would that look like?'. Beth feels that Susan's priorities should be diet and exercise, but resists the urge to take control or steer Susan towards her own preferred option. Susan is relieved that Beth has given her the option and chooses to concentrate on 'losing weight'.

Making a change involves energy, motivation and commitment. There are five stages of change through which clients will pass as they change their behaviour (Prochaska and DiClemente, 1994). Susan is at the 'preparation' stage of change. At this stage it is appropriate to set goals and consider change options.

Using SMART (Specific, Measurable, Attainable, Relevant, Time-based) criteria to set the goal assists with the process. Other goal-setting tools Beth has previously used include 'the stranger test' and 'the dead man's test' (Harai, 2006). In the stranger test the question is asked that if a stranger were to read the goal, would they be able to clearly articulate and understand it. The dead man's test should involve the practitioner guiding the client towards having an action-focused goal as opposed to a goal that might mimic the action of a dead man (e.g. 'not taking medication', 'not being anxious').

Susan is not sure how to start. Beth then outlines the change options which may be helpful:

> There are many options to choose from when making a decision to lose weight. Some people choose to keep a food diary and count calories; others join a weight loss programme and some choose to increase their physical activity.

Susan decides she would like to keep a food diary. Beth and Susan discuss how, when and where the diary will be kept in order that any threats to achievement are identified. Activities to manage challenges are discussed. Susan decides to keep her food diary as a word processor document on her computer. Beth makes an appointment to see Susan in two weeks' time.

Reflective exercise

(a) Consider the benefits of goal attainment.
(b) What practitioner skills are involved in assisting individuals to make plans for change?
(c) What ethical and professional issues may arise in the goal-setting process?

Recommendations

With Susan's decision to change medicines to aripiprazole and her desire to look at a plan to reduce her likelihood of ending up back in hospital, Yvonne suggests that it may be useful to construct a timeline (Ford, 2000). Yvonne explains that this will help to illustrate what is happening during times of being ill as well as times of being well. Initially she suggests a short-term timeline focusing on the recent relapse. Timelines can take a long- or short-term perspective (Pelton, 2009), or even cover a whole life span (Brabban, 2009). Although this timeline takes a short-term perspective it is not implied that it is completed in a short period of time or in a one-off session. It developed in a piecemeal fashion emerging as the therapeutic alliance developed, and depth and meaning was built into the timeline. The format for Susan's timeline example has been taken from the relapse prevention manual

Table 4.5 Short-term timeline.

External events	Changes to thoughts, feeling and behaviours
I returned to university in October 2008	I worried other students knew about my admission to psychiatric hospital. I avoided social situations.
In December 2008 at the time of my assessment submission dates	I felt stressed and didn't sleep well, but despite wanting to complete the assessment items I couldn't concentrate and felt the pressure was overwhelming. I often worked through the night to get all my work done.
Christmas holidays 2008 – Discussed with my parents that I was on the wrong course at Uni but they were angry about this and again threatened to cut me off financially	I felt really trapped and not listened to, like the time I didn't want to go to my uncle's firm for shadowing experience at school. I could not feel really angry with my mum, as she was coping with her own problems. Studying architecture felt repugnant to me. I stopped taking my medicine at this point – I felt 'Why bother? It's only making me very fat and I feel bad enough about myself'.
I returned to university in January 2009	I felt this couldn't go on: I was hardly sleeping or going out of my room and was very suspicious and began again to hear a male voice
Age 20, February 2009 – I was admitted to the psychiatric hospital against my will for the second time	Rather than wait for the lecturer to fail me in the assessment items I confronted him outside Uni and became very angry and then tearful.

Back in the Saddle (Plaistow and Birchwood, 1996). This enables Susan and Yvonne to 'zoom in' to the events surrounding relapse, taking a more detailed and short-term account of key events and providing the opportunity to identify recent times of stress, times of crisis and the early warning signs of relapse. Both Susan and Yvonne hold a copy of the timeline. Susan finds that her memories were quite vivid, but she had some difficulty placing events in the right order. She wonders if her friend Kate can be involved in the sorting out the chronological order of events.

Susan and Yvonne construct the timeline and it becomes clear that there were some key issues during the time she was back at university which she linked to her relapse, and which resulted in readmission to hospital. She was able to track the beginning of the change in her lifestyle with Kate's help and they linked external events to thoughts, feelings and behaviours, as outlined in Table 4.5.

From this short-term timeline an initial relapse prevention plan was constructed (Ford, 2000). The aim is to add to this/refine it over time.

Relapse prevention plan – initial

Relapse signature	**Relapse drill**
I start by having difficulty sleeping	Step 1 – Make time for myself
My concentration starts to reduce	Keep to my bedtime routine
I start to feel that I've got to work harder and harder to keep up	Contact Kate/Yvonne
I start to feel trapped	Step 2 – Increased supportive contact
Start to feel things are out of my control	with Kate and Yvonne
Start to think what's the point?	Consider increase in medicine
I start to feel increasingly suspicious	Step 3 – Increase medicine
Find it difficult to leave my room	Respite in 'Crisis House'
Start to hear a male voice – saying that it's all my fault, I'm useless and that he and other men are going to harm me too	Hospital as a last resort

Triggers

Returning to University to study a course I didn't want to, worrying about what the other students thought about me. Thinking what's the point and going on to stop my medicine.

Both Susan and Yvonne keep a copy of this. Susan finds this process helpful and is further encouraged when Yvonne again reinforces that the aim will be to add more detail/refinement as their work together continues.

Susan successfully switches to aripiprazole and finds that she has the benefits of this medicine without the unwanted weight gain.

Susan asks if a longer timeline covering her whole life (Table 4.6) can be developed sometime. She intimates that she had difficulties in her childhood and wonders if this could have affected her. She would like her friend Kate to be involved in this work, to help her reflect on experiences at university which led up to admission to hospital. Susan, Kate and Yvonne work together over the coming weeks to develop this. This is done gently and sensitively and very much at Susan's pace. Yvonne recognises the need for Susan to lead and control this process. After all, looking back on your life, particularly at difficult times and experiences, can raise lots of emotions, sometimes quite unexpectedly.

As already mentioned, this whole life timeline as shown was constructed over a number of visits, some with Kate present also. Susan also worked on this between these visits and added in about the episode of sexual abuse. This was the first time Susan had disclosed that information, and she admitted that if her uncle had still been alive she would still have felt afraid to speak to anyone. Yvonne reminded Susan about the discussion they had regarding confidentiality at the start of their contact. Yvonne remained calm and accepting, as advocated by Nelson and Hampson (2008), which seemed to reassure Susan, and Susan recounted what had happened. Yvonne asked Susan what problems, if any, she thought the abuse had left her with (Nelson and Hampson, 2008). Susan said that she was feeling a great sense of release even to see the entry about sexual abuse in her timeline and discuss this with Yvonne; however, she said it was difficult to put into words how she felt now, even after the years that had passed. Yvonne acknowledged that many people, despite feeling better after this kind of disclosure, struggled to express how they felt in words. She and Susan explored other avenues of expression and Susan suggested that her interest in art might be her natural form of expression. Yvonne said that she would be interested in Susan starting a portfolio of artwork that represented different points on the timeline so far in her life. Yvonne left Susan's flat after the most recent visit feeling buoyed up and really positive about all the progress that she was making.

Table 4.6 Life span timeline.

External events	Changes to thoughts, feeling and behaviours
I was born in February 1989 – I had two brothers. My mum was a vet and my dad had the farm	
Aged 4, Summer 1993 – I remember not being happy at Nursery School and being picked on by other girls because I came from a posh house	Even at this time I began to realise that although my mum and dad spent loads of time with animals, if they were in pain they didn't seem to see my pain or how upset I was.
Aged 5, August 1994 – I started primary school	It was great to start primary school, and there were some other girls who lived on farms so I was able to fit in better.
Aged 7, May 1996 – I won the painting competition for the whole town	This was a major achievement for me and I began to think that I could be an artist when I grew up. My mum and dad said well done, but made it clear that they had better plans for me and my brothers.
Aged 9, Christmas 1998 – Party at Uncle Peter's house. He offered to show me some of his drawings in his study. Whilst there he sexually assaulted me	Even then I knew that what he had done was wrong and I felt ashamed and guilty. It felt impossible to tell anybody and I did not expect that my mum and dad would listen.
Aged 9–16, 1998–2005 – Things went okay at school	After what happened, somehow it made it hard for me to fit in. Even if I was with other kids at school I felt detached from them. My art really helped to fill out my days and was a good escape. I loved to draw the animals around the farm. When I talked about being an artist I could sense my dad's disappointment.
Aged 16, January 2005 – I was sent to shadow Uncle Peter at his architect's office	He did not assault me again but I felt that even being forced to be at this office was a kind of assault and it seemed to take me right back to being nine years old again.
Aged 18, October 2007 – I started university studying architecture, which was my parents' choice	I was excited to be making a fresh start and leaving home for the first time, despite my reservations about the course, as my preference was art.

Table 4.6 (continued)

Aged 19, Easter 2008 – Returned home. This was the time that my Uncle Peter died. I felt relieved but also paradoxically very upset. Had a big blow-out with my mum and dad because I told them I wanted to switch courses. They threatened to cut me off financially.	Although initially at university I had felt mature and more in control of my life, after this blow-out, I felt about 9 years old.
Aged 19, End of June 2008 – My friend Kate said later that she found me cowering under my bed dishevelled and frightened looking. She was concerned that I would come to harm and contacted Student Services, which then ended up with my admission to hospital against my will.	I felt incredibly stressed about my exams, but it wasn't just the exams: my whole life began to feel unreal and out of control. I never slept for a whole night during this time and often didn't even go to bed as I worked through the night on coursework. I somehow completed enough of my exams before I was admitted to hospital. I really began to feel weird about this time.
Aged 19, October 2008 – I returned to university	I worried other students knew about my admission to psychiatric hospital. I avoided social situations.
Aged 19, December 2008 – The time of my assessment submission dates	I felt stressed and did not sleep well, but despite wanting to complete the assessment items I could not concentrate and felt the pressure was overwhelming. I often worked through the night to get all my work done.
Aged 19, Christmas holidays 2008 – Discussed with my parents that I was on the wrong course at Uni but they were angry about this and again threatened to cut me off financially	I felt really trapped and not listened to, like the time I didn't want to go to my uncle's firm for shadowing experience at school. I could not feel really angry with my mum as she was coping with her own problems. Studying architecture felt repugnant to me. I stopped taking my medicine at this time – I felt 'Why bother? It's only making me fat and I feel bad enough about myself?'.
Aged 19, January 2009 – Returned to university	I felt this could not go on. I was hardly sleeping or going out of my room, and was very suspicious and began again to hear a male voice.
Aged 20, February 2009 – Admitted to the psychiatric hospital for the second time against my will	Rather than wait for the lecturer to fail me in the assessment items I confronted him outside Uni and became very angry and then tearful.

Reflective exercise

Take a moment to reflect on how Yvonne is feeling. How do you think her feelings fit in with a recovery approach?

CHAPTER 5

Interventions

Abstract

Practical interventions to promote concordance include both the individual and family/significant others. Interventions often take place against a background of challenges, for example in relation to memory, mood and thinking. These specific challenges are discussed and illustrated with reference to the three unfolding scenarios – Dougie, Murdo and Susan. When family and friends have a significant role in the person's wellbeing, then whenever possible it is best for them to be involved in the promotion of concordance. For example, it is sometimes difficult to identify the components of a relapse signature subjectively, and the involvement of family friends can help to pinpoint key changes provoking the service user's recollections. The collaborative and ongoing nature of these interventions is stressed.

Key points

- 'Help as required' is a useful maxim in promoting autonomy.
- Service users and their carers should be involved in the risk/benefit analysis of each medicine.
- Whatever best evidence promotes, it is only best evidence if it has resonance and purpose for the individuals involved.
- Psychosocial interventions and medicine-taking can combine well together.
- Concordance working is most successful if/when each member of the multidisciplinary team is committed to it.

Key words

Beliefs, memory, mood, thinking, interventions, collaboration

Objectives

- Illustrate interventions to promote concordance when challenged by problems of memory.

- Illustrate interventions to promote concordance when challenged by problems of mood.
- Illustrate interventions to promote concordance when challenged by problems of thinking.
- Justify the mental health worker's need for clinical supervision.

Introduction

When addressing challenges such as memory loss, mood disorders and problems with thinking it is sometimes too easy for health professionals to dismiss the existing strengths of the individual in order to address the obvious and anticipated problems surrounding concordance in treatment. However, as we have seen, concordance implies partnership and agreement, so why would professionals ignore the ethos of concordance because of a service user's cognitive state? Many people suffer cognitive deficits in their everyday life. Life events ranging from lack of sleep, anxiety, an overload of information either in the home or workplace, a traumatic event or a stressful event can all adversely affect an individual's cognitive state. Yet because these individuals have not been given the label of an illness, it is *not* usual for them to become involved with health professionals and it *is* usual for them to retain autonomy and rely on friends and family to help them through such times.

Thus 'help as required' is a good maxim for health professionals. People with cognitive deficits will have good days and bad days. It is important to remember that good days are characterised by coping being easier and bad days by coping being more difficult. Too often, once a service user has had a 'bad day' the health professionals and/or the family can see this as evidence of 'getting worse'. We have to remember that there are fluctuations in health and illness, and coping strategies help people to remain as independent as possible during the good days and provide a safety net for the bad days.

In some cases, such as those involving the dementia spectrum, people's cognitive abilities will decrease over time, but if strategies to help address cognitive deficits are taught and become routine, there is more chance of the person maintaining an established routine for a longer period of time than if such a routine was not established. In the cases of mood and thinking disorders, routine is useful as an 'automatic pilot response' in times of chaos for the individual. Establishing routines may help to maintain independence.

However, as we have discussed, concordance is not a static agreement between the healthcare professional and the service user – it can be a complicated dynamic agreement between several health professionals, the service user and his or her significant others. It is about knowledge, attitudes, collaboration and belief systems among all or a few players. The three case studies below continue to illustrate how unique every situation is. Best practice is only 'best practice' if it is the best possible interaction/intervention for that service user at that time of his or her illness and unique social circumstances.

Scenario 1: Dougie

Things were getting better, and over the next four months Dougie and his family enjoyed his improved cognitive function, reduced irritability and renewed interest in socialising. Dougie and his wife established a new way of working together and settled into their routine. With the diagnosis of a dementia and the initiation of treatment, there had been discussion about the purpose of the cognitive enhancer, including the fact that it was not a cure and potentially offered just a few years of benefit, the degree of which could not be predicted. But it had to be said that things were better and they were thankful for that.

It had become apparent that for Dougie, Joyce and Chris concordance had become focused upon the therapeutic relationship, with adjustment to Dougie's diagnosis as the key challenge to achieving that concordance. By now, Dougie and Joyce had complete confidence in Chris. They were open about the problems they had and he always seemed to support them to find their own solution that would work for them. Chris was relieved that he was achieving the person-centred care he was aiming for, where Dougie and Joyce were at the centre of their support and everything he did was about what was important for them from their perspective (Scottish Government, 2010). It is important to recognise that in managing dementia, particularly when the person with the dementia is living with either a spouse or relative, the full participation of both (with the necessary consents) in discussions relating to treatments and interventions is critical for concordance.

It had not all been plain sailing though. One problem encountered was that when donepezil was prescribed initially, it was prescribed for night time. Dougie began to experience increased agitation through the night and Chris suggested switching it to the morning, with good effect. A further problem that Dougie had had that was particularly difficult for Joyce to cope with was the fact that he experienced what seemed to be parasomnia or, more specifically, chronic rapid eye movement (REM) sleep behaviour disorder. This resulted in him experiencing vivid and generally violent, threatening and terrifying dreams soon after going to sleep. Joyce, who had moved back into the marital bedroom, had had to resort to sleeping in another room again.

Dougie found these events distressing afterwards; even though he had either only partial or no recollection, it was the effect it had on Joyce and the damage he sometimes caused to his room and property (e.g. throwing the phone across the room to disarm an imaginary gunman) that was worrying. In addition, Chris spoke to a local geriatrician to discuss whether perindopril could be causing Dougie's sleep disturbances. This was discounted initially, but the geriatrician stated he would see Dougie if he needed something different. Chris decided to try a low-dose hypnotic, zolpidem, to see if it could help, and it did. Whether it suppressed his REM sleep during the early part of his sleep is not clear, but both Dougie and Joyce were happy with the beneficial effect.

During this time Chris had asked Dougie about the possibility that his time in the army may have been impacting upon his sleep disturbance and dreams, tentatively offering Dougie an opportunity to discuss it this time, whilst his cognitive skills remained at a level where he could, if needed, participate in a form of post-traumatic stress disorder (PTSD) treatment. It is known that even though Dougie may have managed his symptoms of PTSD in the past, retirement and the changes in his cognition and associated losses could trigger an increase in symptoms or reduce his ability to cope with them (Busuttil, 2002). Dougie made it clear to Chris that this was not an area he wished to revisit, stating that it was a different time and he was a different person. Chris stated that he fully respected this, although that opportunity would remain open if Dougie changed his mind. Chris felt frustrated. He was worried that as Dougie's cognitive decline increased he might experience more profound symptoms and have reduced ability to discuss or process his experiences.

Complications

After four months Dougie experienced a seizure. Joyce was terrified and called their GP, who sent for an ambulance. On admission to accident and emergency, Dougie experienced another, more prolonged, seizure and he was admitted to a medical ward. During his admission the consultant physician discontinued the donepezil, suspecting that it was responsible for the seizures, as seizures are a rare but possible side-effect. Joyce had not given this much thought at the time, as she was more concerned with the seizure. On top of this, Joyce had bumped her leg in her race to get to the phone and she feared that this would be the start of another one of her leg ulcers.

The outcome

Within a few weeks of the discontinuation of donepezil, Dougie, Joyce and their family had noticed a decline in Dougie's cognitive functioning, a loss of volition and withdrawal from social interaction. By now Dougie and Joyce had a good relationship with Chris and he discussed the situation with them. It had been a devastating time for Dougie, who had, with support from Chris, made an appointment for a driver's assessment by the Driver and Vehicle Licensing Agency (DVLA) and had been hopeful about the possibility of driving again. Not only had the seizure meant this was now not going to be possible for Dougie, his memory was getting worse at a faster rate than he had envisaged.

Dougie's story

Dougie felt a huge change in himself when he stopped taking the donepezil – he was worse than he thought and wanted to get back on this tablet, whatever the side-effects. A seizure was nothing compared to how he felt now, he was getting worse and he was frightened. He knew that the 'dementia tablet' was not a cure, but he did know that it made him feel better. It was also helping his condition – without this what would happen to him?

Joyce's story

Joyce was extremely anxious. She was anxious when he was diagnosed with dementia and her anxiety increased when he had a seizure. It was a frightening event, but not half as frightening as the decline she saw in her husband when he had to stop taking his 'dementia tablet'. Dougie was desperate to get back on the tablet, but she knew that he could well have another seizure. Perhaps he could get tablets for seizures? She would ask Chris. She would also ask him to look at the wound on her leg – he was a nurse and would know what to do.

At this stage there is great pressure not only on Chris, but on Dougie and Joyce. If Chris did anything to lose their trust he would also lose the information he needed from them in order to help them cope at home. Dougie and Joyce knew that they were dependent on Chris and were scared that he might leave his post or be transferred to other patients. Such dependency used to be frowned upon, but the essence of a therapeutic relationship is between not only the practitioner and his or her patients, but also the personalities involved and the trust that is earned rather than given.

Action

Chris approached Dr Armstrong, the consultant psychiatrist, and informed her of Dougie's wishes. An appointment was made and Dougie was recommenced on donepezil at 10 mg. Approximately six weeks after recommencing donepezil, Dougie experienced another seizure. Following discussion with the family, Dougie was subsequently prescribed an anti-convulsant: sodium valproate EC 400 mg nocte. The main reason for this was to control the seizures, and although its sedative properties were also discussed, they were considered a bonus rather than a 'side-effect', as Dougie had become increasingly anxious and restless because of his situation. Once it was clear Dougie could tolerate this subtherapeutic dose it was increased to 600 mg. He does still have the occasional seizure, but with Chris's help both he and his family have become more competent at managing them, if and when they occur. As such, much of the initial fear regarding seizures has gone. In short, the family all believe the benefits of Dougie taking the donepezil exceed the risks and distress of the seizures.

Chris also referred Joyce to the district nursing service. Her leg wound showed signs of cellulitis and he felt that Joyce was beginning to struggle with the effects of the last rather traumatic months. He was pleased that Joyce had consulted him about her leg, as she also told him that she had been very stressed about Dougie's fits. This increasing stress had led to her being uncertain that she had remembered to give Dougie all his tablets on a couple of occasions. Chris suggested that she had enough to cope with and recommended the option of using a 'blister pack': a type of seven-day dispensing box which is made up weekly by a participating pharmacist. Both Joyce and Dougie thought this was an excellent idea.

The therapeutic relationship

Chris had now become an integral part in the lives of Dougie and Joyce. They had a trusting and honest relationship with him. Chris was easy to talk to and seemed to know what he was talking about. Dougie, Chris and Joyce had continued to engage in the therapeutic tasks associated with his diagnosis (Weaks *et al.*, 2009). The most significant work had been concerned with Dougie and Joyce establishing their new relationship with each other and with the dementia. Joyce at times wanted to take over, and would then become overwhelmed and irritated with Dougie.

They had both worked to ensure that Dougie established a routine in which he retained all his usual jobs around the house. The sticky notes and the calendar were effective. Joyce had to become accustomed to the fact that the jobs Dougie did might not be as accurate or as timely as they were before. However, the gain was that Dougie was doing them, increasing the sense of reciprocity between he and Joyce, and she was not becoming too overwhelmed by taking on all the household tasks. During these times Chris took the opportunity to introduce reflections upon Dougie's action in relation to his dementia, naturally educating the couple about dementia in a way they were comfortable with. This strategy not only supported a level of normalisation for the couple, but also helped them both to get into a pattern of stopping and thinking, 'Is this the dementia?' when they were becoming upset with each other. They both agreed that sometimes their disagreements were not about dementia.

In addition, Chris offered the couple the opportunity to attend a support group and access information on the Internet, both of which they turned down. Chris discussed with Dougie and Joyce the possibility of Joyce learning cognitive stimulation (Scottish Intercollegiate Guideline Network, 2006) to help Dougie maintain his cognitive skills, and Joyce becoming a full partner in his care. Dougie and Joyce again declined, stating they just wanted to have time to garden, go to the caravan and be with their grandchildren.

Chris found it difficult to accept their rejections of his offered strategies, particularly when the evidence base he was referring to advocated education, support groups and opportunities for psychosocial interventions (NHS Education for Scotland, 2009; Moniz-Cook and Manthorpe, 2009). However, Chris had to accept that whatever the best evidence, such practices will not suit everyone. Dougie had no desire to 'join a club for people with dementia' and both Joyce and Dougie felt that they only wanted their family and friends involved. It was not 'everybody's business'. Chris reflected on what he would want for himself if he were in Dougie's position. He had seen self-help groups work well and was annoyed at Dougie for not giving it a go. Chris would go – or would he? However much he read about empathy, he knew he could only see himself as a devastated soul if he was told he had dementia. Being a professional who advocates services is a far cry from being an individual struggling with a devastating diagnosis. He decided to hold back and just concentrate on being there for Joyce and Dougie. Chris realised, by spending time with Joyce and Dougie, that they were keen to keep as healthy as possible.

One thing they did embrace with enthusiasm was the health promotion elements of Chris's strategies. They completed the Physical Health Check with Chris (Rethink, 2007), made goals to increase their exercise and goals concerned with reducing fat and increasing fruit in their diet. They started walking daily and made it their goal to complete a local 5 kilometre charity walk in the summer. Chris reflected with some bemusement that what had started as health promotion had been developed by Dougie and Joyce into purposeful, pleasurable and social activity, a psychosocial activity reported to have a protective action against depression for the person with dementia and their carer (Moniz-Cook and Manthorpe, 2009; NHS Education for Scotland, 2009). Chris realised that Joyce and Dougie were a team. Self-help groups would have split them into two camps – Dougie would be in a 'users' group and Joyce would be in a 'carers' group. It was not what they wanted. Their original ambition was to have a happy and active old

111

age together, and keeping fit together meant *to them* that they stayed as a team and fought their adversities together. Whatever best evidence promotes, it is only best evidence if it has resonance and purpose for the individuals involved, as discussed in Chapter 1.

Reflective exercise

(a) How do you develop a person's care plan?
(b) How do you draw on the person's existing strengths?
(c) How do you evaluate your care plans?

Scenario 2: Murdo

The following stages of the developing scenario expand upon the previous chapters, focusing on interventions delivered, and demonstrate how each of these interventions weave together to provide a supportive process that enables Murdo to enter into a journey of recovery, and support the establishment of concordance. This begins with an overview of developments so far, highlighting some of Helen's underpinning thinking at the time.

Assessment and recommendations

NICE guidelines (National Collaborating Centre for Mental Health, 2010, p. 5) state clearly that:

> Where possible, the key goal of an intervention should be complete relief of symptoms (remission), which is associated with better functioning and a lower likelihood of relapse.

Helen knew that it was important for Murdo to start taking antidepressants as soon as possible for this to happen, but she also recognized that fluoxetine does take a minimum of 2–4 weeks to start having an effect on mood.

Helen had a long conversation with Murdo and Mary about the medicine she was going to prescribe, explaining that relief of symptoms was an attainable goal, but that it would take a few weeks. Helen's reasons for imparting this information were twofold. Firstly, with concordance in mind, it was important to establish a relationship based on mutual trust; if Helen had led Murdo to believe he would experience immediate relief, Murdo would have had little confidence in the process. Secondly, Murdo's belief at that time was shaped by an illness process. He had strong negative self-concepts coupled with marked biological features.

Together, this can result in a sense of hopelessness. Inclusion and hope are two of the components identified by the Scottish Recovery Network (2006) as being essential to a person's recovery journey, hence Helen's actions for involving Murdo and Mary at the beginning to instil hope (i.e. 'Give the fluoxetine a chance; you will start to feel better soon, but it will take time').

It was Helen's intention to start working with Murdo using some CBT techniques, as it has been evidenced that a combination of CBT and antidepressants gives significant reduction in self-rated depression scores (Fava *et al.*, 2008). Also, NICE Guidance (National Collaborating Centre for Mental Health, 2010) is clear on the need to offer evidence-based stepped care (progressing through stages including medicines and psychosocial and self-help interventions).

However, the first week's session with Murdo and Mary had been exhausting for Murdo. He admitted that he found it challenging, and found the assessment and the timeline difficult to complete. Helen therefore suggested that Murdo and Mary try to relax at home to start with, and that they look together at the booklets that she had given them (on sleep hygiene and on depression). Helen also told them that in subsequent weeks she would be giving Murdo some work to do on his mood in an effort to help him identify and map his progress. Ridge and Ziebland (2006) found that people with depression need to feel that they are taking responsibility for their own recovery. By involving Murdo in these interventions, Helen was hoping to help Murdo experience this process.

When Murdo arrived for his second appointment, he had been taking the fluoxetine for a week. As anticipated, there had been no immediate improvement in his mood, and as discussed in Chapter 4 he was agitated and could not settle in the waiting area. Both he and Mary reported that he had not slept all week.

Assessment

As Helen escorted Murdo and Mary into the consulting room, she could determine a marked change in his demeanour from the previous week. Murdo appeared reluctant to talk at first, and when Mary tried to interject he questioned her intentions. He was able to say that he had not read the leaflets that had been given to him, and that he hadn't been sleeping properly. He was challenging with Helen, and Helen was able to discern that he was suspicious. Helen decided to ask him some of the questions on the team's mental health assessment (Box 5.1) to ascertain what this change in presentation meant for Murdo's health and wellbeing.

Murdo was able to say that he did not feel suicidal, but it became evident through his responses that he was guarded and suspicious. He became agitated when Helen asked if he was hearing voices and said he wasn't prepared to answer 'those sorts of questions'. Mary said that he was uncomfortable when the phone rang, and that if she was speaking on the telephone he would question her to find out if she was discussing his business. She also said that Murdo was reluctant to go outside, even to walk the dog.

Box 5.1 Abridged initial mental health assessment tool (Internal Document, NHS Highland, 2009)

1. **Is there a physical cause for the problem(s)?**
   Is there evidence of medicines and/or alcohol intoxication?
   Is the person physically well enough to be interviewed by mental health staff?
   Background history and general observations
   Does the person pose an immediate risk to self or others?
   Is the person aggressive and/or threatening?
   Does he/she have a history of violence?
   Has the person got a history of self-harm?
   Does the person have a history of mental health problems?

2. **Appearance and behaviour**
   Is the person obviously distressed, markedly anxious or highly aroused?
   Is the person behaving inappropriately to the situation?
   Is the person quiet and withdrawn?
   Is the person inattentive and uncooperative?

3. **Why is the person presenting now? What recent event(s) precipitated or triggered this presentation?**
   What is the person's level of social support (i.e. partner/significant other, family members, friends)?
   Does the person appear to be experiencing any delusions or hallucinations?
   Does the person feel controlled or influenced by external forces?
   Are there major housing or accommodation problems?

Recommendations

Helen ▸ ◂ Murdo

Helen spoke at length with Murdo and Mary, and reassured them by providing information about his situation. She used a combination of reflective and supportive responses to help Murdo share his thoughts and worries about his feelings, and to talk about his fears in general. She explained that his symptoms were consistent with severe depression and that in her experience it was important to prescribe an antipsychotic medicine to augment the antidepressant, as discussed in Chapter 4. This is an extract from their conversation, illustrating reflective and supportive responses:

Murdo: … and mad. Yes, mad, that's how I feel.

Helen: Mad? (Reflective intervention)

Murdo: Yes. Every time Mary looks at me I just know she thinks I'm stupid, I know she wants to leave me.

Helen: That must be very distressing, having those thoughts. (Supportive intervention)

Murdo: Och, I suppose it is. I can't help thinking she's had enough of me. Every time the phone goes, I know she's telling the whole world about me.

Helen: Can you see that some of what you are thinking is part of what has been happening to you; is part of what we think of as depression? Sometimes people with depression, when it is quite severe, they have suspicious thoughts on top of the low thoughts – you know, like the ones you shared last week about feeling worthless – suspicious thoughts like 'Mary is telling everyone about me'. When they have those thoughts, we try another medicine on top of the anti-depressant.

(Supportive, informative intervention. Empathic, staying in person's own frame of reference. Adapted from Heron, 2001).

At this stage in Murdo's care and treatment, Helen felt that he needed some additional support within the community, especially as he was adamant that he did not want an inpatient admission. Her appointments were only offered on a weekly basis because of the way that the service was set up, and they were clinic based. Helen felt that some practical support in the community would help Murdo and

Mary develop coping strategies. To that effect, Helen arranged for a support worker (Catherine) to visit on a weekly basis. Catherine's role was multi-faceted and one of the overall aims of her involvement was to aid the process of concordance.

Both Murdo and Mary appeared overwhelmed by this suggestion, and expressed concern that another person in their midst wasn't something they were really sure about. Helen reflected on this, and recognised that although her intentions were to offer a partnership approach, she had in fact made an autonomous decision.

She therefore explained Catherine's role in more detail, and arranged for them to meet so that Murdo could make an informed choice as to whether or not he wanted her involved in his care.

Because Murdo appeared to be experiencing psychotic symptoms and was reluctant to go outside, Catherine was able to enable him to feel more confident about stepping out. Initially, they took the dog for a short walk along the shore outside their home. Murdo was agitated at times, and Catherine was able to practise some relaxation techniques with Murdo that helped him control his symptoms. He and Catherine developed a close working relationship over the ensuing weeks, and Murdo began to value her input to his recovery journey. Although not qualified in CBT, Catherine has participated in some interpersonal skills training, and in particular has participated in recovery-based training. This stems from the work of Schinkel and Dorrer (2007), which identified a number of recovery-focused qualities in mental health workers:

- Listening skills
- Interpersonal qualities (such as caring, humility, patience)
- Belief in and encouragement of change
- Focus on the individual
- Empathy
- Knowledge about conditions, interventions and resources for recovery
- Bringing about a person's strengths
- Life experience
- Non-judgemental attitude
- Sense of humour

If these qualities are present in a recovery-focused relationship, then Schinkel and Dorrer propose that trust will be established. When alluding to concordance as a relationship, or a process that develops between practitioners and persons receiving their care and treatment, it is more likely to be achieved where trust is established. Catherine encouraged Murdo to share his fears about his situation during their times together; she was also able to draw upon Murdo's strength to overcome them as part of his recovery journey. For instance, on one occasion Murdo was suggesting that he was 'useless'. Catherine asked him how he saw himself as a father, and elicited from him that his children had grown into well-balanced, successful adults, and that they respected him as a role model. Murdo also began to reminisce about his mother and how much he missed her. Catherine listened attentively as the trust between her and Murdo grew and he began to express his feelings more. On another occasion, in week 4, Murdo shared that the tablets (fluoxetine and amisulpiride) 'weren't working'.

Catherine asked him to reflect firstly on what had been said to him when they were first prescribed: he remembered that he was told they don't work immediately. She also asked him to reflect on any changes since starting them. He was able to identify that his sleep had improved slightly since starting the amisulpiride, and that he felt more settled in himself. These interventions from Catherine were crucial in helping Murdo participate in his recovery journey, and in promoting concordance. Without having the chance to air his concerns and reflect on his situation, Murdo might have been tempted to withdraw from the therapeutic relationship. When Catherine reported at the next multidisciplinary team meeting about Murdo's focus on his mother's death this evoked much discussion. The team concluded that perhaps they had given too little attention to the part that grief may have played in the aetiology of Murdo's depressive illness and thanked Catherine both for this information and her role in helping Murdo.

Reflective exercise

What may account for the multidisciplinary team overlooking such a significant part of Murdo's story?

Recommendations: subsequent weeks

As the weeks progressed, Helen started to introduce some CBT techniques to help support Murdo's recovery. This is a form of psychosocial intervention whereby persons can be helped to challenge unhelpful thinking by reformulating their experience, and it is known to be particularly helpful in depression. Helen suggested that Murdo keep a diary of automatic negative thoughts, and then gave him a grid to work with so that he could change them, thereby altering his feelings and behaviours. This is an example of one of the thoughts that Murdo worked on:

Reactions	Situation: I walked by the loch with the dog and saw a neighbour who was on his mobile phone. He ignored me but I felt he was talking about me.	
	Unhelpful	Helpful
Thoughts:	He is talking about me to people	He is so engrossed in his conversation that he didn't notice me
Emotional:	Low, frightened, suspicious	Pleased that he is enjoying his day and his conversation
Physical:	Anxious, restless	None – I feel comfortable
Action:	Stop going out in case I meet others who do the same	Wave across at him; enjoy the rest of my walk with the dog.

At around week 12 Murdo started to have concerns about his medicine. He felt 'stuck' and expressed concern to his wife initially that it wasn't working as well as he had hoped. Mary then brought the subject up in a session with Helen and the consultant when they were undertaking a joint review. Both Helen and the consultant listened to Murdo's concerns and helped him share his experience with them without judging him in any way.

Reflective exercise

(a) What do you think has happened here? For instance, is the feeling of 'being stuck' that Murdo is describing something that Helen should be concerned about? Does it feel like failure of interventions?

(b) Or is it a sign that Murdo is so comfortable in the therapeutic relationship that he is able to share honestly what feels right about his situation and what should change?

(c) How do you feel when people *you* work with tell you that they are making no progress?

This is the second time Murdo has raised this issue of the tablets not working as well as he had hoped. It is now well over four weeks, so any positive effect of the fluoxetine should be apparent by now. From a purely pharmacological perspective, what do you think would be a better drug? Review the BNF to help you with this.

After discussion and reassessment, it was decided to switch from fluoxetine to mirtazapine, with a starting dose of 15 mg at night that was increased to 30 mg after a week. The reassessment included repeating the PHQ-9, which sat at 18 (see previous chapters) and reviewing a mood diary, which Murdo had completed with the help of Catherine. Helen recognised that although fluoxetine and mirtazapine had similar actions, the latter is both a noradrenergic and a specific seratonergic antidepressant (NaSSA). She felt it was worth trying because biologically it hit a second receptor and could therefore enhance the effect of just working on the serotonin mechanism. In terms of discussion, Helen once again spent time discussing the effects and side-effects of the drug, and helped Murdo and Mary share their concerns and ask questions. The fluoxetine was tailed off over a period of 10 days to prevent discontinuation problems.

This episode reflected concordance in action; Deegan and Drake (2006) described how ownership is promoted through the act of collaboration in consultations, and the Medicines Partnership (2003) suggest that a mutually acceptable use of medicines is achieved through the therapeutic alliance.

There are two specific factors within the work carried out with Murdo and with Mary that merit further illustration, as they helped concordance develop and thus contributed to his recovery journey. Firstly, Russell *et al.* (2003) explored an alternative approach to nursing interventions that they propose to help people engage in care activity. They suggested that a 'patient-centred approach involves transferring power and authority away from health care professionals and towards patients'. To that effect, they suggest that nurses take a leadership role within their work that changes focus towards people's *lives*. Helen created a care package with Murdo and Mary that helped Murdo to participate in recovery-focused work within his own environment (such as the walks by the loch). She also encouraged him to be actively involved in decision-making around his medicines and indeed to have the final say.

Secondly, Piat and Sabetti (2009) found that the most important adjunct to medication is communication and a strong therapeutic relationship between service users and care providers. Although there were times when the relationship between Helen, Murdo, Mary (and Catherine) was difficult, such as when Helen made decisions without consultation, it is evident from the progress of their time together and the outcome that this was achieved

Murdo received support from Helen and Catherine for 10 months in total, and at the end he was able to evaluate his experience of receiving care. Murdo shared that he felt Helen and Catherine were 'in his corner', and valued greatly the opportunity for Mary to have been part of his recovery journey.

Scenario 3: Susan

Susan ⊗ Yvonne

Yvonne was feeling satisfied with her progress with Susan and therefore was surprised when, for the next two appointments, Susan was not in when Yvonne visited. At first Yvonne guessed that Susan had forgotten the appointment, but when the next appointment was also missed she began to worry that Susan was becoming unwell again. Yvonne could think of no other reason when things had been going so well. On each visit Yvonne posted a letter through the door saying that she had visited and asked Susan to contact with her. After this had happened for the second time Yvonne telephoned the next morning and Susan picked up the phone. Yvonne was shocked at Susan's dismissive abrupt tone but somewhat relieved when Susan did agree that she could visit later that day.

At this visit Yvonne wanted to convey that she was not blaming Susan for not keeping the appointments, but did want to understand her reasons. Her non-judgemental stance seemed to strike the right chord with Susan who seemed relieved that Yvonne was not angry with her. Susan admitted that she had not done the artwork that Yvonne had advised her to do and therefore felt she had let Yvonne down. Yvonne remembered how satisfied she had been when linking the artwork to the timeline and now felt confused and was embarrassed. Yvonne realised that she had made an assumption and been directive and clearly Susan had not been as enthusiastic as she had been. What Yvonne still did not appreciate, however, was the reason why this had such a major effect on the therapeutic relationship. She asked Susan if she could describe how she felt about their relationship. Susan was very hesitant to enter into this discussion, but encouraged by Yvonne she expressed that she had felt uncomfortable after the last meeting but had to reflect to even understand her own feelings. Susan said she had become upset, and on this recollection she began to cry. She expressed her feeling about not wanting to let Yvonne down but also being upset and disappointed that Yvonne had been so directive. Susan said that although she had not done the artwork around the timeline she did use it on reflection to make sense of how she felt. She was able to see links to past experiences, including her career choice and the sexual abuse. Throughout her life Susan had been made to feel out of control and that her own wishes were not credible. She had not realised, however, just how powerfully this had impacted on her. Reflection on the timeline with Yvonne on this visit helped them both to make sense of all this. Yvonne realised that inadvertently her own interventions had echoed the pattern from Susan's past and this had triggered Susan's avoidance.

Reflective exercise

(a) List all of Susan's experiences which may have contributed to her being unable to directly assert her feelings to Yvonne at the time of being asked to carry out the artwork.

(b) Briefly outline how Yvonne could have kept sensitivity to Susan's feelings and wishes and possibly avoided this roadblock in their concordance working.

(c) Also outline what factors helped this situation to be redeemed and what positive learning can be taken out of this situation for both Susan and Yvonne.

Yvonne decides to take her experiences of working with Susan to Jacqueline, her clinical supervisor. Clinical supervision provides a framework and a process through which nurses can meet regularly with an experienced and suitably trained colleague to explore issues relating to their clinical practice and clinical skill development (Rice *et al.*, 2007). The NMC states that the aims of clinical supervision are to identify solutions to problems, improve standards of patient care and treatment, support clinical skills development, and increase an understanding of the nurse's own clinical practice and wider professional issues (Cutcliffe *et al.*, 2010).

Jacqueline uses the 'double matrix' or 'seven-eyed supervisor' process of clinical supervision (Hawkins and Shohet, 2006; Proctor, 2000). This allows the supervisor and Yvonne to focus on seven aspects:

1. The content of the supervision session
2. The strategies and interventions
3. The therapeutic relationship
4. The therapeutic process
5. The supervisory relationship
6. The supervisor's own process
7. The wider context (organisational issues, social context, professional codes and ethics etc.)

This process allows a clearer focus on the relationship between Yvonne and Susan and overcomes the issues that can often occur in supervision, where the focus can be on just organisational issues to the detriment of some of the key clinical issues. Jacqueline encourages Yvonne to reflect on the issues within her relationship with Susan and the dynamics within that relationship. Jacqueline helps Yvonne to explore the nature of the interpersonal interactions; Yvonne becomes aware that it is her beliefs that ultimately Susan is unable to control, because her illness determines her interpersonal interactions. Yvonne feels appalled at this realisation. Through a process of putting Yvonne in Susan's position, with Jacqueline playing the role of Yvonne and modelling her interactions with Susan, Yvonne recognises how she has disempowered Susan and taken control. Following clinical supervision Yvonne realised that she had inadvertently wrested control away from Susan and that she was empowering herself, rather than working with Susan, to enable her to take control as far as possible over her own life.

At the next appointment Yvonne and Susan took the opportunity to review progress so far and to acknowledge Susan's vulnerability to being marginalised in her own life decisions. Susan also took time to reflect with Yvonne about her contact with the practice nurse, Beth, in relation to her physical health. Susan discusses the goal agreed with Beth that she would 'write a daily food diary for the next two weeks'. Susan highlights that at first she had lots of doubts about whether she would remember to keep the diary, whether she would be honest in her approach to it and also that she was a bit embarrassed as she had been eating a bit more than she previously thought.

Beth had identified that Susan might benefit from having support relating to her goal; highlighting the positive role that families, friends and carers can play in the clients support network (NHS Education for Scotland, 2007). Previous work highlights the improved engagement and outcomes for clients whose families or carers are meaningfully involved (NHS National Treatment Agency for Substance Misuse, 2008).

Susan does not feel that she wants to involve her family and wonders what other support may be available to her. Together, Yvonne and Susan brainstorm 'support in reaching my goal' and produce the following list:

- Affirmations and reminders around her living space, for example putting notes and memory aids in strategic locations.
- Keeping marks or tallies on a calendar or diary.
- Support via email.
- Support via online weight-loss forums. Online virtual networks have previously shown promise, with participants demonstrating significant symptomatic relief and falls in rates of self-harm (Rigby and Ashman, 2008).

■ Support via text messaging. Text message interventions have been used in previous studies, demonstrating positive results (Franklin *et al.*, 2003; Pijnenborg *et al.*, 2010).

From this menu Susan opts to try online weight loss forums as a source of support. Her rationale for this is:

They are available 24 hours a day, no one knows me or my history, they are free, I would not have to even get dressed or leave the house if I did not feel like it and I will pick up useful tips and new knowledge.

Reflective exercise

(a) Do you have any concerns about Susan's choice of support network?
(b) How would you raise these concerns using a recovery-focused approach?
(c) What frameworks or resources would you use to guide you in your decision making?

In light of this Susan was asked to prioritise those control issues that she wanted to address first. Susan expressed her appreciation to Yvonne for helping her make the choice between medicines previously and now wondered if she could take this a step further by in future speaking directly with the prescriber herself. Susan, however, had some misgivings about this because she was unsure how Dr Jones, her psychiatrist, would react to her speaking about her medicine regime when she did not share his view of the diagnosis.

Yvonne asked Susan what would help her have the confidence to speak to Dr Jones, and after some discussion they agreed the need firstly to identify specifically what Susan would like to share with Dr Jones. Susan had used 'brainstorming' techniques before in preparing for essay writing at university and she suggested that they use this to get things out in the open. They wrote down everything that seemed important in any way and from this information they then went on to identify the main areas to be addressed and to express these in terms of questions:

■ How long will I be on my medicine?
■ How will I know when I no longer need medicine?
■ How will I know if I could manage on less medicine or not?
■ How did you come to the decision that I have got schizophrenia?
■ Are there any alternative treatments if I do not want to take this medicine long-term?

Susan said that it felt good to be clear about what her issues were, as she may not have been able to articulate clearly how she was thinking in the stress of an appointment with Dr Jones. Nevertheless, Susan, despite wanting to take this step, still was worried how the appointment would go. Yvonne invited Susan to list her anxieties as a first step to dealing with them.

Anxieties	Approaches
Being in a clinical environment and being kept waiting and feeling my anxiety build up	They agree that Susan's appointments with Yvonne will in future be clinic-based to help her become accustomed to clinical settings. Susan identified that taking a magazine to focus on would help with the waiting.
Forgetting what I want to say and also what Dr Jones says	Susan decides to take her list of questions and a notepad to write down the key points made by the doctor and also to note what actions they both agree on.
Being browbeaten and not listened to because he knows best	They agree to practise the appointment using role play techniques and reviewing by video playback.
Making a fool of myself so that he thinks I am very ill and need to be admitted because I lack insight	They agree to practise the appointment using role play techniques and reviewing by video playback.
Buckling under the pressure and just accepting whatever he says	They agree to practise the appointment using role play techniques and reviewing by video playback.

Susan is sure that Dr Jones will not understand her and that he is going to disagree with her about her diagnosis. Her experiences with her uncle and his abusive behaviour have made her suspicious of males, particularly where they can have power and potential control over her life. She has some preconceived ideas that the psychiatrist will not listen and will only be interested in ensuring that she takes her medicine, regardless of her own thoughts. However, during the initial session with Dr Jones Susan is surprised by his approach; rather than being adversarial and confrontational (as her uncle and her parents had been) he listens actively, demonstrates an interest and respect for Susan and her thoughts and does not disagree with her. This 'rolling with the resistance' (Miller and Rollnick, 2002) proves effective and Susan is given the time, without interruption, to tell him that she is not 'mad' and that there are reasons for the way she has behaved.

The atmosphere in the session is comfortable and Susan feels able to ask Dr Jones how he came to the decision that she has got schizophrenia. Dr Jones is not defensive in his answer; he describes the diagnostic process and how information from interviews with Susan and her family is matched against diagnostic criteria and he shows her the criteria from ICD 10 (WHO, 1992). Dr Jones gives an honest assessment of the diagnostic process and acknowledges that at times it can be uncertain and that without an objective scientific test it can be unreliable. In describing the shortcomings of the diagnostic process he says that there is evidence that many of the symptoms relating to schizophrenia, such as voice hearing and suspicious beliefs, can be caused by a number of factors. He provides a list that includes trauma, a range of biochemical dysregulations, family history, severe emotional disturbance, thinking biases and substance use (Birchwood and Jackson, 2001; Freeman and Garety, 2004; Kingdon and Turkington, 2005). He stresses that everyone has an individual experience of the symptoms and that understanding the individual nature of the experience is more important than using a diagnostic label. Susan asks how this could be done practically, so Dr Jones provides Susan with details about the stress vulnerability model (Zubin and Spring, 1977; Nuechterlien and Dawson, 1984).

Dr Jones explains vulnerability as a concept that can make people prone to or at higher risk of experiencing a psychotic episode and that any significant biological or psychosocial event from the perinatal period onwards can contribute to this vulnerability or proneness. Susan asks if this can be a traumatic life event. Dr Jones acknowledges this and asks Susan if this is the case with her. She says yes, but does not wish to talk about it now. Dr Jones then explains about how the vulnerability is activated through the experience of stress – either long-lasting stress or sudden extreme stress. Dr Jones asks Susan for examples of any stress that she has experienced. Susan says that leaving home and going away to university was very difficult, even apart from the exam stress. She said there was another stress relating to a family member, but she did not want to talk about that.

Susan then asked about treatment options and whether she needed to take the medicine long term. Using the stress vulnerability model as the framework for answering this question, Dr Jones asks Susan what she thinks about perceiving treatments in terms of stress management and stress reduction. Susan agrees that this makes sense and Dr Jones then describes a range of pharmaceutical and psychosocial treatments, such as cognitive behavioural therapy, stress management, solution-focused therapy and interpersonal therapy, that are effective at reducing stress and preventing future episodes of psychosis (Pilling *et al.*, 2002).

125

Susan was pleasantly surprised that the psychiatrist was very willing not to challenge her view that she did not believe that she 'had schizophrenia', although this was still his belief. Together they did agree that it would be useful to look at experiences that contributed to her problems in life and not label these as symptoms or relate them to an illness. This all went smoothly for Susan, who on reflection felt that the work in preparation for this appointment was more useful in giving her the confidence to attend, rather than how to assert herself, because as it turned out the psychiatrist was much more friendly and adaptable to her way of seeing the world than she had ever imagined would be the case when in role play.

Susan felt confident enough to ask how long she would need to keep taking her aripiprazole. Although she had found it useful to deal with edginess, suspiciousness and voice hearing, she wondered if it would be needed for life. Dr Jones listened carefully to Susan and at no time made her feel rushed or out of control. Susan shared her aim to go to art college and he seemed pleased that she had this ambition. They agreed that it would be useful to weigh up when it might be right to consider the prospect of reducing the dose of aripiprazole, and Dr Jones asked Susan if this could be carried out with the help of Yvonne. Susan was pleased at the proposal that she would carry out this discussion with Yvonne, but when agreeing to this she was paradoxically aware of her ambivalence as she also felt some fear about possibly managing without medicine in the future.

Dr Jones sent a letter to Yvonne following his meeting with Susan. At their next appointment Yvonne and Susan reviewed the experience and outcome of the appointment with Dr Jones and what this might mean for the continuing focus for their work together. Susan said that she was keen to continue to work on increasing her confidence/ability to take control of decisions in her own life. She said that she had given a lot of thought to the sexual abuse perpetrated by her uncle and Yvonne's question at the time of disclosing to her: What problems, if any, do you think the abuse has left you with? She said that for her it was very much linked to her need to feel that she could have as much control over her life as possible. At this point she also discussed her parents and their taking of control regarding her career choice and, linked with this, their insistence that she shadow her uncle. Susan reflected on her recent achievements around exerting more control over her life and that being clear about what she wanted and planning how to achieve this, supported by Yvonne, has had a positive impact on her feelings of power and control.

Susan mentioned that she would like to work towards going to art college, an idea which previously her parents had dismissed out of hand. Susan asked Yvonne if they could make a plan towards achieving this goal. To help in making plans to achieve this goal Yvonne supported Susan to complete a Strengths, Weaknesses, Opportunities and Threats (SWOT) analysis (Weihrich, 1982) at their next appointment:

SWOT analysis

Strengths	Weaknesses
I have had previous experience of study at university level Natural artistic ability I'm determined to carry out a long-held ambition	Unsure of my own ability Lack of current portfolio Not able to afford tuition fees
Opportunities	Threats
Worthwhile and fulfilling career Having fun Another chance to make my own decision There is an art college locally	Becoming ill like last time at university Parents' expected response

Susan is encouraged by this process and she and Yvonne decide to use the areas identified to keep focused on working towards her goal. At this point Susan also reflects back to her discussion with Dr Jones about her medicine, how long she would need to take it and when might be a good time to think about reducing/ stopping this. Susan is still keen to try without medicines but is also scared at the possibility of becoming unwell and being detained in hospital and her future plans being thwarted. Yvonne listens attentively to Susan as she deliberates, wondering whether using the approach of writing down the pros and cons and weighing them up might be helpful. Susan is thoughtful and says that in actual fact just hearing herself speak about her medicine – she feels that she is not experiencing any side-effects and the medicine is helpful – means that on balance she feels that the time would not be right to seriously consider a reduction at this point, as she does not want to jeopardise her goal of going to art college. She wonders that maybe once she has got herself established at art college she would like to revisit her decision then. Yvonne is supportive of Susan's decision.

At this point Yvonne raises the possibility of formally screening for potential side-effects of the aripiprazole. Susan is puzzled by this, as she has just told Yvonne that she is not experiencing any side-effects. Yvonne explains that it is acknowledged as good practice to screen for side-effects on a regular basis using a validated assessment. Susan thinks back to the numerous questionnaires and scales she was asked to complete in hospital and is not at all keen. Yvonne does not want to force the issue and suggests that maybe they could look at a scale and use it for discussion. Susan suggests that they re-visit the side-effect profile of aripiprazole and discuss from there. Yvonne is somewhat relieved for two reasons: firstly, that they will be able to have a discussion around side-effects and secondly that she will not have to use the LUNSERS at this point. The Liverpool University Neuroleptic Side Effects Rating Scale (Day *et al.*, 1995) is the assessment used in Yvonne's workplace. Yvonne has been a bit uneasy about her use of this scale, as she has found it difficult to reconcile the use of the 'red herrings' in the scale. She understands why these were included for validation of the scale, and that altering a validated scale/assessment can affect its validity and reliability. However, she worries that she is being disingenuous with service users. Yvonne feels strongly that the she finds that the main benefit of using any scale is about how it promotes discussion, rather than it just being about the completed scale, which in her experience is often just filed and not necessarily discussed or really reviewed. She has not discussed her concerns about the 'red herrings' in her team, as she worries that she may be 'missing the point' and appear really stupid, as she has not heard anyone else have similar concerns or read about any concerns in the literature. She is also concerned that this may be perceived as her questioning her colleagues' practice, and relationships can be tense enough at times. Yvonne decides that she will make a point of discussing this with Jacqueline, her clinical supervisor, at their next appointment.

Yvonne and Susan review the side-effect profile of aripiprazole (BMJ Group and Pharmaceutical Press, 2011b) and Susan identified anxiety and constipation. Susan says that yes, at times she felt a little anxious. However, she felt that this was when she was thinking towards the future, rather than it being her medicine and her fear that she might end up in hospital again. Yvonne discussed that what might be listed as side-effects could also be related to factors other than medicines. Susan had noticed that she had been constipated when initially started on the aripiprazole; however, as she was focusing more on her diet as a result of contact with Beth, the practice nurse, that this had now resolved. Susan shared her relief that her weight had started to reduce – she had now lost 1.5 stones and was feeling very positive about her progress with Beth, with whom she now had monthly appointments. Susan said that she was not feeling so self-conscious now as a result of this weight loss. They agree that the focus of their next appointment will be making plans towards meeting Susan's goal of going to art college.

At their next appointment Susan mentions to Yvonne that she has seen in the local newspaper that an evening art class is available this month, which she plans to attend. Although she has some ambivalence about the pace of this development, as they have not had a chance to do some preparatory work, Yvonne expresses her delight that Susan is taking control of her own life in this way and working so positively to begin to achieve her aim of gaining a place at art college. On her first night at the art class Susan is much more apprehensive than she had anticipated, and finds it difficult to be able to relax.

Mr Piper, the tutor, tries very hard to create a welcoming and encouraging environment but he does make it clear that he is out to see students' work developing. Susan feels satisfied at just getting the first class over and spends much of the next week on a sketch of her family farm and adjacent fields. At the next class Mr Piper gives Susan advice about how to develop perspective when drawing to enhance her sketch, which he describes as very promising. Susan at first takes this at face value, although she does begin to develop a sense of unease over the next few days. She ruminates that Mr Piper did not seem to have given any advice to other class members. She also becomes more convinced that he did not really seem to like her and had looked at her in a way which on reflection seemed critical.

Reflective exercise

For what reasons do you think Susan is particularly sensitive to Mr Piper's comments?

Susan ⊗ Yvonne

On Susan's next visit to the clinic she decides to share her feelings towards Mr Piper with Yvonne. Yvonne's reaction is one of immediate concern. Although she does not voice this straight away, she regrets allowing Susan to attend the evening class so quickly before taking the opportunity to build more resilience with her. Almost before she realises it, Yvonne finds herself trying to persuade Susan not to attend evening class. Yvonne is very concerned that this situation is reminiscent of Susan's previous suspicion of lecturing staff at university. This all 'rang alarm bells' for Yvonne because of the relapse plan work up to that point.

Reflective exercise

Is Yvonne right to feel concerned at this time?

Susan, on the other hand, reacts by becoming overwhelmed by her mixed and conflicting emotions. Once again she is being stopped in her desire to become an artist, and although she has trepidation about going back to the class she does not think it right that Yvonne should decide this. Susan cannot find the words to convey the deep emotions which all this stirs up, and leaves the appointment in tears.

Yvonne takes all this as confirmation that Susan is becoming ill again and she telephones Dr Jones to discuss this. He suggests that they have a joint appointment the following morning. This is arranged and Susan agrees with this because she wants an opportunity to make sense of her own feelings. Dr Jones listens attentively to Susan's story from the start of the art class up to and including her appointment with Yvonne, and takes a guided discovery approach. He uses Socratic questioning to help Susan discover and explore her beliefs about what is happening. Paul (1995) lists the following six Socratic questions: questions which clarify, questions which probe assumptions, questions which probe reasons and evidence, questions about viewpoints, questions which probe implications, and questions of a reflective nature.

Reflective exercise
Give examples of the kind of questions that Dr Jones might have used.

Reflective exercise
Reflect on what might have happened if Dr Jones had taken a risk-aversive view, agreeing with Yvonne, strongly recommending that Susan does not attend the class and advising that it could be a good idea to increase her aripiprazole.

In light of their discussion Dr Jones proposes that it might be useful to review the situation using the stress vulnerability model that they had discussed previously. Together they could see that the art class, although being a positive step, was also a stressor. After some consideration they also agreed that for several reasons Susan might have particular vulnerability to this kind of stressor and therefore be specially sensitised to Mr Piper's comments. Although Susan felt somewhat reassured that her emotions were explained in a way that made them feel normal, she also had not completely lost the notion that Mr Piper was treating her unfairly.

Together, Susan, Yvonne and Dr Jones agree that the art classes should be continued, but also that they should be regarded as a kind of experiment. Although Susan does not want to go back to the art classes, exploration of her thoughts and feelings enables her to draw the conclusion that not going back would be a retrograde step, and that she would not be able to experience the benefits of the learning, development and self-confidence she would gain from attending. She agrees a rationale for a piece of clinical work that will help her manage her thoughts and associated feelings, ultimately realising the latent benefits of attending the art classes.

One of the key principles of cognitive behavioural therapy (CBT) is that of collaborative empiricism. Within the field of CBT, strategies that place people in situations that expose them to anxiety provoking stimuli in order to recognise existing beliefs and/or generate alternative beliefs are categorised as behavioural experiments. These are planned experiential activities designed to test the validity of people's existing beliefs about themselves, other people and the world and to construct and test new more adaptive beliefs (Bennett-Levy *et al.*, 2004).

Collaboration is the key to planning successful experiments. Susan, Yvonne and Dr Jones plan the strategy. For the first part of the strategy they use a modified version of a five-column worksheet for identifying anxious predictions (Fennel, 1999) to structure Susan's reflections regarding her interaction with Mr Piper at the art class (Table 5.1). With prompts from Yvonne, Susan is encouraged to reflect on specific aspects of the experience. Yvonne asks Susan to describe the situation, her range of emotions, her thoughts connected to her emotions and the strength of those thoughts. Yvonne then asks Susan what she predicts will happen and how she would rate her belief in the prediction. To help Susan make a prediction, Yvonne asks Susan to complete sentences that include 'if' and 'then' statements. Some of these statements referred to 'If Mr Piper told me to change the way I paint then I must be a bad artist' and 'If other people heard the criticism then they will know I'm a bad artist'. After some discussion Susan completes the sentence 'If Mr Piper offers some comment

Table 5.1 Completed five-column identifying anxious predictions worksheet (adapted from Greenberger and Padesky, 1995).

Date	Situation	Emotions and body sensations rating (0–100%)	Automatic thoughts	Anxious predictions (rate belief 0–100%
4 July 2011	Art class community college, West Street. Mr Piper makes comments about improving my painting	Anxious (95%) Embarrassed (95%) Heart pounding (95%) Feeling hot and red 100%	'My art work is rubbish' 'I'm worthless' 'Nobody here will want to talk to me'	'His comments were negative' (90%) 'Everyone else heard his comments' (80%) 'Everyone here will know my art work is rubbish' (85%) 'Everyone here will know I'm a fraud' (80%) 'People here will not think I'm worthy – they will not want to talk to me' (85%)

and advice on my artwork then the whole class will know that I'm useless at art'. Susan completes the five-column worksheet.

Susan agrees to attend a few art class sessions and collect further information from what she observes for the worksheet prior to seeing Yvonne for their next appointment, when they will discuss the detail of the worksheet.

Susan ⟶ Yvonne   During the next session Susan and Yvonne work through the information Susan has written into the five-column worksheet. Demonstrating facilitation and partnership working skills is essential, as this allows Susan to develop these alternative perspectives herself, ensuring they are hers and no-one else's. Susan identifies alternative perceptions which could potentially change the prediction she has made about Mr Piper offering her constructive advice about her art work. During the art classes since last seeing Yvonne she observed Mr Piper smile when he looked at her work and murmured 'very good' in a meaningful tone. She then observed that he made constructive comments to three other members of the class about their work. During two other visits he was observed making comments to at least four members of the class, including Yvonne, regarding their work. In each case he made constructive comments and no other members of the class even looked up when he made comments. She was able to reflect that his tone of voice was respectful and his words were very constructive and positive: 'I like the way you have included these colours. Have you thought about bringing other darker colours so that these bring out the brighter colours in the foreground?'. Other members of the class have begun to talk to Susan and ask her about her favourite artists. Two other members of the class commented on the quality of Susan's work. This made Susan feel good about her work.

The next stage of the strategy involves Susan evaluating the evidence that supports her anxious prediction and developing alternative perspectives. Yvonne facilitates this process by asking relevant open-ended guiding questions such as those listed below:

- What is the evidence to support what you are predicting?
- What is the evidence against what I'm predicting?
- What alternative views are there? What evidence is there to support them?
- What is the worst that can happen?
- What is the best that can happen?
- Realistically what is the best that can happen?
- If the worst happens, what can be done about it?
  (Fennel, 1999)

This helps Susan to generate an alternative prediction, different from the one that causes her to think badly about herself and feel anxious. The process also generates prompt questions that she can ask herself. The answers to these questions activate the alternative prediction, making Susan feel more positive and less anxious. Once these are generated Susan is then encouraged to practise using the prompt questions and thinking about the alternative prediction.

The third stage of the strategy is to formalise this alternative prediction and the prompt questions into a structure. Susan is then encouraged to rehearse using the strategy, practising it as role play and then in the 'real life' situation. Susan gives feedback at both stages and slight modifications are made to the strategy with regard to the way in which she will observe for evidence that supports her alternative prediction. On evaluating the strategy, Susan describes a significant reduction in her anxiety and this, together with receiving the benefits of attending the classes, results in her reporting increasing self-confidence.

Yvonne takes the opportunity to look again at her work with Susan with Jacqueline, her clinical supervisor. Yvonne recognises that she had allowed her own anxieties about Susan's behaviour in the past to have blinkered her perspective, rather than looking objectively at Susan's readiness to cope in the current situation. In doing this, Yvonne wrested the control away from Susan, which further fuelled Susan's mixed emotions. Yvonne's initial approach was therefore in danger of becoming a self-fulfilling prophecy. In this case, multidisciplinary working and clinical supervision helped Yvonne to work through a very difficult dilemma with a positive outcome. Susan and Yvonne decide to go back to the work they had already completed on the short-term timeline and relapse prevention work, so that they could refine the details of the kind of situations which might increase Susan's risk and the warning signs that might indicate that Susan is at risk of becoming unwell again, and detail further ways to minimise/manage this risk (Table 5.2). This would help facilitate Susan to have control over her life and not to feel that her life should be risk-free, and also enable her to manage situations as they occur, based on previous learning. Susan and Yvonne worked together over the next six months, focusing on areas that Susan identified as important to her in staying well. Susan developed her own electronic journal, which could be refined over time as a log of the process and content of their work together.

Susan's friend Kate from university was now on placement in a local firm of architects. Susan had valued Kate's help in building a picture of her time at university. Susan was keen for Kate to continue to be involved as a trusted friend who could accompany her when trying out new ways of dealing with social situations. Yvonne emphasised that it was important to remember to relax and have fun, and that sometimes people could become rusty at this. There was a need

Table 5.2 Short-term timeline.

External events	Changes to thoughts, feeling and behaviours
Return to university in October 2008	I worried other students knew about my admission to psychiatric hospital. I avoided social situations.

Agreed actions: I will refer to my journal of the work with Yvonne on how to manage stigma. This will include the rule of thumb that generally it is the case that other people take you as they find you, and it is not useful to avoid social situations based on the assumption that they will know about my past admission.

In December 2008 at the time of my assessment submission dates.	I felt stressed and did not sleep well, but despite wanting to complete the assessment items I could not concentrate and felt the pressure was overwhelming. I often worked through the night to get all my work done.

Agreed actions: I will engage with all academic support from the outset and attempt to pre-empt a feeling of being overwhelmed by tackling workload trimester by trimester in a measured way. I will continue with good sleep hygiene, exercise and relaxation.

Christmas holidays 2008: discussed with my parents that I was on the wrong course at uni but they were angry about this and again threatened to cut me off financially	I felt really trapped and not listened to, like the time I did not want to go to my uncle's firm for shadowing experience at school. I could not feel really angry with my mum as she was coping with her own problems. Studying architecture felt repugnant to me.

Agreed actions: I will remind myself of the value of my own choices and refer to the journal.

Return to university in January 2009	I felt this could not go on. I was hardly sleeping, hardly going out of my room and was very suspicious and began again to hear a male voice.

Agreed action: If I start to experience difficulties sleeping and start to feel suspicious, I will contact Yvonne and we will use the same CBT strategies and approaches we used with the difficulties regarding Mr Piper.

to develop a healthy balance so that everything did not become too serious and introspective, whilst at the same time addressing some key issues. Kate is first and foremost a friend, not a therapist.

Susan expressed concerns about dealing with stigma and her low self-esteem, connected to thoughts that other people would look down on her because she had been admitted to a psychiatric hospital. Together they accessed information showing that, for example, almost anyone could experience behavioural changes associated with psychosis when faced with particular stressors, such as sleep deprivation, isolation, grief, and trauma dislocation. The electronic journal became a personalised stress vulnerability and coping account including examples of information and reflective thoughts. This was also useful for indicating ways in which Susan's decision-making had been driven by her negative thinking as regards stigma and treating this as an opportunity to practise decision-making based on positive assumptions as experiments.

An important area for Susan was the relationship with her parents. Based on the way she had prepared for her first meeting with the psychiatrist, she talked through with Yvonne what she wanted to say and how she would express this. Yvonne then helped to move towards simulating this and practising how to deal with both positive and negative responses. Susan wanted to share with her parents her decision to apply for a place at art college, and she felt this was important for her to demonstrate her own autonomy and to build a new and more equal relationship if possible. She also thought that this was important to demonstrate her own progress to herself.

In addition to all of this work, they decided to embed into the short-term timeline agreed actions of what might be helpful if, in the future, similar types of situation arose, particularly as Susan was enrolling at art college.

It has been quite a journey so far for Susan and Yvonne. They are feeling hopeful for the future, in spite of the potential challenges ahead. We leave them pulling all of their work together into a WRAP – Wellness Recovery Action Plan (Copeland, 2002).

CHAPTER 6

Concordance: the goal of mental health nursing

Abstract

This chapter considers how concordance might be integrated into practice in a systematic manner. It does this by analysing the construction of concordance in current practice in order to offer structured support for its development in the future. It first constructs a conceptual analysis of concordance from practical examples of it discussed throughout this book. It suggests that concordance can be viewed as a composite of knowledge, clinical judgement and person-centred action. In order to provide broader evidence for this view, examples from the narratives developed within this book are presented alongside examples from the literature on mental health nurse prescribing and advanced practice. The chapter then analyses these components of concordance to examine the barriers that may need to be overcome in order to facilitate concordance more widely. It recognises the complexity of concordance, but concludes with a rubric directed towards developing the requisite components in both routine and advanced practice.

Key points

- Concordance is best defined as a composite of what it is *in practice*.
- Concordance entails knowledge, clinical judgement and person-centred care. All components are necessary.
- The barriers to concordance can therefore be understood as barriers to these components.
- These barriers can and should be overcome.
- A framework for surmounting these barriers and hence supporting concordance is articulated.

Key words

Psychotropic medicine, concordance, critical appraisal, knowledge, understanding, clinical judgement, person-centred care, positive risk-taking, collaboration

Objectives

- Develop a theory of concordance in action
- Critically appraise this theory
- Articulate the limits of clinical judgement and critical appraisal
- Articulate the fundamental importance of different health beliefs
- Develop a strategic overview of future support needs requisite to embedding concordance into mental health nursing

The reflections in this chapter are different from the others throughout the book in that they are answered more or less immediately within the text. The reason for this is that the nature of this chapter is to reflect on the book as a whole. So to begin with, consider the following reflection. It is addressed in the next section.

Reflection

Spend some time reflecting on how your understanding of concordance has changed as a consequence of reading the first five chapters of this book. Is there any way this understanding could be translated into a useful practical model for the articulation and strategic development of concordance in practice?

Introduction

This final chapter takes a structured look at the major themes underpinning the principle of concordance. This is to examine how these themes can be articulated by mental health workers and supported by wider organisations.

In order to provide an accessible structure to this discussion we first complete the above reflection in some detail. This is to identify meaningful patterns and commonalities in order to ascertain generalisable aspects of concordance. For example, throughout the unfolding narratives we have seen that concordance entails listening skills, respect, person-centred care and in-depth critical knowledge of medicines. It requires a genuine interest in the recipient of the medicine and a professional self awareness in order to understand the impact of the professional's role on the therapeutic relationship. Whilst it is acknowledged that these issues are intimately interrelated we have summarised these themes under three major headings in order to focus on specific examples of each (Figure 6.1):

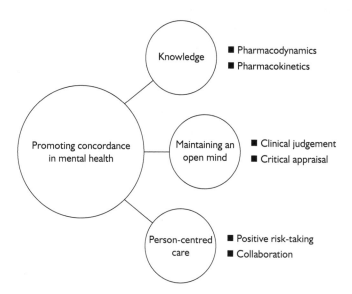

Figure 6.1 Concordance: a framework for educational, professional and strategic support.

- Knowledge
- Maintaining an open mind
- Person-centred care

The first theme is knowledge. Throughout the scenarios, knowledge of pharmacology was expressed. So for example, in Murdo's case knowledge of the pharmacology of antidepressants is essential. In Susan's case we need to understand adverse events associated with olanzapine, while for Dougie's case an understanding of older adult physiology underpins pharmacodynamic considerations. On top of all these, working knowledge of psychosocial interventions has been shown to be invaluable.

Maintaining an open mind has been a consistent theme. It subsumes issues of critical appraisal and clinical judgement, pertaining to the individual and the wider evidence base. For example, we have seen that where advice has been offered outside partnership agreement, things go wrong. In Susan's story, despite Yvonne meaning well, she got carried away with her own agenda. This is an instance of being closed to what was actually required.

Our third theme relates to issues of person-centred care. Person-centred care means ensuring that the outcome of any intervention aligns with what the person actually wants. It requires genuine collaboration and the capacity for positive risk-taking. This requires being comfortable with people holding beliefs different from our own. We have seen many techniques to support this facilitation, from the complex to the straightforward. Socratic questioning is quite difficult to master, for example, but facilitates collaboration. At the other end of the spectrum, and just as importantly, we saw how person-centred care was facilitated in Chapter 5 through simple positive risk-taking by accompanying Murdo outside when he was frightened to go out.

In order to show that these issues are not just common to the unfolding scenarios but also consistent with excellent practice in general, we have sought comparable instances from the literature to illuminate specific coherent connections with the wider evidence base (Snowden, 2011). In order to provide a structure for this discussion we focused on integrating the literature articulating examples of excellent practice from two groups of senior clinical nurses: nurse prescribers and advanced practice nurses. The reason for focusing on these senior clinicians was to show how the themes of knowledge, maintaining an open mind and person-centred care express themselves in this wider group of specialist nurses. The reason for highlighting these commonalities is to show that practising in a concordant manner may be more attainable than some of the policy literature (National Collaborating Centre for Mental Health, 2010) would have us believe.

This chapter is split into two sections. The first specifies the wider evidence for concordance coherent with the emerging themes from this book. The second section reflects on what this means for nurses, educationalists and policy makers wishing to support concordance in practice. The chapter then finishes with a framework summarising the salient aspects from in this evidence. The purpose of this framework is to show future guideline developers that concordance is possible to articulate in practice.

In more detail, the first section of the chapter introduces evidence for the expression of concordance, initially within the nurse prescribing literature and then within the advanced nursing practice literature. It highlights specific instances of the themes of concordance and links them to comparable examples given in the scenarios within the book. This provides evidence of concordance in practice across a range of clinical instances. Elements of person-centred care, professional knowledge and critical understanding are all shown to be related to positive outcomes.

The second section examines these themes in depth in order to show how difficult they can be in practice. The reason for this is to maintain a sense of realism. It is one thing to articulate a thematic analysis, but quite different to operationalise this clinically. An understanding of the structure and function of social process is required, and this analysis is provided in this section. This is important because we need to acknowledge that concordance is difficult to achieve. As discussed in Chapter 1, it would be ideal if every mental health worker could deliver person-centred care in every therapeutic encounter, and be open minded enough to take positive risks grounded in an excellent knowledge base. We know this is not the case, so we need to offer some explanation as to why. If this can be articulated and understood then we have a greater opportunity for the next clinical guideline on medicine management to be led by the principles of concordance as opposed to adherence.

It should be absolutely clear by now that our thesis is that concordance should be the ultimate goal of practice. We will show that the requisite skills *can* be articulated by considering the three interconnected themes discussed here. These themes can therefore be used as a framework to build the necessary support structure to facilitate concordance. The book finishes by articulating this support structure and suggesting further reading.

Section 1: Evidence to support the existence of concordance in practice

Concordance in nurse prescribing

Background

In order to contextualise this discussion we need a brief overview of the relevant prescribing legislation in UK. For an extended discussion pertaining to mental health in particular see Snowden (2008b). In summary, the Medicines and Human Use (Prescribing) (Miscellaneous Amendments) Order of May 2006 effectively meant that in the UK non-medical prescribers, including all registered nurses, could prescribe virtually any medicine for any condition, given that they were trained appropriately and felt competent enough to do so (Department of Health, 2006). Competence is therefore a fundamental issue for individual prescribers, as the onus is on them to articulate and demonstrate their sphere of competence. We will argue here that expression of competence entails the principles of concordance.

In general nursing, prescribing duties have been successfully integrated into various roles, possibly as a consequence of earlier legislation being targeted at supporting restricted prescribing for district nurses and health visitors. General nurses have therefore been prescribing in one form or another for longer. For whatever reason, mental health nurse prescribing (MHNP) has grown slowly in the UK (Hemingway and Ely, 2009). There is an enduring divergence of views on whether mental health nurses should be prescribing or not (Wells *et al.*, 2009). While many mental health nurses have seen prescribing as an opportunity to offer more holistic care (Murray *et al.*, 2007; Laird-Measures, 2010; Grainger and Keegan, 2011) others have had concerns about not being sufficiently competent (Bradley *et al.*, 2007; Kwentoh and Reilly, 2009), and some believe nurses should leave medicine to medics (Patel *et al.*, 2009). Only 1 in 3 MHNPs prescribe once qualified (Jones *et al.*, 2010), suggesting there are indeed some enduring problems between the idea and the enactment of mental health nurse prescribing in practice.

In order to explore these issues from a practical perspective, Snowden and Martin (2010a) studied 40 practising MHNPs in the UK over four years, and concurrently analysed the MHNP literature (Snowden and Martin, 2010b), integrating practical examples of MHNP practice from 13 peer-reviewed case studies. In summary, they found that where the prescribing qualification made life better for individual users of medicines, and the prescriber felt supported by the organisation, prescribing was more easily integrated into existing clinical practice. Successful prescribers were subsequently able to tailor advanced knowledge of pharmacotherapy to the individual needs and understanding of their patients. This is concordance.

However, an unexpected corollary of Snowden and Martin's investigation was that these competent prescribers came to realise, on reflection, that they had not been as competent in medicine management as they had previously believed themselves to be. This claim will be analysed in the final section of this book, as it has strategic consequences for the integration of the principles of concordance in undergraduate nursing. First, it is important to review primary evidence of successful nurse prescribing from a wider sample of nurse prescribers to show how elements of this practice relate to the themes in Figure 6.1.

Evidence for concordance within prescribing practice

Table 6.1 illustrates examples of concordance within prescribing practice from the literature. These examples are set alongside comparable examples of the theme from the unfolding scenarios. The first column entails the thematic structure illustrated in Figure 6.1. The first row of the table gives examples of the theme of knowledge from the case studies and the literature. Knowledge in the chosen examples relates to aspects of relevant pharmacology. We could have chosen any example of knowledge necessary to practise safely, such as legislation or diagnostic issues, but we have chosen pharmacology because of its central importance to safe medicine management.

Table 6.1 Examples of the themes of concordance within the case studies and the literature on nurse prescribing.

Theme	Case study	Literature
Knowledge: e.g. pharmacology	A 'cognitive enhancer', donepezil is a specific and reversible inhibitor of acetylcholinesterase (AChEI) (Grainger and Keegan, 2011). Its use is predicated on the belief that a significant decline in neurons containing the neurotransmitter acetylcholine (McGleenon et al., 1999) is a significant factor in the disease process of Alzheimer's type dementia (Chapter 4, Scenario 1).	The typical antipsychotics have an affinity for blocking the flow of dopamine in the mesolimbic and nigrostriatal dopamine pathways. The nigrostriatal dopamine pathway has a role in assisting the brain to coordinate bodily movements. It has been suggested that when hypodopaminergia occurs in the nigrostriatal dopamine pathway as a consequence of taking antipsychotic medication, then the patient is likely to develop EPSE (Jones et al., 2006).
Maintaining an open mind: clinical judgement	Helen began to suspect that there might be some initial challenges to developing the partnership necessary to complete a comprehensive assessment of Murdo's health and wellbeing due to the apparent lack of verbal response (Chapter 4, Scenario 2). She encouraged him to tell his story and helped him construct a timeline (Ford, 2000). These can span a short or long term, and help the service user focus on events that may be part of their un-wellness or their recovery.	'…there are moments when you clue into somebody's beliefs, where they are at that moment, and when they're in the mood to discuss. They recognize that you are in the mood to discuss too and you're giving them the time, space and opportunity. There are other times when you can ask the best questions in the world and they don't want to go there' (Practice nurse 3, cohort 1, one month interview) (Latter et al., 2010, p. 1134).
Critical appraisal	Helen was aware of research which suggested that full remission of depression is an attainable goal, but for some patients, combination and augmentation strategies using atypical antipsychotic medication early in treatment may increase the likelihood of this remission taking place (Kennedy and Lam, 2003) (Chapter 4, Scenario 2).	Nurse prescribers believed that they were practising certain fundamental principles of concordance... [this was not] borne out by findings from the observation of practice in this study. [This aligns with the finding that] nursing students often claim an easy allegiance to principles of 'new paradigm' health education, but that implementing the principles in practice often proves a more difficult task (Latter et al., 2007, p. 16).

Table 6.1 (continued)

Theme	Case study	Literature
Person-centred care: positive risk-taking	Yvonne, the CPN, discusses these issues with the wider multidisciplinary team, who are at first not keen to consider alternatives because olanzapine has been successful in symptom management. However, they agree that a change of medication could be considered and so Yvonne suggests Susan try aripiprazole because it is weight neutral (BMJ Group and Pharmaceutical Press, 2011b). Yvonne advocates for involving Susan fully in this decision and proposes to do this on her next visit (Chapter 4, Scenario 3).	Unlike previous contact with the mental health services, David (the subject of Jones et al.'s case study) has agreed and continues to work with services. David initially requested that our work with him focus on supporting him in his long-term aspirations to reduce his dose of olanzapine and eventually withdraw from treatment completely. We agreed to support David in this option, though outlined the potential risks and what we could do to minimise these risks. Following his recent CMP review, David requested that we continue to support him with his current treatment plan of 7.5 mg. He has now been well for 12 months (Jones et al., 2006).
Collaboration	(Example of where collaboration breaks down)\ Yvonne felt satisfied with her progress with Susan and therefore was surprised when for the next two appointments Susan was not in when Yvonne visited. Yvonne telephoned the next morning and Susan picked up the phone. Yvonne was shocked at Susan's dismissive and abrupt tone but somewhat relieved when Susan did agree that she could visit later that day (Chapter 5, Scenario 3).	[nurse prescribing] moves away from unilateral decision-making and it genuinely is a collaborative process between patient, nurse and doctor... (Oldknow et al., 2010).

Discussion of concordance themes in Table 6.1

One of the first things to note is the contextual nature of all these contributions. The knowledge examples are not simply expressions of knowledge for its own sake, but are applied to the setting. The case study discussion of the pharmacodynamics of acetylcholinesterase inhibitors precedes a discussion of the impact of that medicine on Dougie, and its likely effects. It provides evidence of the underpinning theory of neural degeneration associated with a diagnosis of Alzheimer's disease. Without this knowledge it would be impossible to administer the medicine safely in any meaningful way. Likewise, Jones *et al.*'s (2006) discussion of the underlying mechanism of iatrogenic movement disorders demonstrates an awareness of the risks of antipsychotic medicines. This suggests that the nurses will know what to look for in terms of side-effects and monitor accordingly. All of this may seem perfectly obvious, but as in Chapter 2 we would state that person-centred care is utterly incomplete without a critical *contextual* understanding of the pharmacology underpinning the interventions applied.

As in Figure 6.1, 'Maintaining an open mind' entails two subcategories: clinical judgement and critical appraisal. The example chosen from the nurse prescribing literature elucidates a situation that will probably be familiar to most mental health workers. The nurse recognises that sometimes people are in the mood for a deep discussion of issues and sometimes they are not (Latter *et al.*, 2010). Allowing someone to engage at their own pace is essential. The Murdo scenario example is related, in that Helen 'suspects' there may be some initial challenges to developing a partnership. Both examples show quite clearly that assessment is not simply about the quality of the assessment tool, although this is an essential component. It is also about the clinical skills of the person doing the assessment. Remember how Yvonne jumped ahead without Susan in Chapter 5? It could be argued this was poor clinical judgement. There are claims that clinical judgement may be related to a type of emotional intelligence (Codier *et al.*, 2010), and this will be discussed in the following section.

The other subtheme of 'maintaining an open mind' is critical appraisal. Critical appraisal is the capacity to balance available evidence. In other words, in order to understand the likelihood of a certain intervention being successful the evidence for that intervention needs to be understood within context. In the case study example Helen suggests that there may be a likelihood of remission being enhanced through augmentation of treatment with antipsychotic medication in the early stages. This is grounded in high-quality cited evidence and is a potentially important intervention pertinent to the current context.

However, whilst this example shows why it is relatively straightforward to incorporate high-quality evidence, the literature example was chosen to illustrate the necessity for criticism. This important example introduces a potential fly in the ointment. In their study examining concordance in practice Latter *et al.* (2007) found that concordance is a lot easier to assimilate into language than it is into practice. In other words, although nurses believed they were applying principles of concordance within their prescribing activity their behaviour suggested a much more directive approach. This is extremely pertinent to this book and will also be discussed in more detail shortly.

In the examples of 'positive risk-taking' the goal for both David and Susan was reduction and ultimately cessation of olanzapine. These related examples begin to show just how difficult concordance is. Although both expressed the desire to stop taking the medicine, in Susan's scenario the multidisciplinary team is reluctant and in David's case, the vignette shows the anxiety of the team through their focus on risk *management.* Both result in positive outcomes, but it is interesting to see the role that risk plays in these journeys. A wider reading of both these cases shows the anxiety to be a function of clinician disquiet premised on the assumption that all is currently well.

In other words, listening to what people actually want may be uncomfortable for clinicians, who may not historically have taken much notice of 'side-effects', given that as far as they were concerned the primary problem was under control. Subjectively unpleasant effects were tolerated for the greater good. However, as discussed in Chapter 2, the notion of side-effect is potentially disingenuous, and an improved understanding of just how unpleasant these medicines can be has driven a more sympathetic view, certainly within the literature (Bentall, 2003). Weight gain and akathisia are highly distressing. A quick trawl through the internet sees many instances of users of antipsychotics describing akathisia as a living hell. However, it would be equally disingenuous to suggest that stopping the drug is always the best solution. Positive risk-taking then, like concordance, is a lot easier to say than do.

The case study example of collaboration was chosen as an illustration of what can happen when collaboration goes wrong. It is a particularly striking example of what happens when good intentions outrun the person they are intended to help. Yvonne is oblivious to her actual impact on Susan throughout this time. This is because the proposed care is no longer person-centred. As you saw in the previous chapters the situation is rescued, but this period was avoidable. There are parallels with much of the literature on paternalism, and it raises interesting ethical issues regarding the function of caring when it is dissociated from the recipient of the care. These ethical issues simply do not arise where collaboration is maintained.

The example from the literature is much more straightforward and simply entails a statement of the function and form of collaboration within this particular team. It describes who the collaboration is between and favourably contrasts this with a unilateral approach to decision-making. There are many comparative examples, whereby collaboration is seen as a universal good. This is virtually undisputed within the literature but, as we have seen, it is a lot easier to say than do.

Concordance in advanced nursing practice

Background
This part of Section 1 takes a similar approach to the previous one in that it compares examples of aspects of concordance from the unfolding scenarios with examples of concordance from the advanced practice literature. This is to show the breadth of concordance and the necessity to recognise its value beyond mental health nursing. That is, concordance is not just a topic worth elaborating for mental health services but for medicine management in general. First, a brief discussion of the concept of advanced practice is needed to define the scope of this section for an international audience.

As with the rest of this book we will be focusing mainly on UK nursing literature, so some differences need to be clarified. Unlike the USA, for example, there is no nationally recognised Advanced Nurse Practitioner (ANP) role in UK. Nursing in UK is regulated by the Nursing and Midwifery Council. The NMC protects the public by registering all suitably qualified nurses as fit for practice in one of four branches: adult, mental health, children and learning difficulty. Despite the content and skills differences of these four branches, all registered nurses abide by the NMC's Code of Conduct, which informs the public what level of skill and expertise they may expect from a qualified nurse.

The NMC further recognises three recordable qualifications: teaching, specialist practice and prescribing. However, despite protracted discussion aimed in a general sense at integrating these recordable skills into a registration for advanced nurse practice, there is no consensus on what competencies the public should expect from such a practitioner. The UK definition of ANP therefore differs across the country, and there are currently a multitude of advanced nursing roles, all with different titles, responsibilities and remuneration. For the purpose of this chapter, we will use the broad term of advanced practice to include all advanced clinical roles, such as nurse consultants, modern matrons, specialist practitioners and any other advanced role, such as clinical nurse specialist. This decision was not taken to make any statement on the advanced nursing debate within the UK, but simply to ensure that the literature search included evidence about concordance from as wide a range of advanced nurses as possible.

Evidence for concordance within advanced nursing practice

In order to source appropriate evidence from the advanced practice literature we looked for examples of positive outcomes as a function of partnership working within the thematic structure illustrated in Figure 6.1. There was a lot of this evidence, so to keep the discussion manageable we focused on just two specialities: diabetes and oncology nursing. As in the previous example, case study literature or reflective examples of clinical practice were sought to maintain focus on descriptions of nursing in action. Table 6.2 summarises some of the examples from this literature combined with aspects from the case studies, as in Table 6.1.

Discussion of concordance themes in Table 6.2

The discussion on knowledge within Table 6.2 relates to pertinent knowledge for the particular speciality. Consequently, we have three different examples of context-specific knowledge. Within the literature the examples show a diabetic nurse helping to manage some unpleasant effects for a grateful recipient and a cancer nurse studying risk through knowledge of heredity. In Murdo's scenario we show further detail from the example given in Table 6.1, where Helen integrates knowledge of appropriate assessment with classification of depression and augmentation of therapy. As in the mental health nurse prescribing example, none of the subsequent skills discussed would be effective without this level of context coherent knowledge.

The examples in the clinical judgement section were chosen for their diverse but related set of approaches to exercise an open mind. All demonstrate awareness of the likely needs of the person, which is essentially grounded in awareness that people respond differently at different times and circumstances. Murdo's scenario shows that the application of clinical guidelines requires an open mind to the possibility that the process needs to be tailored to individual needs. Helen realises that Murdo and Mary are exhausted and discusses a different strategy with them. Specialist nurse 3 in Latter *et al.*'s (2010) study demonstrates a deep awareness of the importance of listening to what the person is actually saying. She has chosen to pay attention to the words the person is using as a technique to better understand what is happening. Perhaps the clearest example is practice nurse 6. Through a simple question 'What are your priorities today?' she conveys the message that she is open, receptive and interested.

Table 6.2 Examples of the themes of concordance within the case studies and the literature on advanced nursing practice in cancer and diabetes.

Theme	Case studies	Literature
Knowledge	*Knowledge of medicine management* All of the interventions involved full assessment. Initially, in order to determine the severity of Murdo's depression, Helen used the PHQ-9 assessment rating scale as seen in Table 4.3 on pages 85 and 86. Because Murdo scored 22, Helen prescribed a course of antidepressants (fluoxetine 20 mg), and after a week introduced amisulpride (200 mg b.d. for 3 days, then increased to 400 mg b.d. as Murdo tolerated it) (Chapter 5, Scenario 2).	*Knowledge of diabetes* 'I get these terrible itchy legs with the diabetes and she cured that. Took her a while to do it trying out different drugs but she eventually came up with the right combination and she cured it... She explained a lot of things that to be quite honest I didn't really realize' (Stenner *et al.*, 2011, p. 41). *Knowledge of heredity in cancer* But I do remember there were two... sisters who were grown up.... They came back here to ask about themselves... and I just came to talk to them and their fear: was it hereditary?.... It was either their mother or their sister who had died here, and then their grandmother had had it as well. So I thought well, there is something here... (Lillie *et al.*, 2011).
Maintaining an open mind: clinical judgement	NICE guidance (2010) is clear on the need to offer evidence-based stepped care (progressing through stages including medicines, psychosocial and self-help interventions). However, the first week's session with Murdo and Mary had been exhausting for him. He admitted that he found it challenging, and found the assessment and the timeline difficult. Helen therefore suggested that Murdo and Mary try to relax at home to start with, and that they look together at the booklets that she gave them (on sleep hygiene and on depression) (Chapter 5, Scenario 2).	'I'm trying to listen to the patient's words more carefully. I'm trying to listen to the words that they're choosing to use, because that could be very informative and can really highlight what's going on' (Diabetes specialist nurse 3, cohort 2, 1 month interview) (Latter et al., 2010, p. 1133). 'I always, now, open up a consultation with "what are your priorities today?" So that just flows now naturally and has been very useful' (Practice nurse 6, cohort 3, 1 month interview) (Latter *et al.*, 2010)

Table 6.2 (continued)

Theme	Case studies	Literature
Critical appraisal	Spielmans et al. (2011) suggest that psychotherapies and pharmacotherapy yield roughly similar efficacy in the short-term treatment of depression, with psychotherapies showing some advantage at long-term follow-up. Helen therefore decided to introduce some supportive therapies to Murdo's care situation that would begin to empower him to participate in the recovery process (Chapter 5, Scenario 2).	Diabetes care and research are changing so much that there is never a feeling of stagnation (Llahana and Hamric, 2011, p. 21). 'So the evidence that chemotherapy's beneficial in Hodgkin's disease is probably pretty overwhelming: but in many, the evidence is by nature, ... weak.... I mean if evidence and things were proven or not proven, ... you could (do) medicine pretty well by computer.... Chemotherapy is being increasingly applied... irrespective of any evidence of response' (medical interview 9) (McCullough et al., 2010, p. 485).
Person-centred care: positive risk-taking	Because Murdo appeared to be experiencing psychotic symptoms and he was reluctant to go outside, Catherine was able to support him to feel more confident about stepping out. Initially, they took the dog for a short walk along the shore outside his home. Murdo was agitated at times, and Catherine was able to practise some relaxation techniques with Murdo that helped him control his symptoms. He and Catherine developed a close working relationship over the ensuing weeks, and Murdo began to value her input to his recovery journey (Chapter 5, Scenario 2).	'It makes me feel happy that I am in control of what I want to do. They [nurses] can make suggestions on what I tell them, but it's not written in stone that I am saying you will do, or have, this. I have an involvement in what I do' (Stenner et al., 2011, GP6p2, p. 43).
Collaboration	Susan and Yvonne construct the timeline and it becomes clear that there were some key issues during the time she was back at university, which she linked to her relapse. She was able to track the beginning of the change of her lifestyle (Chapter 4, Scenario 3).	The main purpose of an oncology nurse navigator (ONN) is education regarding the effects of treatment and management strategies, as well as education of next steps to follow and resources available to get through treatment. An ONN must be available to patients for questions and be able to direct them to the correct answers and resources (Swanson and Koch, 2010, p. 72).

Reflective exercise

Just for a moment consider how would you feel if someone asked you this. We believe these types of question communicate genuine interest in a clinically useful way. Another medicine-related example may be 'What do you believe this medicine will do for you?'.

The evidence for the function of collaborative exploration of health beliefs will be analysed in the next section.

In terms of critical appraisal, the examples from the literature illustrate the limits of evidence, both in terms of keeping up with it (Llahana and Hamric, 2011) and applying it in a clinically useful manner (McCullough *et al.*, 2010). In the first instance, Llahana and Hamric (2011) explored the development of the diabetic specialist nurse (DNS) role in order to ascertain the process through which competent practice was developed. Whilst some may find the endless updating of knowledge exhausting, they suggested that these nurses found the integration of new evidence a stimulus against complacency. They explained successful functioning in relation to 'good communication and support, recognition and positive feedback from colleagues, management and patients'. This suggests quite clearly that there is an important social aspect to the capacity for critical appraisal and that good communication and organisational support are essential.

The comment from the study by McCullough *et al.* (2010) goes to the heart of the limits of evidence-based practice. Practice should always be led by evidence. There is no place for any other type of reasoning. However, there will always be gaps in the evidence, so clinical work will never be entirely evidence-based. The case study example shows that this should not prevent critical judgement. Despite equivocal evidence for pharmacotherapy and psychotherapy in the cited study, Helen takes this as an opportunity to offer both. The safe application of evidence in these instances depends to a large extent on how informed the recipient is. We would argue that this is a function of person-centred care.

That is, we saw previously that positive risk-taking sometimes leads into unknown territory. However, because this was an open, honest process the risk was mitigated. The same is true in the examples we discuss in this section. Of particular relevance to our thesis is the work of Stenner *et al.* (2011). They have a significant body of work investigating the role of the diabetic nurse prescriber, a role that straddles both specialism and medicine management, and therefore worthy of deeper discussion here. The example we have given in Table 6.2 shows a person expressing the autonomy and control facilitated by their nurse. Although this person recognises that the nurse is well placed to make suggestions, they are quite clearly at the centre of this relationship, in charge and pleased to be so (Stenner *et al.*, 2011).

Throughout their body of work Stenner *et al.* (2011) present empirical evidence that people prefer services where their lifestyle factors and opinions are considered by healthcare professionals within a partnership approach. Specifically, in the cited study they show how the consultation style of the nurse prescribers was recognised and appreciated by people who subsequently felt listened to and valued as individuals. As a consequence they felt free to discuss anything they felt to be important within the consultation and developed improved understanding of their condition and its successful management as a consequence. This is a perfect example of risk management through improved communication, and could therefore be viewed as a method of facilitating positive risk-taking. Importantly, they found that where people perceived the nurse to be genuinely concerned for their wellbeing this both inspired them to reciprocate efforts to improve their health and was seen as therapeutic in itself.

This aspect of positive risk-taking will be discussed in detail in the next section. However, the parallels with the unfolding scenarios developed in this book should hopefully be clear. The Murdo example of positive risk-taking in Table 6.2 parallels the qualities highlighted by Stenner *et al.* (2011). Murdo feels valued as a function of Catherine being genuinely interested. This stemmed from a practical solution (going out for an accompanied walk) aimed at facilitating positive risk-taking.

The final thematic category is collaboration. In the previous section we looked at an outcome of breakdown in care to show that negative consequences can be seen as a function of breakdown in collaboration. We also saw that collaboration is seen as a universal good in nursing. To complete the picture here we show examples of positive actions that support collaboration in practice.

Within the cancer specialist literature, Swanson and Koch (2010) showed that specialist nursing in cancer can reduce distress and hence improve quality of life. Theirs is an interesting paper, as the specialist nurse is referred to as a 'navigator' (Oncology Nurse Navigator; ONN), with the expressed aim of helping people through their individual journey in a structured manner. In other words, their dedicated role was related to collaboration. The most interesting aspect of this paper from a concordance perspective was the multifaceted role of the navigator. Depending on the person's needs the nurse could and did provide physical, educational, emotional and practical support, or some combination of these. The very existence of this role is arguably positive from an organisational perspective. It says to the person with cancer that the organisation recognises that the journey is complex and frightening and that they are concerned enough to do something about it. After Stenner *et al.* (2011) (above), this recognition is likely to be positive in itself.

The case study has an equally overt demonstration of collaboration, but this time focuses on a therapeutic technique discussed throughout the book: timelines. The *act* of constructing a timeline together is also inherently positive (Marland *et al.*, 2011a). This shared journey into Susan's past not only identifies events in her past that may be relevant to her present, but also demonstrates that Yvonne wants to help.

Summary of Section I

This section has presented evidence that the themes articulated throughout this book are pertinent to nursing and medicine management more widely. If concordance is construed as a composite of the themes illustrated in Figure 6.1 then it seems that these themes are coherent with excellent nursing practice in oncology, diabetes and mental health. If this is a generalisable claim then concordance begins to become demystified. It is simply a composite of these themes. However, demystifying concordance is only the first step. In order to support its wider evolution into everyday language and practice we need to review these individual themes in some depth. This is the main purpose of the next section.

Before we can do this we briefly need to reflect on the quality of the information and the analysis we have conducted so far. This is because despite the apparent existence of certain patterns and connections this is clearly just one part of the story. For example, the evidence for advanced nurses applying critical appraisal skills in a consistent manner is far from convincing. The evidence for coherent application of knowledge in medicine management in mental health is equally slim. There are other forces at work and they need to be articulated. This is also an aim of the next section.

In brief, all we are claiming in this chapter is that we have ascertained patterns within and beyond the case studies presented here that may help identify support needs. Interested readers are encouraged to study the primary sources to develop their own critical viewpoints. Although we would consider it unlikely, other readers could view the literature and case studies in a different manner.

However, we maintain that Figure 6.1 is clinically useful because there *is* convincing evidence that person-centred care and critical application of pharmacological knowledge facilitate concordance. As a 'best practice' aspiration then, the model is useful. There is evidence for it. The next section therefore provides a critical look at the evidence for and against the *themes* within the model. By understanding this wider context we can better identify and articulate clinical, theoretical and support needs requisite to the facilitation of concordance.

Section 2: Critical appraisal of the components of concordance

This section takes a critical look at the themes of knowledge, maintaining an open mind and person-centred care. They are discussed in turn along with their subcategories as highlighted in Figure 6.1. The purpose of this is to show the strengths and weaknesses of these concepts. The rationale for this is to articulate the best way to support them in practice. That is, we are assuming that a deeper critical understanding of these themes will more likely lead to a coherent strategy to support their development in practice. The chapter finishes by integrating the salient aspects of these analyses into a framework to support concordance by developing specific clinical, educational and strategic goals. This framework concludes the book. We will closely examine what we mean by 'maintaining an open mind' and 'person-centred care', but first we consider 'knowledge'.

Knowledge

Without knowledge it is doubtful any of the other themes would remain meaningful. There is evidence this knowledge is not as good as it should be. Recall at the beginning of Section 1 that we said we would discuss the claim that mental health nurses may not understand medicines as well as they think they do. This claim developed from analysis of statements such as:

> It's learning around medication that changes. The classic thing that [nurse prescribers] say is that they used to understand medication and now they REALLY understand. They didn't previously take on the responsibility. That seems to change the way they act. (Snowden and Martin, 2010a, p. 547)

This statement was taken from a study of nurse prescribers reflecting on their journey to becoming competent prescribers. On reflection, this and other prescribers within the study came to recognise that they had not been as competent in medicine management as they had previously believed themselves to be. We have since discussed this hypothesis personally with many other practising MHNPs who have confirmed that this is pertinent to them. Although this is only one study and some anecdotal evidence, it is a claim worth discussing because it fits with wider commentaries on the current status of medicine management within undergraduate mental health nurse education. For example, Hemingway *et al.* (2011) present evidence that medicine management has not been prioritised to the extent that it needs to be within pre-registration training, or indeed within current practice. This is widely agreed (Department of Health, 2006; Jones *et al.*, 2010), so it is worth considering how this position has developed.

First of all, we must be clear that there is no evidence to support any assumption that knowledge of medicines by mental health nurses was ever any better than it is now. Nevertheless, it is probably fair to say that in recent years knowledge of medicines has not held the central place it did in earlier mental health nurse training. For example, summative assessment in psychiatric nurse training in the early 1980s entailed a final written exam and four practice-based assessments: teaching, management, therapeutic intervention and the medicine round. The medicine round was invariably assessed by a scary and very knowledgeable charge nurse/ward sister who knew how everything within the drug trolley interacted with everything else, and expected the student to know too. At least that was our personal experience and we have not forgotten it yet.

Teaching medicine management is no longer like this, and quite rightly so. The assessment discussed above was not focused centrally on the person in receipt of the medicine. However, as the recipient of the medicine has rightly become the focus of attention the more mundane aspects of medicine taking, such as what medicines do, how and why, has perhaps diminished too far. In other words, the diminution of the importance of psychopharmacology can be viewed as a paradoxical artefact of person-centred care. For example, the credibility of medicine in mental health has been challenged by progressively eloquent deconstructions of the medical model (Bentall, 2003; Moncrieff, 2007) and sophisticated criticism of classification of mental illnesses (Kutchins and Kirk, 1997). These critiques have engendered a mistrust of 'treatment' within psychiatry. At the same time the increasing recognition of the limits of reductionist biology and hence pharmacology (Noble, 2002, 2006) has been paralleled with the rise of evidence-based alternatives to medicines, such as cognitive behavioural therapy (Hall and Iqbal, 2010). All of these developments appear to be grounded in the ethics of human rights (Barker, 2011), which offers further moral credibility to non-medical perspectives of mental health.

Nurse education has evolved in parallel with the zeitgeist. According to Skingsley *et al.* (2006) the prominence now given to psychosocial interventions within mental health nursing education has led to the neglect of biological approaches in preregistration education. If this is true, it is out of step with public action. That is, psychotropic prescribing has continued to rise year on year

(Information and Statistics Division, 2011), making medicines the most widely utilised intervention in mental health by some margin. In other words, mental health nurse training has quite rightly been driven by the recovery agenda, but this agenda needs to recognise that more people than ever take psychotropic medicines, and so medicine management needs to also be at the front of this agenda.

It is important to be absolutely clear that the claim that mental health nurses may not understand medicines as well as they think they do is taken from anecdotal evidence and an inference from a single study. Mental health nurses may be entirely competent. However, if it is generalisable to any degree then people prescribed psychotropic medicines may not be as well supported as they could be. Novice mental health nurses may be subsequently having their pharmacology knowledge assessed by nurses who themselves are not only busy and over-stretched (Hemingway *et al.*, 2011), but are not as knowledgeable as they think they are (Snowden and Martin, 2010a). This creates a tension with the NMC requirement regarding evidence of competence in drug administration:

> The administration of medicines is an important aspect of the professional practice of persons whose names are on the Council's register. It is not solely a mechanistic task to be performed in strict compliance with the written prescription of an independent/supplementary prescriber. It requires thought and the exercise of professional judgement... (Nursing and Midwifery Council, 2010, p. 1).

Whilst it is fair to acknowledge that some Higher Education Institutes have recognised the issue and take a highly structured approach to medicine management in mental health (Hemingway and Ely, 2009), there is no explicit directive for them to do so. The professional directive is that competence in medicine management be assessed as one of the skills clusters (Nursing and Midwifery Council, 2010; Table 6.3 shows the relevant conditions of entry to the register). There is evidence to suggest that training pertinent to clinical practice is best managed within this setting (Reid-Searl *et al.*, 2010), and so it makes sense for medicine skills to be assessed in practice. But as already stated, this is problematic if the trainers are not up to the task.

This book suggests therefore that there should be an explicit academic component to developing competence in medicine management. We also agree with Hemingway *et al.* (2011) that a stepped approach to medicine management is sensible. For example, the University of the West of Scotland, along with its clinical partners in NHS Ayrshire and Arran and Greater Glasgow and Clyde have

Table 6.3 Essential Skills Clusters: Medicine Management (Nursing And Midwifery Council, 2010, p. 35).

36. People can trust the newly registered graduate nurse to ensure safe and effective practice in medicines management through comprehensive knowledge of medicines, their actions, risks and benefits.

First progression point	Second progression point	Entry to the register	Indicative content
	1 Uses knowledge of commonly administered medicines in order to act promptly in cases where side effects and adverse reactions occur.	2 Applies knowledge of basic pharmacology, how medicines act and interact in the systems of the body, and their therapeutic action.	Related anatomy and physiology. Drug pathways, how medicines act.
			Impacts of physiological state of patients on drug responses and safety, for example the older adult, children, pregnant or breast feeding women and significant pathologies such as renal or hepatic impairments.
		3 Understands common routes and techniques of medicine administration including absorption, metabolism, adverse reactions and interactions.	Pharmacodynamics – the effects of drugs and their mechanisms of action in the body.
			Pharmacotherapeutics – what are the therapeutic actions of certain medicines. Risks versus benefits of medication.
		4 Safely manages drug administration and monitors effects.	Pharmacokinetics and how doses are determined by dynamics and systems in the body.
		5 Reports adverse incidents and near misses.	Role and function of bodies that regulate and ensure the safety and effectiveness of medicines.
		6 Safely manages anaphylaxis.	Knowledge on management of adverse drug events, adverse drug reactions, prescribing and administration errors and the potential repercussions for patient safety.

developed a level 9 (final year undergraduate or postgraduate) module designed to improve knowledge and skills in medicine management for registered nurses. The content of the course matches the indicative content of the skills cluster in Table 6.3, with specific focus on psychotropic medicines.

In terms of delivery, theory on pharmacokinetics and pharmacodynamics is presented alongside case studies, such as those developed within this book. This module is designed to bridge the gap between basic undergraduate skills, such as drug calculations, and advanced clinical practice, like prescribing. Perhaps such a stepping stone may not only objectively improve medicine management knowledge for these nurses, but also offset the finding by Jones *et al.* (2010) that only 1 in 3 MHNPs prescribe once qualified. That is, these nurses may be better equipped to go on to become prescribers because their knowledge and insight into that knowledge will be better aligned than current prescribing course attendees. This is being evaluated (Snowden and Barron, 2011).

Maintaining an open mind

A mind is like a parachute; it doesn't work if it's not open (Frank Zappa)

The reason it is important to maintain an open mind is to acknowledge the possibility that we might be wrong. This is very important in a clinical context as we need to be alert to signs and signals that may otherwise be ignored because they don't fit with what we have already decided to believe. There are many theories of learning that explain how we process information. One that neatly explains a theory of the mechanism of why this process sometimes goes wrong is cognitive dissonance. Cognitive dissonance was initially described by Festinger in 1954 (Kruger and Dunning, 1999). It describes the psychological discomfort felt when new information fails to align with existing beliefs. It assumes that people have to make sense of new information within an existing belief structure, so if something does not fit, either the information or the belief structure needs to change.

Most people are capable of going some way to changing their view of the world in the light of new evidence. However, some people are better at this than others and some information is easier to assimilate than other information. A well-worn example is that most people used to believe that the Earth was the centre of the Universe. As a result of observations by Copernicus and others, most people eventually came to accept that the Earth was not the centre of the Universe. However, this information was more difficult to assimilate for some people than others, with the level of difficulty partly related to the strengths of belief and the amount of effort invested in the original belief.

Considering the Earth to be the centre of the Universe may seem silly now, but cognitive dissonance has good explanatory power relevant to examples today. It explains why extremist thought is not amenable to change. For example, cognitive dissonance explains the endurance of conspiracy theories. From a cognitive perspective conspiracy theories can never be disproved if the underlying assumption that there *is* a conspiracy theory is unshakeable. All new information is simply assimilated within that belief. In Copernicus' case then, for many people the Earth remained at the centre of their Universe, and they came to believe instead that Copernicus was simply wrong (Principe, 2011).

Of clinical relevance is the capacity to recognise and react to new information in a clinically constructive manner. As far back as 1991 Harrison recognised that cognitive dissonance could be a factor in nurses underestimating the pain that their patients endured. Harrison suggested that because nurses were ineffective at reducing the pain they played down its severity. Whilst this cognitive strategy reduced the dissonance for the nurses, it was not the best outcome for the patients.

It has to be acknowledged that this is a theoretical explanation, but the literature on cognitive dissonance is extensive and compelling. We therefore need to be aware of such possibilities affecting our own belief systems and take steps to mitigate them. Without understanding our own beliefs and the impact they have on the therapeutic relationship, concordance is unlikely to be optimal. There are two techniques pertinent to enhancing clinical awareness. We will discuss the place of critical appraisal in relation to research shortly. First we will look at clinical judgement. It will be seen that the evidence for this is poor. In other words, as soon as people move away from evidence they are left with constructs such as intuition, or emotional intelligence. Like cognitive dissonance, these constructs are self-protective rather than clinically demonstrably useful, and therefore not necessarily conducive to best practice. We would urge caution in relying on this type of knowledge. Clinical supervision may offer some protection in this regard, but again the evidence is poor.

The purpose of segregating this discussion on maintaining an open mind into separate components is primarily to highlight the fundamental importance of critical appraisal skills. However, it would be disingenuous to consider lack of evidence as *no evidence* for the value of clinical judgement. There is certainly a place for it, as discussed below, but its limits need to be understood, mitigated and managed. The first part of this section therefore breaks the discussion on clinical judgement down into summaries of the utility of assessment tools, the lack of evidence for intuition, emotional intelligence and clinical experience; and finishes by suggesting these limitations can be offset to a degree through structured reflection on practice. In other words, maintaining an open mind for the purpose of facilitating concordance is dependent upon evidence-based interventions. The art of critical appraisal finishes this section.

Clinical judgement

Clinical judgement integrates tacit knowledge with best evidence to meet the specific needs of the person (Thornton, 2006). This is a widely cited understanding of evidence-based practice:

> Evidence-based [practice] is the integration of best research evidence with clinical expertise and patient values. (Sackett *et al.*, 2000, p. 3)

Clinical judgement is therefore the art of balancing research and experience with the situation in hand. We will discuss how to critically appraise research in the next section. Here we will concentrate on the more difficult aspect of applying the results of that appraisal. Good clinical judgement can be considered a function of two related elements: the quality of clinical assessment tools and the quality of the clinician using them.

The reason we use assessment tools is to maximise pertinent information and minimise error. We need to be able to define and agree what we are talking about in order to have a meaningful conversation with others. In other words, clinical judgement is facilitated and enhanced with appropriate assessment tools. The better the assessment tool the better the conversation.

For example, in Section 1 we introduced evidence of concordance from the oncology nursing literature. A significant and well-validated tool supporting this process was the distress thermometer (DT) (Mitchell, 2007). The DT is a screening tool (Richardson *et al.*, 2006). It has been validated in a wide range of studies and is reliable. This is extremely important as the quality of the assessment method dictates the quality of the information returned. In short, participants rate their distress, tick any problems they have, and finally indicate and rank their three most pressing problems in priority order.

The fact that the tool has been extensively tested in a wide population is essential, as we now know that it is a clinically meaningful measure of distress in this population (Mitchell, 2010). Without this process any clinical judgements made would not be as robust. However, assessment tools also present significant opportunity to enhance clinical judgement. For example in cancer care the distress thermometer (DT):

> ...brought up issues during consultations which might not normally have been discussed, enabling [nurses] to use consultation time more effec-

tively by focusing on patient concerns. It also demonstrated to patients and their carers that the health care team were interested in all aspects of patient wellbeing. (Lynch *et al.*, 2010)

In other words, as we saw in the unfolding scenarios using timelines (Marland *et al.*, 2011a), the *act* of gathering high-quality information fulfils a dual role. Completing the DT not only indicates clinical levels of distress, but also appears to have the potential to function as a sign that the clinicians knew what they were doing and were interested. The impact of this is both simple and effective. The statement below is from a person who had filled out the distress thermometer before a consultation. By systematically organising her thoughts she noticed she had got more out of this consultation than usual, thereby facilitating clinical judgement:

I think [the DT] was pretty helpful because [the consultant] did explain a lot more that day we went there... sometimes you get there and your mind goes blank anyway, and you forget what you were gonnae ask... if we didn't have the [DT] form a lot of things [we] spoke about in the waiting room wouldn't have come up. As I say, [the consultant] seemed to explain a wee bit more, well a lot more to us about my situation. (Interview 8) (Snowden *et al.*, 2011)

Nurses have seen the potential here and taken the function of the DT further still. The example of collaboration in Table 6.2 related to the Oncology Nurse Navigator was also taken from a study that used the DT as a method of assessment. In their study, like Lynch *et al.* above, Swanson and Koch used the distress thermometer not only to identify relevant aspects of distress but to support people appropriately. In other words, although the DT was developed as a screening tool to identify clinical levels of distress, advanced nurses have used it to facilitate clinical judgement directed towards practical ends.

Parallels can easily be drawn with the case studies that weave through this book. That is, the act of assessment in these cases has become an overt demonstration of the desire not just for information but a means of facilitating personally relevant clinical information. The assessment method signals that the nurse is open to receive personally relevant information.

However, we also discussed earlier that there are occasions when even the best assessment tool is not enough. Sometimes people do not or cannot engage. One of us remembers as a clinician being asked to formally assess, at his home, a man who the GP suspected of having severe depression. Upon meeting him it was immediately obvious that he would be unable to complete any assessment, as he was so unwell. He was asked (without formal assessment) if he would come into hospital and he did. Completing an assessment in this case would not have been showing clinical interest. In fact it would have conveyed the opposite. So how do we know when to skip the algorithms and take alternative action?

In Section 1 we introduced the notion of emotional intelligence. We need to discuss this a little further here, as it would seem intuitive that this may be a necessary component of clinical judgement. We would also imagine that clinical experience would play a role, and related to this we need to look at the role of reflection on good practice. We will briefly discuss these in turn.

Emotional intelligence

In coming to a decision we use more than cognitive processes according to proponents of emotional intelligence (EI). Bar-On (1997) defined emotional intelligence as 'an array of non-cognitive capabilities, competencies and skills that influence one's ability to succeed in coping with environmental demands and pressures'. He believed that emotional intelligence develops and changes over time, and can be improved through training. It entails aspects such as reality testing, independence and emotional self-awareness. In order to test these ideas he developed the Emotional Quotient Inventory (EQI) as a self-report questionnaire that divides emotional intelligence info five composite components and 15 content subscales.

van Dusseldorp *et al.* (2011) used the EQI to study emotional intelligence in mental health nurses. This was the first study in the mental health nurse population and they found that mental health nurses scored significantly higher on EI than the general population. However, although they found other significant differences amongst the subscales, they measured so many variables that this may have been a chance finding. In other words, although it may be intuitively appealing to speculate that mental health nurses gain emotional intelligence over time or that clinical experience would be related to EI, this was not found in this study. Perhaps all that can be said from this particular study is that people with a higher emotional intelligence are drawn to the profession of mental health nursing in the first place.

It is also interesting to note that other work found unexpected consistencies across different age groups in terms of EI (Hess *et al.*, 2010). That is, where older people would have been expected to outperform younger ones on this measure it turned out this was not the case. Work on EI, in particular in relation to mental health nursing, is therefore a work in progress. Emotional intelligence as defined by Bar-On may or may not be correlated with clinical judgement. It is probable that the model of EI may need to be refined (Codier *et al.*, 2010) to better establish the influence of EI in clinical judgement. In other words, although we perhaps want to consider ourselves 'emotionally intelligent', there is no evidence as yet to support that assertion in any clinically relevant manner.

Clinical experience

> For the vast majority of day-to-day clinical decision-making situations, the 'evidence' for decision-making is experiential knowledge. (Thompson, 2003)

It is intuitive to assume that clinical judgement improves with experience. However, this assumes that peoples' *learning* improves from experience. Thompson's thesis is that this is not necessarily so, and this appears to correlate with van Dusseldorp's findings on emotional intelligence above. Thompson points out that nurses use cognitive shortcuts, or 'heuristics', in order to manage everyday clinical judgements. He then goes on to show that these shortcuts lead to error. Essentially he is arguing that evidence-based practice should supersede cognitive shortcuts. He recommends a version of probabilistic reasoning. Instead of relying on previous experience, clinical judgement should entail a rational balance of the likelihood of an action being the best one. Any other way of coming to a clinical judgement introduces bias and error.

If this is true then there may be times when clinical experience works against accurate clinical judgement. However, this is very difficult to address in the rational manner that Thompson suggests, because most people don't think probabilistically (Isaacs *et al.*, 2009). So, although Thompson makes a persuasive case, probably of more use from a pragmatic perspective is to recognise the limitations of such intuitively plausible constructs, such as emotional intelligence and clinical experience and use structured reflection on practice in order to offset these clear limitations.

Reflection on practice

There are many models of reflection that have been validated, many of them cyclic, such as Gibbs cycle of reflection or Kolb's model in Figure 6.2. Some are context-specific. For example Lasater's Clinical Judgement Rubric (Lasater, 2011) is designed to help facilitate the development of clinical judgement. This may be useful in supporting a general discussion on the development of these skills from a novice perspective. However, it may be more useful to incorporate this discussion within a critical incident review. Remember in Chapter 5 that clinical supervision was structured in this manner. In general there is some evidence that

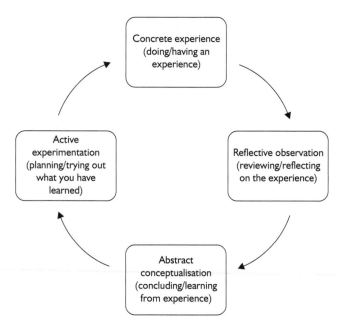

Figure 6.2 Kolb's learning cycle.

contextualising, structuring and personalising learning is effective. Action learning sets are a good example of this technique (Rivas and Murray, 2010).

Action learning sets

Action learning sets (ALSs) were developed as a process by McGill and Beaty (2001). People form a group or 'set' with the purpose of discussing issues of concern relating to practice. The process entails one member presenting an issue whilst the rest of the set enable or assist the presenter to explore the issue by asking clarifying, thought-provoking and open-ended questions. During the session the presenter may reflect on previously unexplored potential actions and make preliminary commitments towards experimenting them into action. Learning occurs not only for the presenter but also for other members in the set, as they themselves critically reflect. The process is based upon Kolb's (1984) learning cycle (Figure 6.2). Observing and reflecting on an experience leads to new planned behaviour about the way forward for a future situation.

It is difficult to find any rigorous assessment of action learning sets in the literature at present. That is, their impact on clinical outcomes has not been systematically studied. The tone of the current literature is that it is a useful model of reflection, and Young *et al.* (2010) claim care has improved as a consequence.

Clinical supervision

The most popular definition of clinical supervision is:

> an intervention provided by a more senior member of a profession to a more junior member or members of that same profession. This relationship is evaluative, extends over time, and has the simultaneous purposes of enhancing the professional functioning of the more junior person(s), monitoring the quality of professional services offered to the clients, she, he, or they see, and serving as a gatekeeper for those who are to enter the particular profession (Bernard and Goodyear, 2004, p. 8).

Clinical supervision has been around longer than action learning sets, so the evidence for its efficacy is deeper and broader. It is also equivocal, however. Buus and Gonge (2009) carried out a systematic review and methodological critique of the clinical supervision research in mental health nursing. They reviewed 35 papers in total and concluded, rather like the action learning set literature, that clinical supervision is broadly viewed as a good thing, supporting the need for structured reflection in a general sense. However, in their well-conducted study they concluded that a lack of uniformity of definition of clinical supervision and the methodological weaknesses of the studies made it difficult to support that conclusion. For example, the most popular definition quoted above failed all four necessary tests of a good definition: precision, specification, operationalisation and corroboration (Milne, 2007). This is one of the reasons it is difficult to discuss the literature on clinical supervision.

This is not to say that clinical supervision does not have a positive impact on clinical judgement. One of the main reasons for Buus and Gonge's (2009) reticence was the difficulty of separating out the effect of clinical supervision from any other variable within the included studies. In other words, clinical supervision *may* have been the reason behind care improvements; it was just impossible to tell with the research designs used. At present, it is fair to say that further research is required to identify the impact of clinical supervision on care.

In summary then, clinical judgement entails the use of the most appropriate assessment tools in conjunction with a critical understanding of their strengths and limitations, and when to use them.

> Participant 01: people react differently to different things and you don't always know everything that's going on so you make judgements based

on the evidence that you've got and information that you've got but you, you know, you can never know, so it's always about doing the best you can at that time. (Robertson and Collinson, 2011)

In order to be able to do the best you can at any time you need to be able to find and critically appraise appropriate sources of information in order to apply them. In maintaining an open mind to the end of concordance this skill should be prioritised every time. The next section will briefly discuss this issue.

Critical appraisal skills

Nurses find the application of evidence-based practice difficult, which may be why they rely on less robust methods of decision-making, as highlighted above. To some it is an issue of confidence:

> Don't trust enough of the knowledge I've accumulated, when others with long experience come with well formulated arguments. (Graue *et al.*, 2010, p. 13)

For others it relates to the perceived relevance of evidence in day-to-day work:

> Of the 90% of respondents who indicated they had access to electronic resources for research, 42% answered that they seldom needed research evidence to support their nursing role regardless of their work setting. (Beke-Harrigan *et al.*, 2008)

For more it is a matter of prioritising other tasks, with lack of time being cited most frequently as a reason for not engaging (Graue *et al.*, 2010). Running through all of these is the consistent theme that nurses find critical appraisal difficult to do. It is important to recognise that this difficulty is not confined to nurses. The art of critical appraisal is beyond the scope of summarising here. Instead we direct the reader to Trisha Greenhalgh's *How to Read a Paper* (2010). Currently in its fourth edition, this is an excellent resource. In this book we focus on the necessity for critical appraisal in order to make the case that critical appraisal skills are relevant to everyday work.

This case can be made easily by considering some of the difficulties highlighted above. Glasziou and Haynes (2005) beautifully articulated the numerous pitfalls between even the best quality evidence and clinical practice. These pitfalls include issues such as awareness, applicability and acceptance of evidence. Figure 6.3 summarises the salient points of their paper and we will discuss this now, as it illustrates the importance of critical appraisal within the process.

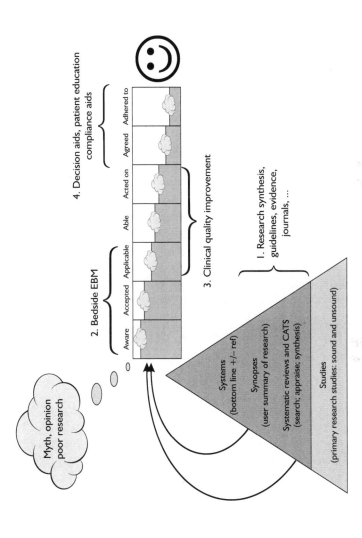

Figure 6.3 The research to practice pipeline (Glasziou and Haynes, 2005). New research, of varying soundness, is added to the expanding pool and enters practice either directly or is reviewed, summarised and systematised (delay) before entering practice, with leakage occurring at each of several stages between awareness and patient outcome. Different knowledge translation disciplines focus on different parts of the pipeline (1–4).

Figure 6.3 shows Glasziou and Haynes' (2005) interpretation of the journey between research and real-world outcomes. It is a drawing of the 'theory–practice gap'. The pyramid on the left shows varying types and quality of evidence coming into the consciousness of clinicians (the 'aware' box at top left of the pipeline). This then has to fight for space with myth, opinion and poor research evidence (intuition and emotional intelligence, for example) all the way through various stages within the process until it becomes routine practice itself. This journey entails numerous transitions where research can get lost, all with their differing risks and challenges. For example, a new method of working may make it all the way to be agreed on by all the appropriate stakeholders, yet still not be adhered to. The reasons for this are rarely related to open hostility or opposition to best practice, but more often simple process issues.

In other words, translating research into practice is extremely difficult. This is why it is absolutely fundamental that only the best research enters this pipeline in the first place. Note at the bottom of the pyramid that both sound and unsound studies vie for attention just like all the other research. We cannot rely on others to tell the difference. Understanding the difference between good and poor research is an essential skill for every nurse. It is impossible to maintain a truly open mind without this skill. It is highly recommend that you read and apply Greenhalgh (2010).

Person-centred care

Once we have the best evidence and knowledge at hand it has to be applied in context. This is person-centred care, which is our third and final concordance theme. Here we will discuss two essential and related components illustrated in Figure 6.1 and discussed throughout: collaboration, and first, positive risk-taking.

Positive risk-taking

The example given in Table 6.1 from the literature entailed Jones *et al.* (2006) listening and supporting David through a potentially risky endeavour, namely reducing his medicine. The outcome is positive for all. This is not always the case.

Promoting safety and positive risk-taking is the ninth 'Essential Shared Capability (ESC)' (NHS Education for Scotland, 2011). The ESCs underpin undergraduate mental health nurse education in that they define the values required of every mental health nurse. *Promoting safety and positive risk-taking* is expanded in the following terms: 'Using available resources and support to achieve the desired outcomes and to minimise potential harmful outcomes'. In other words, despite being labelled as *positive* risk-taking, its focus is actually skewed towards risk minimisation.

The zeitgeist for quantifying and avoiding risk at all cost is grounded in managerialism, an essentially paternalistic position (Keevers *et al.*, 2008). Organisations insure against risk and insurers guarantee that their own risk is mitigated by only insuring safe practice. Organisations and individuals are not compensated if they operate outside these margins. As a consequence, the capacity for risk-taking has to be considered within these limits. In this context person-centred care can be seen to conflict with a risk averse culture.

For example, the clinicians in Robertson and Collinson (2011) study on positive risk-taking referred to operationalising risk as *gambling*, an inherently risky activity. Whilst not gambling could be regarded as safe, it may not allow for the exercise of truly individual choice as promoted in ESC 9. At its worst, the needs of the organisation conflict with individual care. To be clear, we are not talking here about necessary restriction, where someone may need to have their rights temporarily curtailed for their own or others' safety. We are discussing everyday risk.

There are demonstrably negative consequences of an inherently risk-averse culture. For example, consider the following statement from a doctor in charge of medicine management at a nursing home:

> We very rarely go and see what we can remove from their list or try to rationalize it. Just tend to add on and they end up on massive amounts. (GP6) (Hughes and Goldie, 2009)

This is a doctor discussing their own behaviour as if they have no control over it. In order to clarify the impact of this admission the statement needs to be connected to the attitudes of the residents of that care home in order to understand the full consequences of that behaviour:

> I just take what I am given. I believe in doing what I am told. (R5)

> I'm completely happy because I feel that the people who are giving me the medicine know what they are doing and what I require and I accept that, so I just take what they give me – implicitly, without question. (R8) (Hughes and Goldie, 2009, p. 512)

This is resonant with the medicine-taking decision-making category of deferential compliance expounded by Marland and Cash (2005). Because compliance is guaranteed in this population, medicine-taking behaviour is seen as unproblematic (risk-free) by the doctors and nurses in this study (Hughes and Goldie, 2009). This is despite the fact that these clinicians recognise the lack of autonomy of the recipients (p. 513), and therefore the responsibilities they have for these residents. Further, the healthcare professionals in this study expressed the desire to be patient (resident)-centred, and *actually believe they are*. Yet risk-taking within this population doesn't even extend to rationalising 'massive amounts' of medicines.

We acknowledge therefore that risk-taking is culturally difficult at present. Whilst it is clearly positive in individual contexts, such as those discussed within this book, the reality is that any risk-taking that backfires may have serious consequences for the clinicians involved. It would be disingenuous not to acknowledge how entrenched this position has become. Positive risk-taking is therefore a function of a highly self-aware and skilled clinician working within a supportive and reflective organisation. Given that this is in place, subsequent capacity for positive risk-taking can be understood as a function of the quality of the therapeutic relationship:

> Participant 10: I think one situation with someone I am familiar with I am ok and I go so far in terms of risk-taking, someone I don't I probably am more cautious. (Robertson and Collinson, 2011, p. 155)

Collaboration

We have seen that collaboration is broadly seen as a universal good. However, collaborating does not necessarily save time. In many instances it may take more time, and there is evidence that some nurses feel that they don't have the skills to operate in this manner (Snowden *et al.*, 2011). Clinicians may fear opening 'cans of worms' they feel unable to manage (Latter *et al.*, 2010). However, there is evidence that this anxiety is unrelated to the evidence for collaboration. For example, collaborating did not take any longer than treatment as usual in a study of distress management (Snowden *et al.*, 2011). Further, if a collaborative consultation opens up a 'can of worms' this is often neither unwelcome, inappropriate nor unmanageable:

> I've opened a can of worms with some patients. I had been labouring under the misapprehension that they were actually managing quite well, that they understood what they were doing, that they were taking their medications... I'm now, in a sense, creating work for myself [but] I've found that's not the case. I've had to start working harder with them and getting to grips with what exactly is going on... I'm hoping that in the end, in the long term, it will actually reduce work, I mean its short term misery for long term gain so it's fine. (Community matron 1, cohort 2, 1 month interview) (Latter *et al.*, 2010, p. 1135)

Of course, some people may want to keep their cans of worms firmly closed and we would defend their right to do so. As in Marland and Cash's (2005) typology it is also important to recognise that people may not expect or want anything to do with medicine-taking decisions (Manias, 2008). For example, Stenner *et al.* (2011) found that regardless of the level of information patients wanted, when it came to making decisions about treatment, most preferred the nurse to use their professional judgement to offer the best treatment option for them. This makes knowledge of medicines' actions and interactions even more important, as in these cases the person is relying on the health professional to tell them everything they need to know. These 'passive compliant' people (Marland and Cash, 2005) still need to understand and be understood. However, although this is increasingly recognised as a worthy aim there is consistent evidence that nurses may not be giving people as relevant information about medicines as they think they are (Ekman *et al.*, 2007).

For example, Latter *et al.* (2007) examined medicine management by nurses. They wanted to analyse collaboration, and recalled that in 2000 nurses confined their practice of education about medicines to simple, one-way information-giving about the name, dosage and timing of administration of the medicine. They subsequently found that although the rhetoric of medicine-taking had changed considerably by 2007, the activity of one-way communication persisted. They concluded that the

> paradigm shift to a concordance model that emphasizes partnership through explanation of the risks and benefits of treatment options and fully informed patients able to make decisions about treatment options, was not yet integrated into practice. (Latter *et al.*, 2007)

This is particularly relevant to our book, as we have tried to show that the language of medicine management needs to be consistent with practice. Returning to the terminology of adherence may therefore be coherent with this agenda, but it does nothing to facilitate and embed genuine collaboration.

In an attempt to address this Latter *et al.* (2010) found nurse prescribers could be taught skills to further improve their communication skills. Latter *et al.* focused on teaching nurses how to elicit patients' *beliefs* about their medicines in order to better support their medicine-taking. The results were significant, and showed that there is considerable room for improvement in this area. Latter *et al.* conclude that the clinical consequence of better dialogue is unknown, and this is wholly consistent with a cautious interpretation of their results. However, there is broader evidence in support of the power of aligning treatment with beliefs.

Consider the placebo effect. Benedetti has spent an entire research career trying to understand the neurobiological underpinnings of this mechanism and produced some fascinating findings. For example, he has shown that if people take diazepam without knowing then it has no anxiolytic effect. He has also shown that pain can be reduced in people who believe they are receiving pain-relieving medication even when they are receiving opioid-blocking medication, as long as the person administering the medicine also believes it will relieve the pain (Benedetti *et al.*, 2005). This would suggest that the beliefs of *everyone* involved in medicine management have an impact on the efficacy of that medicine.

This is work in progress, but there is an important issue relevant to concordance. Whilst we do not understand why, there is evidence that medicine-taking behaviour that aligns with people's beliefs about the medicines is never trivial, and appears to exert a physical impact. This may go some way to explaining the efficacy of homeopathy for example. Many studies have shown that homeopathic tablets themselves contain nothing therapeutic and are no better than placebo (Goldacre, 2009). They are sugar pills. Their method of manufacture entails dilution of such magnitude there are no known physical laws that support the existence of them containing anything therapeutic.

However, recall the earlier discussion on cognitive dissonance. This would predict that someone who values the laws of physics would subsequently discount the therapeutic value of a sugar pill, regardless of the ritual performed to make it. Nevertheless, someone who believes strongly in the power of homeopathy would probably instead doubt the power of known physics to explain how it works. Goldacre falls into the first camp and the vast majority of people who value physics and the rationality of probability would likely follow him. However, we have also seen that a significant proportion of people are not necessarily rational in this manner, and subsequently view the world in less rigorous ways. Homeopathy exploits this doubt, which is essentially grounded in the truism that there are limits to human knowledge.

Therefore, although there is nothing in the pills, homeopathy as an intervention may be effective in a certain population of people, or at certain points in people's lives. This has consistently been shown to be a function of the consultation process. For example, in a rheumatology trial homeopathic consultation was shown to be beneficial (Brien *et al.*, 2011), whereas the homeopathic remedy alone was not. This is a consistent finding within this literature, illustrating the power of *collaboration*, a fundamental tenet of homeopathic consultations.

Skilled clinicians therefore need to understand the importance of their own beliefs within this collaborative process. Unlike Goldacre, who dismisses homeopathy as nonsense, we would suggest that finding out that someone believes in homeopathy tells you a great deal about the person you are collaborating with. This does not require a value judgement. In fact, we would argue that challenging this view may not be therapeutically justified. Perhaps all you will succeed in doing is removing a vestige of hope. We acknowledge that this is a moral minefield, in that colluding with beliefs you do not share is disingenuous. However, tolerance of different beliefs does not require collusion, and we do not believe there is any disingenuous function of attempting to establish a middle ground towards the end of clinical improvement. Remember Chapter 5, where Susan and the psychiatrist were able to discuss symptoms and classification of schizophrenia. There was no collusion here, just a mutual exploration of each other's understanding.

All this leads to agreeing with Latter *et al.* (2007), who suggest that we need to develop further educational approaches that would help facilitate *genuine* concordance. This is about stepping outside any semblance of paternalism and maintaining an open mind to the end of supporting person-centred care. In Latter *et al.*'s (2007) language it entails facilitating the 'more radical elements associated with fully informed patients choosing their preferred treatment options'. We would argue that concordance should not be radical, it should be the norm.

Conclusion

We have seen that concordance is complex. It is a normative concept which describes an ideal, and ideals are difficult to achieve. However, they are not always unattainable, and can be approached in a systematic manner once their complexity and in particular their utility is understood.

In order to break it down we have suggested that this complexity can be understood as a composite of some familiar themes, illustrated in Figure 6.1. The first and most obvious theme was knowledge. Any medicine management requires an in-depth knowledge of what the medicine is, what it is for and how it works. The other themes are irrelevant without this and vice versa. The second theme related to the qualities of the clinician. In order to apply knowledge in a comprehensible manner clinical judgement needs to be combined with critical appraisal skills in order to facilitate the best application of evidence-based practice. The third and final theme related to the focus of care. The knowledge and clinical judgement in the previous themes need to be individualised to the person receiving the medicine. We have seen how complex this is. It involves understanding people as they see themselves, because this is predictive of how they will respond to treatment. Treating people in a manner coherent with how they would want to be treated involves levels of collaboration and risk-taking that are rarely seen, and only possible within an entirely supportive organisational structure.

When summarised in this way it becomes quite clear why concordance is so hard to achieve. Risk-taking is frowned upon (Robertson and Collinson, 2011), collaboration is rarely as good as nurses think it is (Latter *et al.*, 2007), and clinical judgement has been shown to be grounded in irrational thought (Thompson, 2003). Nurses do not engage with evidence as much as they claim to (Nolan and Bradley, 2008), and nurses' knowledge of medicines in mental health also leaves room for improvement (Ndosi and Newell, 2009).

However, all is not lost. Person-centred care is at the forefront of modern mental health nursing (Scottish Government, 2010) and a significant driver of latest UK NHS strategy (Department of Health, 2010). Mental health nurses are demonstrably good at understanding people with severe mental health problems (Shattell *et al.*, 2006). They are more engaged with clinical supervision and other means of reflective practice than ever before (Severinsson and Sand, 2010), and the gap in knowledge of medicines is increasingly recognised and managed (Hemingway *et al.*, 2011). If these findings are indicative of a larger trend then they are all moving in the right direction. We will therefore finish the book on a positive note with a rubric to support the evolution of genuinely collaborative care grounded in the evidence for concordance in practice.

Recommendation

There is considerable evidence that when people are listened to and genuinely made the focus of the process they have better health (Department of Health, 2010). These are aspects of concordance. This book has shown different pathways to attaining concordance, and this final chapter has broken down the process into manageable components. We therefore finish by articulating the action needed to support progress within these components in order to better facilitate concordance as the endpoint of an intervention. In this way you will have the best chance of offering meaningful help to people that is personally relevant to them, grounded in the best evidence and delivered in a practical, caring manner. You will be able to reflect on this process with all relevant parties in a comprehensible manner.

Table 6.4 is broken down into the themes discussed throughout this chapter, and the clinical, theoretical and strategic actions needed to facilitate concordance. For example, the clinical column specifies the competencies necessary to attain these goals in practice. We have separated these competencies into those required of all nurses and those for advanced practice. This is to show how these basic skills can be developed and built upon. Requisite support needs are likely to differ at different points within a nursing career. For the purpose of simplicity we have reduced this to a distinction between the knowledge, skills and support needs of *all* nurses, and the comparable needs of advanced nurses.

Next to this is a column detailing the theoretical knowledge needed to support these competencies. These are all summaries of themes developed in detail throughout this book. The final column describes the support structure that organisations need to offer to facilitate this process in practice. These issues should all be familiar by now as they have been discussed in detail. However, it is important to see how they all fit together to the end of supporting concordance in action.

Table 6.4 therefore summarises the action required to support concordance in practice. It has been developed from the perspective of the clinician, as we have assumed that these people are most likely to be the first to recognise the value of concordance to practice. However, the wider purpose of this table is to offer a starting point for the systematic development of concordance. It could be used as a discussion document for any clinician, organisation, or education facility wanting to support the concordance agenda. These partners could come together with a clear idea of the paths each needs to take.

Concordance is best practice. It is realistic and achievable. It is better than adherence, which we would argue is not best practice in itself. From a purely objective perspective the evidence would suggest it is unachieveable. Fifty per cent of people do not adhere to prescribed medicines. However, when concordance is achieved adherence naturally follows, as the mutual agreement, and not the outcome of this agreement, has been prioritised. This is why current national guidelines for medicine management (National Collaborating Centre for Mental Health, 2010) have to evolve to recognise this, as they presently have these fundamental priorities the wrong way round.

Table 6.4 Support structure for the components of concordance.

Theme	Clinical (what do I need to do?)	Theoretical (what do I need to know?)	Strategic (What organisational support do I need?)
Knowledge: Pharmacology			
All nurses	Develop enough knowledge to safely administer medicine in line with NMC administration statement	Enough about medicines and diagnostics to exercise professional judgement	Formal medicine management training at undergraduate level. CPD
Advanced	Develop NMC competence in specialist area	Detailed critical understanding of aetiology, medicine actions and interactions	Nurse Prescribing course and ongoing structured support from multidisciplinary colleagues
Maintaining an open mind: Critical appraisal			
All nurses	Continually update skills and knowledge in relation to pertinent evidence	How and when to apply systematic critical appraisal to clinical information	Systematic organisational engagement with evidence-based practice e.g journal clubs
Advanced	Articulate, apply and contribute to the evidence within your own specialist area	Practical research skills training	Organisational support for research/ clinical linkages
Maintaining an open mind: Clinical judgement			
All nurses	Critically apply evidence-based practice	How and when to apply systematic critical appraisal to clinical information	Clinical supervision and systematic reflective practice
Advanced	Generate evidence-based practice	Practical research skills training	

Table 6.4 (continued)

Person-centred care: Positive risk-taking

All nurses	Apply safe clinical principles of risk management in practice	Critical understanding of MHA, RRR and ESCs	RRR revisited embedded within organisation. Open culture
Advanced	Demonstrate specialist application of these principles in complex circumstances	Specialist practice, knowledge of MHA case law. Critical understanding of ethics applied to mental health	Support for Specialist Practice Qualification/Clinical doctorate/ masters

Person-centred care: Collaboration

All nurses	Enact person-centred values within all practice	Critical understanding of the centrality of person-centred care	RRR revisited embedded within organisation. Open culture
Advanced	Specialist practice, e.g. developing a novel medication regime grounded in individual health beliefs	Critical understanding of the impact of collaboration	Support for Specialist Practice Qualification/Clinical doctorate/ masters

Further reading

We hope you have found this book practically useful and thought provoking. We have attempted to make concordance accessible, moral and practical. In this we have had to make shortcuts and sacrifice certain detail for the sake of sticking to the main stories. We would therefore like to finish by providing some recommendations for further reading for those interested in pursuing some relevant and interesting threads in more detail.

Prescribing and Mental Health Nursing (2008) by Austyn Snowden

This book is separated into two parts. The first focuses on the history and development of mental health nursing and prescribing rights more generally. Of particular relevance is the discussion on the historical development of psychiatric medicines. The book shows the largely fortuitous nature of these developments. It illustrates how medicine treatment of certain patterns of distress led to the clustering of these symptoms for the purpose of psychiatric classification, rather than the other way round. For example, panic disorder did not exist as a distinct concept until a medicine was found to have subdued a cluster of symptoms previously thought to be aspects of anxiety. Unsurprisingly, this medicine remains the mainstay of treatment for panic disorder.

The second part of the book looks at the evidence for medicine treatment of certain classifications of disorder. It focuses on the avoidance of 'side-effects' in that each chapter has a section entitled 'what's the worst that can happen?'. These issues are essential knowledge within any concordant discussion on medicine taking. They establish the parameters of risk that may need to be discussed.

The Music of Life (2006) by Denis Noble

This wonderful little book articulates with great clarity the limits of any reductionist view of biology. Professor emeritus Noble is a geneticist at the forefront of studies of the human genome and is therefore perfectly placed to explain exactly what we can and can't conclude from this work. There are many of these types of books out there attempting to explain how everything fits together, and nearly all end up tying themselves in knots with the circularity of the puzzles they create for themselves. Noble's position is refreshingly scientific yet simultaneously humble and articulate. His rejection of top down and bottom up explanations of behaviour in favour of 'middle out' multi-level processes leaves considerable room for an evidence-based explanation of the importance of concordance within a purely biological narrative.

The Myth of the Chemical Cure (2007) by Joanna Moncrieff

Moncrieff presents a lucid and compelling deconstruction of the classification of mental illness. She does this by focusing on the actions of psychiatric medicines in isolation from their contextualised purpose. She argues strongly against any disease based representation of 'mental illness' and presents evidence to support her position. There are limits to her position, and like any radical perspective she can be criticised for minimising the potential benefit of the treatments she criticises. Nevertheless, her account provides a coherent challenge to modern psychiatry, and should be critically appraised by anyone working within the system. The idea for presenting Chapter 2 as a 'value-free' account of medicines originates in this book.

How to Read a Paper, 4th edn (2010) by Trish Greenhalgh

Although not possessing the snappiest title, this little book is the bible of critical appraisal. It is written in a comprehensible manner and is required reading for all students undertaking research in mental health in UWS. It covers analysis of complex papers in a straightforward and thoroughly accessible manner. Many students have commented how easy the art of critical appraisal becomes once they have read this book. Critical appraisal is a fundamental skill.

Placebo Effects (2009) by Fabrizio Benedetti

The notion of value judgements is further examined here in great detail through the construct of the placebo effect. The idea that a placebo effect is a worthless effect, that it is 'all in the mind' and therefore somehow less worthy than a real, physical effect is beautifully challenged within this body of work. Not only does Professor Benedetti show that this thinking is wrong, but that the biological assumptions are more complex than these simplistic ideas would suggest. Placebo effects are 'real' effects. Linking this to the ideas expressed in Noble's book, it seems there is a further role for concordance based around Benedetti's findings. If beliefs play such a demonstrable role in biological outcomes, as demonstrated here, then aligning treatment with expectations is essential. This is concordance.

Suggested responses to reflective exercises

Chapter 1

Reflective exercise: p. 2
Reflect on what concordance means to you and in your own words define concordance.

Suggested response
Maybe you have not come across this term before, or maybe it is familiar term but you have not been able to define it clearly. It is also not uncommon for people to use the term *concordance* as a more modern and acceptable word for compliance. They may therefore say or write *concordance* but think of *compliance*. In other words they may be using *concordance* as a synonym for *compliance*. As you will learn soon, however, concordance when defined is essentially a process of collaboration. Concordance does not refer to a person's medicine-taking behaviour but rather to the nature of the relationship between service user and mental health worker, which should be akin to a consultation between equals (Royal Pharmaceutical Society of Great Britain and Merck Sharpe and Dohme 1996). The term concordance means 'together-heart' and implies agreement on a contract (Treharne *et al.*, 2006; Snowden, 2008a). Concordance is based on shared decision-making, and for decisions to be shared mental health workers need to discuss options in a way that elicits the person's point of view.

Reflective exercise: p. 4
Think about what you value most in life. Would it be possible without the freedoms implied by Repper and Perkin's components of recovery?

Suggested response

Most of the hobbies and interests and ways that people choose to spend their leisure time would be difficult to imagine without the freedoms explicit in this list. These terms are closely connected to the concept of wellbeing.

- Hope
- Meaning and purpose
- Control and choice
- Self-management
- Risk-taking
- Relationships
- Inclusion

Reflective exercise: p. 12

Think back to your last contact with health services as a patient. Did you perceive care to be centred on your needs?

Suggested response

If you responded positively try to summarise what happened that led you to come to this conclusion. Unfortunately for many people the experience of healthcare is one centred on routine, systems and staff needs and often seems to be delivered almost without regard to the patient.

Chapter 2

Reflective exercise: p. 49

Choosing a particular medicine to prescribe involves careful consideration of the biological effects of the medicine and the context in which it will be taken. Such considerations must include the pharmacokinetics and pharmacodynamics of the medicine as well as the effects the medicine is expected to produce. The *BNF* is an essential starting point for gathering the information needed to make these choices.

Consider the following possible substitutions of some of the medicines being prescribed for the service users in this book.

Dougie: temazepam instead of zolpidem

Suggested response

The medicines belong to different classes of hypnotic but do they still have similar effects in terms of efficacy, pharmacodynamic/pharmacokinetic issues (e.g.

duration of action), side-effect profiles, cautions, contraindications etc. We must also remember that temazepam is a Schedule 3 controlled drug and that there may also be local rules regarding its use.

Murdo: trazodone instead of fluoxetine

Suggested response
Trazodone is a tricyclic-related antidepressant, whereas fluoxetine is an SSRI. These different classes of drug are generally considered to have similar efficacy in terms of treating depression, so the basis of the choice between the medicines is likely to come down to the side-effects profiles and the 'state of play' in terms of the person's condition. As an example, trazodone, which has sedative properties, may be preferable in someone who is agitated, whereas fluoxetine may be better if the person is withdrawn.

Susan: haloperidol instead of aripiprazole

Suggested response
Aripiprazole is an atypical antipsychotic, whereas haloperidol is a typical antipsychotic. When the newer atypical medicines where first produced it was hoped that they would show greater efficacy than the older typical ones; however, long-term analysis of the effects has struggled to find any real difference in terms of efficacy. The argument for using atypicals thus rests on the belief that they are less likely to induce serious motor side-effects than the typicals, though this is also debatable. Again therefore the choice of medicine boils down to what effect(s) one is trying to achieve/alleviate and the state of the person's condition.

Chapter 3

Reflective exercise: p. 59
(a) Consider how you make first contact with people from your service.
(b) Are there any barriers or challenges service users may face by your approach?
(c) Are you confident that you lay positive foundations for the therapeutic alliance through that first contact?
(d) What would you have done differently for Dougie and Joyce?

Suggested response
(a) Sometimes methods for first contact can create barriers for people being referred to the service. Some evidence-based methods can make people with memory problems unable to access the service. For example, methods for reducing missed appointments, such as letters inviting people to make their

own appointments, may result in them not responding if a person is scared or is experiencing cognitive problems. Missed appointments should always be investigated. Some service design or function may also create barriers, such as the focus upon baseline assessment at the first meeting and passing elements of the person's journey to other departments or organisations.

(b) Maybe introductions and supporting the person to tell their story should be the main aim of the first meeting. Having one clinician to support the person through key stages of their journey should also be considered. Asking for the person's expectations of your visit – what they have already been told or know – can be a good place to start, as we are aware reasons for referral to community mental health teams are not always clearly articulated. Chris found that working with Dougie needed to be at his pace and aimed at initially addressing fears for Dougie and Joyce, the service imperatives of providing a diagnosis and commencing cognitive enhancers were not Dougie and Joyce's imperatives.

(c) Dougie's story is real in describing the struggle that people can experience with themselves and their partners/children with the onset of memory difficulties. The issue of timeliness of contact with a specialist memory assessment service is relevant and this negotiation process clearly needs to have started between Dougie and his GP (de Lepeleire *et al.*, 2008). It is important that people get the facts early on (since some people with mild memory problems do not go on to develop more significant problems and some do) so as to inform their choice over the next steps. Barker (1997) describes the extent to which people are enabled (or not) to consent to mental health assessments before they are completed and questions whether the implications of the assessments are discussed and disclosed by the practitioner before they are undertaken (de Lepeleire *et al.*, 2008).

Reflective exercise: p. 60

Can you think of any reasons why Murdo may find it particularly difficult to grieve the death of his father?

Suggested response

Murdo is emotionally inhibited (Bowlby, 1980) and finds it difficult to express his feelings verbally. He has very high standards in his life and likes control order and security all of which are threatened by the Frank's death. As Worden (1991) poignantly states '...the intensity of grief is determined by the intensity of love' and Murdo felt a strong love for his mother and father.

Reflective exercise: p. 61
Why is it significant that Murdo does not seem to be getting back to normal one year after his mother's death?

Suggested response
Although grief reactions vary, after one year it is usual to have at least begun to resume normal patterns of behaviour and have located the deceased in the past (Worden, 1991). Although Murdo was very much aware that he was not getting through the time of mourning, he was not able to move on in resolving his grief.

Reflective exercise: p. 63
Consider why Susan's mum might describe her as being manipulative.

Suggested response
This statement may reflect more on her mother's values than Susan's behaviour. The mother thinks that she and Susan's father have done all they can for Susan and they have provided a perfect opportunity for Susan to work with Uncle Peter. Susan's mother and father have a perception that parents should have a controlling influence and have become used to this through their experience with Susan and her siblings. Nevertheless words such as 'manipulative' can have a negative effect on those to whom they are applied as labels.

Reflective exercise: p. 65
(a) Consider why Susan might be feeling embarrassed being admitted to hospital again.
(b) Consider why Susan might be feeling upset that she has been given a diagnosis of schizophrenia.

Suggested response
(a) Based on her life experience that successful people should be self-reliant and good at coping, and also her recent experience of admission that she had wanted to 'sweep under the carpet' as a one-off event, Susan now faces the prospect of seeing herself starting a career as a 'mental patient.'
(b) This diagnosis confirms Susan's worst fears that she has a permanent and incurable disease.

Chapter 4

Reflective exercise: p. 75

(a) What does your assessment process look like?

(b) Do you ask for and get feedback on your assessment process to inform development of your practice?

(c) How 'strengths-based' is your assessment?

Suggested response

(a) Many services use a standardised format for comprehensive initial mental health assessments, including standardised risk assessments and other assessments such as for falls and nutrition. The requirement to complete all of this essential documentation does not always sit easily with a collaborative person-centred approach to assessment.

(b) It is important to obtain feedback from service users and carers on their experience and perception of the assessment process. It will be important to clearly identify the purpose, scope and content of assessment before it is undertaken, to promote choice for the service user and understanding through negotiation of the likely outcome of the assessment process. Clinical supervision can provide a useful forum to evaluate your practice and review completed assessments, to explore the extent to which strengths as well as deficits are identified. Feedback can be obtained through informal discussion at the end of an assessment or more formally through mechanisms such as an anonymous questionnaire which has a code to identify the specific practitioner and a pre-paid reply envelope. Dougie's story also reflects the reality of completing cognitive assessments that can expose, embarrass and worry people, while striving to balance this through working with the person to recognise their strengths, abilities and opportunities and to capitalise on these. As this indicates, most diagnostic processes continue to seek deficits and problems, not strengths and opportunities.

(c) Strength-based assessments focus upon what skills the person has and seek to amplify and support adaptation of these strengths to the person's changing circumstances. As discussed above, many assessment strategies do not focus upon strengths identification; deficit assessment is often the current approach, due, understandably, to having to gain baselines for commencement of treatment and to being able to monitor the effectiveness of the prescribed medication. In taking a strengths-based approach one of the questions Chris may ask Dougie and Joyce is how they have managed so far in the face of their described challenges, and then going on to amplify these evolving strengths by asking, 'What else do you do that helps you deal with these problems?'.

A naive curiosity about Dougie's life, current situation and helpful and unhelpful reactions to his symptoms will be Chris's greatest ally in moving towards a person-centred strengths-based approach. Continuing to ask about strengths and coping will help Chris and Dougie to draw out the details of Dougie and Joyce's problem-solving abilities and resources, and their priorities for the next step.

Reflective exercise: p. 78

(a) What other questions can you list which set a collaborative tone to your discussion?
(b) What would you ask if a client was unable to articulate their needs or was not clear on what they wanted?
(c) How do you support elements of the psychological tasks and stages in your practice?

Suggested response

(a) Examples of collaborative questions:
- How has this week been?
- And what has helped you do all of that?
- What else?
- What would you most like to be doing next (week/month)?
- What will help you achieve this?
- Is there anything you can do now to work towards this?

(b) Where a person is unable or unclear about what they want or what needs they feel they have, time is their best support. For the worker to engage at a level and pace they need makes sure the worker is ready willing and able when the person becomes ready.

(c) The worker should also consider creative and supportive methods to enable people to express themselves. Emotional Touchpoints (Dewar *et al.*, 2002) and Talking Mats are just two methods to enable and support communication.

Finding a practical task or activity which can be completed side by side with people has been found to support engagement and assist people to speak about their concerns in a manner which is found to be more natural than speaking one-to-one opposite each other. Something that the person used to do or still does or would like to try can be explored as a potential joint activity. Post-diagnostic support has always been of vital importance, but as memory services have developed, the need for psychological support has become more apparent. There are a number of post-diagnostic support frameworks and theories to draw from and training available for mental health workers to access to develop their psychological knowledge and skills. The essence underpinning any approach to psychological adjustment to diagnosis is the person-centred approach and staying in step with the process of the adjustment the person is experiencing. We found that Dougie relaxed and appreciated time with Chris when they were 'talking cars', and these conversations provided appropriate breaks in talking about dementia. These discussions also gave opportunity for the layers of the therapeutic relationship to be repeatedly overlaid and built upon in addition to amplifying Dougie's strengths and capabilities.

Do you use a therapeutic model to support you in your day-to-day working with people with dementia? What underpinning philosophy or theoretical perspective do you use to guide your partnership working? In Dougie's story we use the psychological stages and tasks model as an underpinning framework for Dougie, Joyce and Chris. There are, however, alternatives, and the choice of which to use should be indicated by client need. NHS Education for Scotland and Scottish Recovery Network (2008) in their educational resource explore the use of cognitive behavioural therapy, supportive psychotherapy, counselling approaches and group work approaches to working with people post-diagnostically.

Reflective exercise: p. 88

(a) Why do you think Murdo became so distracted at the end of this session?
(b) Do you think the questioning and assessment process in general had anything to do with it?

Suggested response

(a) Murdo was clearly exhausted, as is often the case with significant depression. He had poor concentration, and it is possible that Helen was expecting too much of him in the first instance.
(b) Helen had a 'formula' from which she was working, had a routine on which she was basing her assessment, and somewhere in the process she had lost touch with the impact that her interventions were having on Murdo. This merits critical reflection in clinical supervision, out of which learning will come for Helen.

Reflective exercise: p. 90

(a) What do you think of Helen's initial approach here – i.e. going ahead and saying she would arrange for Catherine's involvement without prior discussion with Mary and Murdo?
(b) Where does that sit with fostering concordance?

Suggested response

(a) The intentions here are sound; however, it is necessary within concordance working to keep the individual, wherever possible, at the heart of any decisions about them.

(b) If we describe concordance in terms of a relationship that is fostered between a prescriber and person who is in a treatment situation, then the aim is for informed choice to drive the decision-making on the part of the person. Murdo should be in the position where he has the choice whether or not to accept Catherine's involvement in his care. Helen, however, has leapt ahead and made the decision based on her knowledge that Catherine's involvement could make a difference. On reflection, through supervision, she was able to acknowledge that this is a paternalistic approach and is not in keeping with the nature of concordance

Reflective exercise: p. 96

(a) Have you been in a similar situation recently and if so how did this make you feel?

(b) What concerns did you have?

(c) What could Beth have done or said to improve the situation?

Suggested response

(a) Feelings may have included anxiety, anger or despair. You may have felt that it would be difficult to challenge the situation.

(b) Concerns may have related to unanswered questions about what information was being collected, for example: Who would see the notes? What was being written? Who would it be shared with? Was it accurate? Did the record reflect the nature, impact and meaning the events held?

(c) Prior to recording, Beth could have provided Susan with a summary of what she wished to record. A summary also has the additional benefit that it demonstrates listening and assists the client in organising their experience (Rosengren, 2009). The summary can also be an opportunity to use affirmations and summarise strengths.

Reflective exercise: p. 97

(a) Consider the benefits of goal attainment.

(b) What practitioner skills are involved in assisting individuals to make plans for change?

(c) What ethical and professional issues may arise in the goal-setting process?

Suggested response

(a) Goal attainment impacts positively on confidence, motivation and self-efficacy.

(b)

- Self awareness of any 'roadblocks to communication' (Gordon, 1970, in Rosengren, 2009). These may include giving advice, persuading, judging, analysing or moralising.
- Reflection in action.
- Observation of service user feedback (fidgeting, tiredness, changing the subject, blaming others, interrupting). If these occur it may be a sign that the service user is not ready to make plans for change.
- Communication of opportunities for choice and control.

(c)

- Having a concern about the service user's choice of goal.
- Having a personal investment or judgement in relation to the chosen goal.
- Power imbalances.
- Dissonance between where the service user believes they should be and where the practitioner wants them to go.

Reflective exercise: p. 103

Take a moment to reflect on how Yvonne is feeling. How do you think her feelings fit in with a recovery approach?

Suggested response

Yvonne is thinking that she is working in partnership with Susan and using a strengths based approach.

Yvonne's thinking is not in keeping with a recovery approach because she is taking control and being directive, however well-intentioned she may be. The power and control are not with Susan. Yvonne has inadvertently stumbled on an issue which is particularly sensitive for Susan.

Chapter 5

Reflective exercise: p. 112

(a) How do you develop a person's care plan? How do you draw on the person's existing strengths?

(b) How do the people you work with know what their responsibilities are and know what yours are?

(c) How do you evaluate your care plans?

Suggested response

(a) Many people within the community may have a plan of care but not have a copy of it or understand what it is and what their role is in their own care. There are clear expectations from service users' feedback that they should be full partners in any care they receive and that includes fully negotiating their plans of care, including co-writing or writing that care plan. The mental health worker's role during this process can be to support informed decision-making, providing a range of options for the person to choose from and construct their care plan with. Care planning for people with dementia can often be based on risk reduction and supporting the carer to become a partner in care. The person with dementia must remain central to care planning; supporting them through the use of appropriate psychosocial interventions to retain current skills or develop additional coping skills and strategies is essential. Becoming a burden or being over-indebted to other people without choice and control has been asserted to be a cause of depression in older people, and one way to avoid this is by taking a strengths-based approach.

(b) Service users have fed back that they often do not know what the role of a mental health worker is, what their role in the wider team is and how they can be of support to them. Many service users, when asked, were not aware of professional codes of conduct or local policies and procedures of service and care delivery.

(c) If the development of care plans has been through participation and partnership working, the methods of evaluation will be based on their initial expression of need. There will be quantitative objective assessment data which can inform how medicines may be working, which is appropriate to ensure effectiveness and appropriateness. The person-centred goals set by the person and or their carer give the mental health worker a benchmark to evaluate the care plans in partnership with the person. For Dougie, one of his goals was initially to be able to use his car and then later to be able to have usefulness and value within his home and his relationship with his wife. That would be what needs to be evaluated and only Dougie and Joyce could say how that was going for them.

Reflective exercise: p. 117

What may account for the multidisciplinary team overlooking such a significant part of Murdo's story?

Suggested response

Murdo was unwell and distressed and the team's priority had been to commence a medicine regime. Murdo met the criteria for major depressive episode and it is sometimes the case in the assessment process that significant threads in the aetiology of illness can be overlooked when the emphasis is on diagnosis and not the person's story.

Reflective exercise: p. 118

(a) What do you think has happened here? For instance, is the feeling of 'being stuck' that Murdo is describing something that Helen should be concerned about? Does it feel like failure of interventions?

(b) Or is it a sign that Murdo is so comfortable in the therapeutic relationship that he is able to share honestly what feels right about his situation and what should change?

(c) How do you feel when people *you* work with tell you that they are making no progress?

Suggested response

(a) What Murdo is going through is not a 'failure of the interventions'. Depression is a challenging, distressing condition to experience, and is equally challenging for both those staff charged with helping and the carers. What Murdo is experiencing here is simply a reflection of him starting to recognise that this is going to be a long process. He is possibly looking back with some frustration that his experience is not improving quickly.

(b) However, it is certainly a sign that he is working well with his wife, his CPN and his support worker. He obviously feels settled in the relationship with those individuals and is able to voice his concerns and feelings without feeling that he is somehow going to burden them with his problems.

(c) Consider this question in light of your reflection on the Murdo scenario and relate to your own practice.

Reflective exercise: p. 121

(a) List all of Susan's experiences which may have contributed to her being unable to directly assert her feelings to Yvonne at the time of being asked to carry out the artwork.

(b) Briefly outline how Yvonne could have kept sensitivity to Susan's feelings and wishes and possibly avoided this roadblock in their concordance working.

(c) Also outline what factors helped this situation to be redeemed and what positive learning can be taken out of this situation for both Susan and Yvonne.

Suggested response

(a) List:

- Susan's relationship with her parents had wrested control away from her in respect of her artwork, as they were adamant that she should not pursue art as a career and insisted she pursue architecture instead.
- Her parents insisted that Susan go for work experience with her uncle despite her not wanting to do this.
- Susan had previously been sexually abused by her uncle and close contact with him was abhorrent to her.
- Susan always had art as something which was a personal passion, but she had not been able to fulfil this because of issues of power and control.
- Susan resented once again someone else attempting to take control of her personal interests.
- Previous negative experience with health professionals.

(b) Yvonne could have been sensitive to Susan's verbal/non-verbal messages and picked up her resentment earlier. Yvonne could have firstly asked for Susan's suggestions about the timeline construction. If it then seemed appropriate Yvonne could have raised using the artwork as a possibility, but then checked with Susan what her thoughts and feelings were about this.

(c) This situation was redeemed because they had built a strong relationship initially. How Yvonne behaved at this stage was an aberration in her overall approach. Susan was able to make links about why she felt so strongly and therefore realised that the issue transcended her work with Yvonne and was derived from past experiences, which Yvonne was not aware of. Yvonne took this issue to clinical supervision and this allowed her to take a step back and review the whole situation. Yvonne persevered with Susan's non-attendance. Susan had a willingness to work through this difficult situation. Neither Yvonne nor Susan gave up on each other or blamed each other.

Reflective exercise: p. 123

(a) Do you have any concerns about Susan's choice of support network?
(b) How would you raise these concerns using a recovery-focused approach?
(c) What frameworks or resources would you use to guide you in your decision making?

Suggested response

(a) If you had concerns relating to the safety of online forums you could offer these concerns in a recovery-focused way (supporting choice and control).

(b), (c)   One approach could be to use the Elicit–Provide–Elicit method (Rollnick *et al.*, 1999). This method starts by asking service users what they already know (Elicit):

> What do you know about online forums? (Genuine interest expressed, affirming client's knowledge)

The practitioner can then add to this (Provide):

> I wonder if you would be interested in hearing about other forums people have used. (Supports choice, offers control, conveys respect)

The practitioner can then ask for the service user's opinion:

> What do you think of those examples? (Elicit)

Statements of concern could also be offered using normalising techniques to support formulation of the statement:

> There are some really good forums and some not so good ones. I am concerned and wondered if we could discuss this. (Offers choice)

> Sometimes when looking for good resources a menu or checklist can help make decisions about which sites to use. Would either of those approaches be useful to you?

Other more formal frameworks or grids may also help you in deciding whether to raise your concerns. These include your professional code, ethical grids (for example Seedhouse, 1998) or the use of a process-based approach, such as the 10 Pointers to good process in values-based practice (VBP) (Woodbridge and Fulford, 2004).

The 10 pointers to good process in VBP are as follows:

Practice skills
Awareness: being aware of the values in a given situation.
Reasoning: thinking about values when making decisions.
Knowledge: knowing about values and facts that are relevant to a situation.
Communication: using communication to resolve conflicts/complexity.

Models of service delivery
User-centred: considering the service user's values as the first priority.
Multidisciplinary: using a balance of perspectives to resolve conflicts.

Values-based practice and evidence-based practice
The 'two feet' principle: all decisions are based on facts and values.
Evidence-based practice and values-based practice therefore work together.
The 'squeaky wheel' principle: values shouldn't just be noticed if there's a problem.
Science and values: increasing scientific knowledge creates choices in healthcare. This can lead to wider differences in values.
Partnership: in VBP decisions are taken by service users working in partnership with providers of care.

Reflective exercise: p. 129
For what reasons do you think Susan is particularly sensitive to Mr Piper's comments?

Suggested response
Susan has made a great effort just to get to this class. In Susan's upbringing her opinion has tended to be subjugated. Generally, art has been a personal passion and way of expressing her independence which, however, has also been suppressed and ridiculed. She is therefore very sensitive to any perceived criticism. Her relationships with significant males in her life have been difficult, as illustrated by her father, her uncle and her tutor at university.

Reflective exercise: p. 129
Is Yvonne right to feel concerned at this time?

Suggested response
It is understandable that Yvonne feels concerned given Susan's timeline and the behaviours which have been associated with relapse. Yvonne, however, seems not to be in step with the deeper meanings of this situation for Susan.

Reflective exercise: p. 130
Give examples of the kind of questions that Dr Jones might have used.

Suggested response
For example, using the list of Socratic questions, a question which clarifies Susan's attitude towards Mr Piper is asked initially. Should this attitude be negative about Mr Piper, a second question could then be asked to probe assumptions about Mr Piper. The third question elicits reasons and evidence for Susan holding these

assumptions. The fourth question asks for Susan's viewpoint or perspective of what would be the best course of action; for example, whether or not to return to Mr Piper's class. A fifth question probes possible implications and consequences of returning or not returning to the class. A sixth question allows a deeper level of reflection for Susan and gives Dr Jones a clearer picture of Susan's overall perceptions. Thereafter, together Susan, Yvonne and Dr Jones agree a course of action which they each feel comfortable with.

Reflective exercise: p. 130

Reflect on what might have happened if Dr Jones had taken a risk-aversive view, agreeing with Yvonne, strongly recommending that Susan does not attend the class and advising that it could be a good idea to increase her aripiprazole.

Suggested response

This view would not be unrealistic in contemporary practice and in some ways is justifiable. However, in a recovery-oriented approach positive risk-taking is important, so that feelings of disempowerment are not compounded. Everyone's life involves disappointments, setbacks and challenges, and overcoming these and learning to cope builds resilience and increases coping and self-esteem. If these opportunities are denied, people with mental health difficulties may then find that positive development is systematically curtailed. There is, ironically, a risk that Susan may disengage from contact with Yvonne and Dr Jones and revert to being cast in the role of the non-compliant patient. This would build on her non-compliant daughter role and would be regressive and detrimental to her mental wellbeing. The sad thing is that being risk-averse in this way may perversely increase the risk of relapse.

References

Abarca, J., Colon, L., Wang, V., Malone, D., Murphy, J. and Armstrong, E. (2006a) Evaluation of the performance of drug–drug interaction screening software in community and hospital pharmacies. *Journal of Managed Care Pharmacy*, **12**(5), 383–9.

Abarca, J., Malone, D., Skrepnek, G., Rehfeld, R., Murphy, J., Grizzle, A., Armstrong, E. and Woosley, R. (2006b) Community pharmacy managers' perception of computerized drug–drug interaction alerts. *Journal of the American Pharmacists Association*, **46**(2), 148–53.

American Psychiatric Association (2000) *Diagnostic and Statistical Manual of Mental Disorders*, 4th edn. Text Revision (DSM-IV-TR). American Psychiatric Association, Washington.

Appleby, B. S., Roy, P., Valenti, A. and Lee, H. B. (2007) Diagnosis and treatment of depression in Alzheimer's disease: impact on mood and cognition. *Panminerva Medica*, **49**(3), 139–49.

Baker, J. and Fletcher, J. (2009) Problem solving in medicines management. In: *Medicines Management in Mental Health Care* (eds. N. Harris, J. Baker and R. Gray), pp. 208–22. Wiley-Blackwell, West Sussex.

Banning, M. (2007) Medication review for the older person. *Reviews in Clinical Gerontology*, **17**(1), 25–32.

Barker, P. (1997) *Assessment in Psychiatric and Mental Health Nursing: in Search of the Whole Person*. Stanley Thornes, Cheltenham.

Barker, P. J. (2011) *Mental Health Ethics: the Human Context*. Routledge, London.

Bar-On, R. (1997) *The Bar-On Emotional Quotient Inventory (EQ-i): a Test of Emotional Intelligence*. Multi-Health Systems, Toronto.

Beke-Harrigan, H., Hess, R. and Weinland, J. A. (2008) A survey of registered nurses' readiness for evidence-based practice: a multidisciplinary project. *Journal of Hospital Librarianship*, **8**(4), 440–8.

Benedetti, F. (2009) *Placebo Effects*. Oxford University Press, Oxford.

Benedetti, F., Mayberg, H. S., Wager, T. D., Stohler, C. S. and Zubieta, J. K. (2005) Neurobiological mechanisms of the placebo effect. *The Journal of Neuroscience*, **25**(45), 10390–402.

References

Bennett-Levy, J., Butler, B., Fennell, M., Hackmann, A. Mueller, M. and Westbrook, D. (eds.) (2004) *Oxford Guide to Behavioural Experiments in Cognitive Therapy*. Oxford University Press, New York.

Bentall, R. P. (2003) *Madness Explained: Psychosis and Human Nature*. Penguin, London.

Bernard, J. and Goodyear, R. (2004) *Fundamentals of Clinical Supervision*. Pearson Education, Boston.

Birchwood, M. and Jackson, C. (2001) *Schizophrenia*. Psychology Press, Hove.

BMJ Group and Pharmaceutical Press (2011a) *British National Formulary: BNF 61, March 2011*. [Online] Available: http://bnf.org/bnf/bnf/current/56911.htm [accessed: 23 August 2011].

BMJ Group and Pharmaceutical Press (2011b) *British National Formulary: BNF 61, March 2011*. [Online] Available: http://bnf.org/bnf/bnf/current/128396.htm [accessed: 23 August 2011].

Bowlby J. (1980) *Attachment and Loss: Loss, Sadness and Depression*. Basic Books, New York.

Brabban, A. (2009) Why me? Why now? Understanding vulnerability from a cognitive perspective. In: *Back to Life, Back to Normality: Cognitive Therapy, Recovery and Psychosis* (eds. D. Turkington, D. Kingdon, S. Rathod, S. Wilcock, A. Brabban, P. Cromarty, R. Dudley, R. Gray, J. Pelton, R. Siddle and P. Weidon), pp. 127–38. Cambridge University Press, Cambridge.

Bradley, E., Hynam, B. and Nolan, P. (2007) Nurse prescribing: reflections on safety in practice. *Social Science & Medicine*, **65**(3), 599–609.

Breggin, P. R. (1993) *Toxic Psychiatry: Drugs and Electroconvulsive Therapy; the Truth and the Better Alternatives*. HarperCollins, London.

Brien, S., Lachance, L., Prescott, P., McDermott, C. and Lewith, G. (2011) Homeopathy has clinical benefits in rheumatoid arthritis patients that are attributable to the consultation process but not the homeopathic remedy: a randomized controlled clinical trial. *Rheumatology*, **50**(6), 1070–82.

Brown, C., Bannigan, K. and Gill, J. (2009) Questioning: a critical skill in postmodern health-care service delivery. *Australian Occupational Therapy Journal*, **56**(3), 206–10.

Brown, W. and Kandirikirira, N. (2007) *Recovering Mental Health in Scotland. Report on Narrative Investigation of Mental Health Recovery*. Scottish Recovery Network, Glasgow.

Brownlowe, K. and Sola, C. (2008) Clozapine toxicity in smoking cessation and with ciprofloxacin. *Psychosomatics*, **49**(2), 176.

Burnard, P. (2002) *Learning Human Skills: An Experiential and Reflective Guide for Nurses and Health Care Professionals*. Butterworth-Heinemann, Oxford.

Busuttil, W. (2004) Presentations and management of post-traumatic stress disorder and the elderly: a need for investigation. *International Journal of Geriatric Psychiatry*, **19**(5), 429–39.

Butler, R., Hatcher, S., Price, J. and von Korff, M. (2007) Depression in adults: psychological treatments and care pathways. *BMJ Evidence Centre*. [Online] Available at http// clinicalevidence.bmj.com [accessed 16 April 2011].

Buus, N. and Gonge, H. (2009) Empirical studies of clinical supervision in psychiatric nursing: a systematic literature review and methodological critique. *International Journal of Mental Health Nursing*, **18**(4), 250–64.

Carpenter, W. T., Jr and Heinrichs, D. W. (1983) Early intervention, time-limited, targeted pharmacotherapy of schizophrenia. *Schizophrenia Bulletin*, **9**(4), 533–42.

Charles, C., Gafni, A. and Whelan, T. (2004) Self-reported use of shared decision-making among breast cancer specialists and perceived barriers and facilitators to implementing this approach. *Health Expectations*, **7**(4), 338–48.

Cheston, R. and Bender, M. (1999) *Understanding Dementia: the Man with the Worried Eyes*. Jessica Kingsley, London.

Clarke, L. (2011) A commentary on books, awards and warnings: with passing reference to a frog. *Journal of Psychiatric & Mental Health Nursing*, **18**(3), 274–6.

Clarke, S., Oades, L., Crowe, T., Caputi, P. and Deane, F. (2009) The role of symptom distress and goal attainment in promoting aspects of psychological recovery for consumers with enduring mental illness. *Journal of Mental Health*, **18**(5), 389–97.

Clyne, W., Granby, T. and Picton, C. (2007) *A Competency Framework for Shared Decision Making with Patients: Achieving Concordance for Taking Medicines*. National Prescribing Centre Plus, Liverpool.

Codier, E., Muneno, L., Frankey, K. and Matsuura, F. (2010) Is emotional intelligence an important concept for nursing practice? *Journal of Psychiatric & Mental Health Nursing*, **17**(10), 940–8.

Copeland, M.E. (2002) *Wellness Recovery Action Plan*. Available: http://www.spsychserv. com/Client%20Resources/WRAPworkbook-adults.pdf [accessed 16 September 2011].

Corrigan, P. W., Liberman, R. P. and Engel, J. D. (1990) From noncompliance to collaboration in the treatment of schizophrenia. *Hospital & Community Psychiatry*, **41**(11), 1203–11.

Craddock, N., Antebi, D., Attenburrow, M. J., Bailey, A., Carson, A., Cowen, P., Craddock, B., Eagles, J., Ebmeier, K., Farmer, A., Fazel, S., Ferrier, N., Geddes, J., Goodwin, G., Harrison, P., Hawton, K., Hunter, S., Jacoby, R., Jones, I., Keedwell, P., Kerr, M., Mackin, P., McGuffin, P., MacIntyre, D. J., McConville, P., Mountain, D., O'Donovan, M. C., Owen, M. J., Oyebode, F., Phillips, M., Price, J., Shah, P., Smith, D. J., Walters, J., Woodruff, P., Young, A. and Zammit, S. (2008) Wake-up call for British psychiatry. *British Journal of Psychiatry*, **193**(1), 6–9.

Cramer, J. A. and Rosenheck, R. (1998) Compliance with medication regimens for mental and physical disorders. *Psychiatric Services*, **49**(2), 196–201.

References

Cutcliffe, J., Hyrkas, K. and Fowler, J. (2010) Clinical supervision: origins, overviews and rudiments. In: *Routledge Handbook of Clinical Supervision: Fundamental International Themes* (eds. L. Cutcliffe, K. Hyrkas and J. Fowler), 2nd edn. Routledge, London.

Day, J. C., Wood, G., Dewey, M. and Bentall, R. P. (1995) A self-rating scale for measuring neuroleptic side-effects: validation in a group of schizophrenic patients. *British Journal of Psychiatry*, **166**(5), 650–3.

Deegan, P. and Drake, R. (2006) Shared decision making and medication management in the recovery process. *Psychiatric Services*, **57**(11), 1636–9.

Deegan, P. E. (1988) Recovery: the lived experience of rehabilitation... psychiatrically disabled adults. *Psychosocial Rehabilitation Journal*, **11**(4), 11–19.

Deegan, P., Rapp, C., Holter, M. and Riefer, M. (2008) A program to support shared decision making in an outpatient psychiatric medicine clinic. *Psychiatric Services*, **59**(6), 603–5.

De Lepeleire, J., Wind, A. W., Iliffe, S., Moniz-Cook, E. D., Wilcock, J., Gonzalez, V. M., Derksen, E., Gianelli, M. V. and Vernooij-Dassen, M. (2008) The primary care diagnosis of dementia in Europe: an analysis using multidisciplinary, multinational expert groups. *Aging and Mental Health*, **12**(5), 568–76.

Department of Health (2006) *Improving Patients' Access to Medicines: A Guide to Implementing Nurse and Pharmacist Independent Prescribing Within the NHS in England.* Department of Health, London.

Department of Health (2010) *Equity and Excellence: Liberating the NHS.* Retrieved from: http://www.dh.gov.uk/prod_consum_dh/groups/dh_digitalassets/@dh/@en/@ps/documents/digitalasset/dh_117794.pdf [accessed 10 September 2011].

Department of Health, Sainsbury Centre for Mental Health and National Institute of Mental Health in England (2004) *The Ten Essential Shared Capabilities for Mental Health Practice (ESC).* London, HMSO.

Dewar, B., Mackay, R., Smith, S., Pullin, S. and Tocher, R. (2010) Use of emotional touchpoints as a method of tapping into the experience of receiving compassionate care in a hospital setting. *Journal of Research in Nursing*, **15**(1), 29–41.

Ekman, I., Schaufelberger, M., Kjellgren, K., Swedberg, K. and Granger, B. (2007) Standard medication information is not enough: poor concordance of patient and nurse perceptions. *Journal of Advanced Nursing*, **60**(2), 181–6.

Elwyn, G., Laitner, S., Coulter, A., Walker, E., Watson, P. and Thomson, R. (2010) Implementing shared decision making in the NHS. *British Medical Journal (Overseas & Retired Doctors Edition)*, **341**(7780), 971–3.

Evans, J. (1992) Healthy minds. *Nursing Times*, **88**(16), 54–6.

Even, C. and Weintraub, D. (2010) Case for and against specificity of depression in Alzheimer's disease. *Psychiatry and Clinical Neurosciences*, **64**(4), 358–66.

Farmer, A. (2010) Antipsychotic medicine and their use in first episode psychosis In: *Promoting Recovery in Early Psychosis: a Practice Manual* (eds. P. French, J. Smith, D. Shiers, M. Reed and M. Rayne), pp. 73–82. Wiley Blackwell, Chichester.

Faulkner, A. (1998) Experts by experience: strategies for living project. *Mental Health Nursing*, **18**(4), 6–8.

Fava, G. A., Ruini, C., Rafanelli, C., Finos, L., Conti, S. and Grandi, S. (2004) Six-year outcome of cognitive behavior therapy for prevention of recurrent depression. *American Journal of Psychiatry*, **161**(10), 1872–6.

Fennell, M. (1999) *Overcoming Low Self-esteem – A Self-help Guide Using Cognitive Behavioral Techniques*. Robinson Publishing, London.

Fenton, W. S., Blyler, C. R. and Heinssen, R. K. (1997) Determinants of medication compliance in schizophrenia: empirical and clinical findings. *Schizophrenia Bulletin*, **23**(4), 637–51.

Fisher, D. (2003) People are more important than pills in recovery from mental disorder. *Journal of Humanistic Psychology*, **43**(2), 65–8.

Fisher, D. B. (2008) Promoting recovery. In: *Learning about Mental Health Practice* (eds. T. Stickley and T. Basset). John Wiley & Sons, Chichester.

Fleeman, N., McLeod, C., Bagust, A., Beale, S., Boland, A., Dundar, Y., Jorgenson, A., Payne, K., Pirmohamed, M., Pushpakom, S. Walley, T., de Warren-Penny, P. and Dickson, R. (2010) The clinical effectiveness and cost-effectiveness of testing for cytochrome P450 polymorphisms in patients with schizophrenia treated with antipsychotics: a systematic review and economic evaluation. *Health Technology Assessment*, **14**(3), 1–182.

Folstein, M. F., Folstein, S. E. and McHugh, P. R. (1975) Mini-mental state: a practical method for grading the cognitive state of patients for the clinician. *Journal of Psychiatric Research*, **12**(3), 189–98.

Ford, B. (2000) *Coping with Setbacks and Staying Well. Training Manual*. York Health Services NHS Trust, York.

Franklin, V., Waller, A., Pagliari, C. and Greene, S. (2003) 'Sweet talk': text-messaging support for intensive insulin therapy for young people with diabetes. *Diabetic Technology and Therapeutics*, **5**(6), 991–6.

Freeman, D. and Garety, P. A. (2004) *Paranoia: The Psychology of Persecutory Delusions*. Maudsley Monograph 45. Psychology Press, Hove.

Gadkari, A. S. and McHorney, C. A. (2010) Medication nonfulfillment rates and reasons: narrative systematic review. *Current Medicine Research and Opinion*, **26**(3), 683–705.

Gamble, C. (2006) Building relationships: lessons to be learnt. In: *Working with Serious Mental Illness: a Manual for Clinical Practice* (eds. C. Gamble and G. Brennan), 2nd edn, pp.73–83. Edinburgh, Elsevier.

References

Glasziou, P. and Haynes, B. (2005) The paths from research to improved health outcomes. *Evidence Based Nursing*, **8**(2), 36–8.

Goldacre, B. (2009) *Bad Science*. Harper Perennial, London.

Grainger, M. and Keegan, K. (2011) New agents in the management of Alzheimer's disease: a case study. *Nurse Prescribing*, **9**(1), 12–18.

Graue, M., Bjarkøy, R., Iversen, M., Haugstvedt, A. and Harris, J. (2010) Integrating evidence-based practice into the diabetes nurse curriculum in Bergen: perceived barriers to finding, reading and using research in practice. *European Diabetes Nursing*, **7**(1), 10–15.

Gray, R., Leese, M., Bindman, J., Becker, T., Burti, L., David, A., Gournay, K., Kikkert, M., Koeter, M., Puschner, B., Schene, A., Thornicroft, G. and Tansella, M. (2006) Adherence therapy for people with schizophrenia. European multicentre randomised controlled trial. *British Journal of Psychiatry*, **189**(6), 508–14.

Gray, R., Wykes, T. and Gournay, K. (2002) From compliance to concordance: a review of the literature on interventions to enhance compliance with antipsychotic medication. *Journal of Psychiatric and Mental Health Nursing*, **9**(3), 277–84.

Greenberger, D. and Padesky, C. (1995) *Mind Over Mood: Change How You Feel by Changing the Way You Think*. Guilford Press, London.

Greenhalgh, T. (2010) *How to Read a Paper: the Basics of Evidence-based Medicine*, 4th edn. Wiley-Blackwell, Chichester.

Haddad, P., Dursun, S. and Deakin, B. (2004) *Adverse Syndromes and Psychiatric Drugs. A Clinical Guide*. Oxford University Press, Oxford.

Hall, K. and Iqbal, F. (2010) *The Problem with Cognitive Behavioural Therapy*. Karnac Books, London.

Harai, H. (2006) MI for anxiety. *MINT Bulletin*, **13**(1), 37.

Harding, C. M. and Zahniser, J. H. (1994) Empirical correction of seven myths about schizophrenia with implications for treatment. *Acta Psychiatrica Scandinavica Supplementum*, **90**(384, suppl.), S140–S146.

Harrison, A. (1991) Assessing patients' pain: identifying reasons for error. *Journal of Advanced Nursing*, **16**(9), 1018–25.

Harrison, G., Hopper, K., Craig, T., Laska, E., Siegel, C., Wanderling, K., Dube, C., Ganev, K., Giel, R., van der Heiden, W., Holmberg, S., Janca, A., Lee, P., Leon, C., Malhotra, S., Marsella, A., Nakane, Y., Sartorious, N., Ken, Y., Skoda, C., Thara, R., Tsirkin, S., Vijoy, K., Dermot, W. and Wiersma, D. (2001) Recovery from psychotic illness: a 15 and 25 year international follow-up study. *British Journal of Psychiatry*, **178**(6), 506–17.

Hawkins, P. and Shohet, R. (2006) *Supervision in the Helping Professions*, 3rd edn. Open University Press, Maidenhead.

Hayes, N. and Orrell, S. (1998) *Psychology: an Introduction*. Addison Wesley Longman, Harlow.

Haynes, R. (1979) Determinants of compliance: the disease and the mechanics of treatment. In: *Compliance in Health Care* (eds. R. B. Haynes, D. W. Taylor and D. L. Sackett), pp. 49–62. Johns Hopkins University Press, Baltimore.

Haynes, R. B., Taylor, D. W. and Sackett, D. L. (eds.) (1979) *Compliance in Health Care*, pp. 49–62. Johns Hopkins University Press, Baltimore.

Healthcare Commission (2007) *Talking About Medicines. The Management of Medicines in Trusts Providing Mental Health Services*. Healthcare Commission, London.

Healy, D. (2008) *Psychiatric Drugs Explained*, 5th edn. Churchill Livingstone, Edinburgh.

Healy, D. (2009) 'Trussed in evidence? Ambiguities at the interface between clinical practice. *Transcultural Psychiatry*, **46**(1), 16–37.

Helman, C. (2007) *Culture, Health and Illness*, 5th edn. Hodder Arnold, London.

Hemingway, S. and Ely, V. (2009) Prescribing by mental health nurses: the UK perspective. *Perspectives in Psychiatric Care*, **45**(1), 24–35.

Hemingway, S., Stephenson, J. and Allmark, H. (2011) Student experiences of medicines management training and education. *British Journal of Nursing*, **20**(5), 291–8.

Heron, J. (2001) *Helping the Client: a Creative, Practical Guide*. Sage, London.

Herz, M., Lamberti, J., Mintz, J., Scott, R., O'Dell, S., McCartan, L., and Nix, G. (2000) A program for relapse prevention in schizophrenia: a controlled study. *Archives of General Psychiatry*, **57**(3), 277–83.

Herz, M. and Melville, C. (1980) Relapse in schizophrenia. *American Journal of Psychiatry*, **137**(7), 801–5.

Hess, T. M., Beale, K. S. and Miles, A. (2010) The impact of experienced emotion on evaluative judgments: the effects of age and emotion regulation style. *Aging, Neuropsychology & Cognition*, **17**(6), 648–72.

Hewitt, J., Coffey, M. and Rooney, G. (2009) Forming, sustaining and ending therapeutic interactions, In: *Mental Health Nursing Skills* (eds. P. Callaghan, J. Playle and L. Cooper), pp. 63–73. Oxford University Press, Oxford.

Hickie, I. (2002) Preventing depression: a challenge for the Australian community. *Medical Journal of Australia*, **177**(suppl.), S85–S86.

Horne, R., Weinman, J., Barber, N., Elliott, R., Morgan, M., Cribb, A. and Kellar, I. (2005) *Concordance, Adherence and Compliance in Medicine Taking: Report for the National Co-ordinating Centre for NHS Service Delivery and Organisation R & D (NCCSDO)*. NHS, London.

Hughes, C. M. and Goldie, R. (2009) I just take what I am given: adherence and resident involvement in decision making on medicines in nursing homes for older people: a qualitative survey. *Drugs & Aging*, **26**(6), 505–17.

Information and Statistics Division. (2011) *Antidepressant Prescribing Statistics*. [Online] Available: http://www.isdscotland.org/isd/information-and-statistics.jsp?pContentID=3671&p_applic=CCC&p_service=Content.show& [accessed 11 April 2011].

Isaacs, S., Ploeg, J. and Tompkins, C. (2009) How can Rorty help nursing science in the development of a philosophical 'foundation'? *Nursing Philosophy*, **10**(2), 81–90.

Jack, K. and Smith, A. (2007) Promoting self awareness in nurses to improve nursing practice. *Nursing Standard*, **21**(32), 47–52.

Jackson, S. E. (1983) Participation in decision making as a strategy for reducing job-related strain. *Journal of Applied Psychology*, **68**(1), 3–19.

Jeste, D. V., Gladsjo, J. A., Lindamer, L. A. and Lacro, J. P. (1996) Medical comorbidity in schizophrenia. *Schizophrenia Bulletin*, **22**(3), 413–30.

Jones, M., Bennett, J., Gray, R., Arya, P. and Lucas, B. (2006) Pharmacological management of akathisia in combination with psychological interventions by a mental health nurse consultant. *Journal of Psychiatric and Mental Health Nursing*, **13**(1), 26–32.

Jones, M., Robson, D., Whitfield, S. and Gray, R. (2010) Does psychopharmacology training enhance the knowledge of mental health nurses who prescribe? *Journal of Psychiatric and Mental Health Nursing*, **17**(9), 804–12.

Kalbe, E., Kessler, J., Calabrese, P., Smith, R., Passmore, A. P., Brand, M. and Bullock, R. (2004) DemTect: a new, sensitive cognitive screening test to support the diagnosis of mild cognitive impairment and early dementia. *International Journal of Geriatric Psychiatry*, **19**(2), 136–43.

Keady, J. and Gilliard, J. (2001) The early experience of Alzheimer's disease: implications for partnership and practice. In: *Dementia Care: Developing Partnerships in Practice* (eds. T. Adams and C. Clarke), pp. 227–56. Baillière-Tindall, London.

Keevers, L., Treleaven, L. and Sykes, C. (2008) Partnership and participation: contradictions and tensions in the social policy space. *Australian Journal of Social Issues*, **43**(3), 459–77.

Kemp, R., Hayward, P. and David, A. (1997) *Compliance Therapy Manual*. Institute of Psychiatry, London.

Kennedy, S. and Lam, R. (2003) Enhancing outcomes in the management of treatment resistant depression: a focus on atypical antipsychotics. *Bipolar Disorders*, **5**(suppl.), S36–S47.

Kenten, C., Bowling, A., Lambert, N., Howe, A. and Rowe, G. (2010) A study of patient expectations in a Norfolk general practice. *Health Expectations: an International Journal of Public Participation in Health Care and Health Policy*, **13**(3), 273–84.

Kingdon, D. G. and Turkington, D. (2005) *Cognitive Therapy of Schizophrenia*. Guilford Press, New York.

Kleiman, A. (1980) *Patients and Healers in the Context of Culture: an Exploration of the Borderland Between Anthropology, Medicine, and Psychiatry*. University of California Press, Berkeley.

Kolb, D. A. (1984) *Experiential Learning: Experience As the Source of Learning and Development*. Prentice Hall, Englewood Cliffs.

Kroenke, K., Spitzer, R. L. and Williams, J. B. W. (2001) The PHQ-9: Validity of a brief depression severity measure. *Journal of General Internal Medicine*, **16**(9), 606–13.

Kruger, J. and Dunning, D. (1999) Unskilled and unaware of it: how difficulties in recognizing one's own incompetence lead to inflated self-assessments. *Journal of Personality and Social Psychology*, **77**(6), 1121–34.

Kutchins, H. and Kirk, S. A. (1997) *Making Us Crazy: DSM: The Psychiatric Bible and the Creation of Mental Disorders*. Free Press, New York.

Kuyken, W., Padesky, C. A. and Dudley, R. (2009) *Collaborative Case Conceptualization : Working Effectively with Clients in Cognitive-behavioral Therapy*. Guilford Press, New York.

Kwentoh, M.-L. and Reilly, J. (2009) Non-medical prescribing: the story so far. *Psychiatric Bulletin*, **33**(1), 4–7.

Laird-Measures, J. (2010) Prescribing for depression: a case study. *Nurse Prescribing*, **8**(11), 525–31.

Lasater, K. (2011) Clinical judgment: the last frontier for evaluation. *Nurse Education in Practice*, **11**(2), 86–92.

Latter, S., Maben, J., Myall, M. and Young, A. (2007) Perceptions and practice of concordance in nurses? Prescribing consultations: findings from a national questionnaire survey and case studies of practice in England. *International Journal of Nursing Studies*, **44**(1), 9–18.

Latter, S., Sibley, A., Skinner, T., Cradock, S., Zinken, K., Lussier, M., Richard, C. and Roberge, D. (2010) The impact of an intervention for nurse prescribers on consultations to promote patient medicine-taking in diabetes: a mixed methods study. *International Journal of Nursing Studies*, **47**(9), 1126–38.

Legare, F., Ratte, S., Grave, L. K. and Graham, I. (2008) Barriers and facilitators to implementing shared decision-making in clinical practice: update of a systematic review of health professionals' perceptions. *Patient Education and Counseling*, **73**(3), 526–35.

Lillie, A. K., Clifford, C. and Metcalfe, A. (2011) Caring for families with a family history of cancer: why concerns about genetic predisposition are missing from the palliative agenda. *Palliative Medicine*, **25**(2), 117–24.

Llahana, S., and Hamric, A. (2011) Developmental phases and factors influencing role development in diabetes specialist nurses: a UK study. *European Diabetes Nursing*, **8**(1), 18–23, 23a.

Lynch, J., Goodhart, F., Saunders, Y. and O'Connor, S. J. (2010) Screening for psychological distress in patients with lung cancer: results of a clinical audit evaluating the use of the patient Distress Thermometer. *Supportive Care in Cancer*, **19**(2), 193–202.

Maidement, A. (2004) User perspective – the good psychiatric nurse. In: *Mental Health Nursing Competencies for Practice* (eds. S. Kirby, A. Hart, D. Cross and G. Mitchell), pp. 46–55. Palgrave Macmillan, London.

Mandrioli, R., Mercolini, L. and Raggi, M. A. (2008) Benzodiazepine metabolism: an analytical perspective. *Current Drug Metabolism*, **9**(8), 827–44.

Manias, E. (2008) Complexities of communicating about managing medications – an important challenge for nurses: a response to Latter *et al. International Journal of Nursing Studies*, **45**(7), 1110–13.

Marland, G. R. and Cash, K. (2001) Long term illness and patterns of medicine taking: are people with schizophrenia a unique group? *Journal of Psychiatric and Mental Health Nursing*, **8**(3), 197–204.

Marland, G. R. and Cash, K. (2005) Medicine-taking decisions: schizophrenia in comparison to asthma and epilepsy. *Journal of Psychiatric and Mental Health Nursing*, **12**(2), 163–72.

Marland, G. R., McNay, L., Fleming, M. and McCaig, M. (2011a) Using timelines as part of recovery-focused practice in psychosis. *Journal of Psychiatric and Mental Health Nursing*. [Online] Available: doi/10.1111/j.1365-2850.2011.01738.x/pdf.

Marland, G. R., McNay, L., McCaig, M. and Snowden, A. (2011b) Medicine taking and recovery-focused mental health practice. *British Journal of Wellbeing*, **2**(2), 21–5.

Matchar, D. B., Thakur, M. E., Grossman, I., McCrory, D. C., Orlando, L. A., Steffens, D. C., Goldstein, D. B., Cline, K. E. and Gray, R. N. (2007) Testing for cytochrome P450 polymorphisms in adults with non-psychotic depression treated with selective serotonin reuptake inhibitors (SSRIs) Evidence Report/Technology Assessment No. 146. AHRQ Publication No. 7-E002. [Online] Rockville, MD: Agency for Healthcare Research and Quality. Available: http://www.ahrq.gov/downloads/pub/evidence/pdf/cyp450/cyp450.pdf [accessed: 23 August 2011].

McCullough, L., McKinlay, E., Barthow, C., Moss, C. and Wise, D. (2010) A model of treatment decision making when patients have advanced cancer: how do cancer treatment doctors and nurses contribute to the process? *European Journal of Cancer Care*, **19**(4), 482–91.

McGill, I. and Beaty, L. (2001) *Action Learning: a Guide for Professional, Management and Educational Development*, 2nd edn. Kogan Page, London.

McGleenon, B. M., Dynan, K. B. and Passmore, A. P. (1999) Acetylcholinesterase inhibitors in Alzheimer's disease. *British Journal of Clinical Pharmacology*, **48**(4), 471–80.

Medicines Partnership (2003) *Project Evaluation Toolkit*. Medicines Partnership, London.

Millan, B. (2001) *Report on the Review of the Mental Health (Scotland) Act 1984*. [Online] Available: http://www.scotland.gov.uk/health/mentalhealthlaw/Millan/Report/rnhs.pdf [accessed: 27 August 2011].

Miller, W. R. and Rollnick, S. (eds.) (2002) *Motivational Interviewing: Preparing People for Change*, 2nd edn. Guilford Press, New York.

Milne, D. (2007) An empirical definition of clinical supervision. *British Journal of Clinical Psychology*, **46**(4), 437–47.

Mioshi, E., Dawson, K., Mitchell, J., Arnold, R. and Hodges, J. (2006) The Addenbrooke's Cognitive Examination Revised (ACE-R): a brief cognitive test battery for dementia screening. *International Journal of Geriatric Psychiatry*, **21**(11), 1078–85.

Mitchell, A. (2007) Pooled results from 38 analyses of the accuracy of distress thermometer and other ultra-short methods of detecting cancer-related mood disorders. *Journal of Clinical Oncology*, **25**(29), 4670–81.

Mitchell, A. J. (2010) Short screening tools for cancer-related distress: a review and diagnostic validity meta-analysis. *Journal of the National Comprehensive Cancer Network*, **8**(4), 487–94.

Moncrieff, J. (2007) *The Myth of the Chemical Cure: a Critique of Psychiatric Drug Treatment*. Palgrave Macmillan, London.

Moniz-Cook, E. and Manthorpe, J. (2009) Early Psychosocial Intervention in Dementia, Evidence-based Practice. Jessica Kingsley, London.

Moore, R. (2011) Conference Address: *Rights, Relationships & Recovery 5 years on ... delivering the RRRs*. One Day Conference, Tuesday 22 March 2011, Beardmore Conference Centre, Clydebank.

Murray, S. A., Kendall, M., Grant, E., Boyd, K., Barclay, S., and Sheikh, A. (2007) Patterns of social, psychological, and spiritual decline toward the end of life in lung cancer and heart failure. *Journal of Pain and Symptom Management*, **34**(4), 393–402.

Mushlin, A. and Appel, F. (1977) Diagnosing potential noncompliance. Physicians ability in a behavioural dimension of medical care. *Archives of Internal Medicine*, **137**(3), 318–21.

Myers, L. and Midence, K. (1998) Methodological and concepts and issues in adherence. In: *Adherence to Treatment in Medical Conditions* (eds. L. Myers and K. Midence), pp. 1–24. Gordon and Breach: London.

National Audit Office (2007) *Improving Services and Support for People with Dementia*. Stationery Office, London.

National Collaborating Centre for Mental Health (2010) *Depression: the Treatment and Management of Depression in Adults (update)*. National Clinical Guidance 90. National Institute for Health and Clinical Excellence, London.

National Institute for Health and Clinical Excellence (2006) *Obesity: Guidance on the Prevention, Identification, Assessment and Management of Overweight and Obesity in Adults and Children*. NICE clinical guideline 43. National Institute for Health and Clinical Excellence, London.

National Institute for Health and Clinical Excellence (2010) *The Treatment and Management of Depression in Adults (Updated Edition)*. National Clinical Guidance 90. National Collaborating Centre for Mental Health, London.

National Institute for Health and Clinical Excellence (2011) *Donepezil, Galantamine, Rivastigmine and Memantine for the Treatment of Alzheimer's Disease. Technology Appraisal Guidance*. TA217. National Institute for Health and Clinical Excellence, London.

Ndosi, M. E. and Newell, R. (2009) Nurses' knowledge of pharmacology behind drugs they commonly administer. *Journal of Clinical Nursing*, **18**(4), 570–80.

Nelson-Jones, R. (2008) *Basic Counselling Skills: a Helper's Manual*, 2nd edn. Sage, London.

Nelson, S. and Hampson, S. (2008) *Yes You Can: Working with Survivors of Childhood Sexual Abuse*. Scottish Government, Edinburgh.

NHS Education for Scotland (2009) *An Educational Resource to Support Early Interventions for People Receiving a Diagnosis of Dementia*. NES, Edinburgh.

NHS Education for Scotland (2011) *The 10 Essential Shared Capabilities for Mental Health Practice: Learning Materials (Scotland)*. Edinburgh, NHS Education for Scotland.

NHS Education for Scotland and Scottish Recovery Network (2008) *Realising Recovery Learning Materials*. NHS Education for Scotland/Scottish Recovery Network, Edinburgh.

NHS National Treatment Agency for Substance Misuse (2008) *Supporting and Involving Carers. a Guide for Commissioners and Providers*. [Online]. Available: http://www.drugscope.org.uk/Resources/Drugscope/Documents/PDF/Good%20Practice/supportingcarers.pdf [accessed 3 May 2011].

Noble, D. (2002) The rise of computational biology. *Nature Reviews. Molecular Cell Biology*, **3**(6), 459–63.

Noble, D. (2006) *The Music of Life. Biology Beyond the Genome*. Oxford University Press, Oxford.

Nolan, P. and Bradley, E. (2008) Evidence-based practice: implications and concerns. *Journal of Nursing Management*, **16**(4), 388–93.

Nose, M., Barbui, C. and Tansella, M. (2003) How often do patients with psychosis fail to adhere to treatment programmes? A systematic review. *Psychological Medicine*, **33**(7), 1149–60.

Nuechterlein, K. H. and Dawson, M. E. (1984) A heuristic vulnerability/stress model of schizophrenic episodes. *Schizophrenia Bulletin*, **10**(2), 300–12.

Nunes, V., Neilson, J., O'Flynn, N., Calvert, N., Kuntze, S., Smithson, H., Benson, J., Blair, J., Bowser, A., Clyne, W., Crome, P., Haddad, P., Hemingway, S., Horne, R., Johnson, S., Kelly, S., Packham, B., Patel, M. and Steel, J. (2009). *Clinical Guidelines and Evidence Review for Medicines Adherence: Involving Patients in Decisions About Prescribed Medicines and Supporting Adherence.* National Collaborating Centre for Primary Care and Royal College of General Practitioners, London.

Nurse Education Scotland (2008) *The 10 Essential Shared Capabilities.* Retrieved from http://www.nes.scot.nhs.uk/media/5844/module2-the10essentialsharedcapabilities.pdf. [accessed 16 September 2011].

Nursing and Midwifery Council (2008) *The Code: Standards of Conduct, Performance and Ethics for Nurses and Midwives.* NMC, London.

Nursing and Midwifery Council (2010) *Standards for Medicines Management.* [Online] Available: http://scholar.google.com/scholar?hl=en&btnG=Search&q=intitle:Standards+for+medicines+management#4 [accessed 8 December 2010].

O'Connor, A., Jacobsen, M. J. and Stacey, D. (2011) *Ottawa Personal Decision Guide.* Available: http://decisionaid.ohri.ca/docs/das/OPDG_2pg.pdf [accessed 21 March 2010].

Oldknow, H., Bottomley, J., Lawton, M., McNulty, C. and Earle, E. (2010) Independent nurse prescribing for older people's mental health. *Nurse Prescribing,* **8**(2), 66–9.

Otto, M. W., McHugh, R., Simon, N. M., Farach, F. J., Worthington, J. J. and Pollack, M. H. (2010) Efficacy of CBT for benzodiazepine discontinuation in patients with panic disorder: further evaluation. *Behaviour Research and Therapy,* **48**(8), 720–7.

Page, S., Hope, K., Maj, C., Mathew, J. and Bee, P. (2011) Doing things differently – working towards distributed responsibility within memory assessment services. *International Journal of Geriatric Psychiatry.* [Online]. http://onlinelibrary.wiley.com/doi/10.1002/gps.2716/pdf [accessed: 27 August 2011].

Park, L. C. and Lipman, R. S. (1964) A comparison of patient dosage deviation reports with pill counts. *Psychopharmacologia,* **6**(4), 299–302.

Patel, M., Robson, D., Rance, J., Ramirez, N., Memon, T., Bressington, D. and Gray, R. (2009) Attitudes regarding mental health nurse prescribing among psychiatrists and nurses: a cross-sectional questionnaire study. *International Journal of Nursing Studies* 46(11): 1467-1474.

Paterson, J. G. and Zderad, L. T. (1988) *Humanistic Nursing.* National League for Nursing, New York.

Patrick, H. (2006) *Mental Health, Incapacity and the Law in Scotland.* Tottel Publishing, Edinburgh.

Paul, R. (1995) *Critical Thinking: How to Prepare Students for a Rapidly Changing World.* Foundation for Critical Thinking, Santa Rosa.

Paul, R. and Elder, L. (2006) *Thinker's Guide to the Art of Socratic Questioning.* Foundation for Critical Thinking, Dillon Beach.

Pelton, J. (2009) Where do I begin? (...or so many problems, so little time!). In: *Back to Life, Back to Normality: Cognitive Therapy, Recovery and Psychosis* (eds. D. Turkington, D.

Kingdon, S. Rathod, S. Wilcock, A. Brabban, P. Cromarty, R. Dudley, R. Gray, J. Pelton, R. Siddle and P. Weidon), pp. 11–22. Cambridge University Press, Cambridge.

PHQ-9 available at http://www.pfizer.com/. Copyright ©1999 Pfizer Inc.

Piat, M. and Sabetti, J. (2009) The importance of medication in consumer definitions of recovery from serious mental illness: a qualitative study. *Issues in Mental Health Nursing*, **30**, 482–90.

Pijnenborg, G. H. M., Withaar, F. K., Brouwer, W. H., Timmerman, M. E., van den Bosch, R. J. and Evans, J. J. (2010) The efficacy of SMS text messages to compensate for the effects of cognitive impairments in schizophrenia. *British Journal of Clinical Psychology*, **49**(2), 259–74.

Pilling, S., Bebbington, P., Kuipers, E., Garety, P., GedMurdo, J., Orbach, G. and Morgan, C. (2002) Psychological treatments in schizophrenia: I. Meta-analysis of family intervention and cognitive behaviour therapy. *Psychological Medicine*, **32**(5), 763–82.

Plaistow, J. and Birchwood, M. (1996) Back in the saddle: a guide to relapse prevention. In: *Early Intervention in Psychosis: a Guide to Concepts, Evidence and Interventions* (eds. M. Birchwood, D. Fowler and C. Jackson), pp. 239–44. Wiley, Chichester.

Principe, L. M. (2011) *Scientific Revolution: a Very Short Introduction*. Oxford University Press, New York.

Prior, T. I. and Baker, G. B. (2003) Interactions between the cytochrome P450 system and the second-generation antipsychotics. *Journal of Psychiatry Neuroscience*, **28**(2), 99–112.

Prochaska, J. and DiClemente, C. (1994) *The Transtheoretical Approach: Crossing Traditional Boundaries of Therapy*. Krieger, Malabar.

Proctor, B. (2000) *Group Supervision: a Guide to Creative Practice*. Sage, London.

Rapp, M. A., Schnaider-Beeri, M., Wysocki, M., Guerrero-Berroa, E., Grossman, H. T., Heinz, A. and Haroutunian, V. (2011) Cognitive decline in patients with dementia as a function of depression. *American Journal of Geriatric Psychiatry*, **19**(4), 357–63.

Raptopoulos, A. (2010) The road to recovery. In: *Mental Health, Service User Involvement and Recovery* (ed. J. Weinstein), pp. 88–100. Jessica Kingsley, London.

Reid-Searl, K., Moxham, L., Walker, S. and Happell, B. (2010) Whatever it takes: nursing students' experiences of administering medication in the clinical setting. *Qualitative Health Research*, **20**(7), 952–65.

Repper, J. and Perkins, R. (2003) *Social Inclusion and Recovery: A Model for Mental Health Practice*. Baillière Tindall, Edinburgh.

Repper, J. and Perkins, R. (2009) Recovery and social inclusion. In: *Mental Health Nursing Skills* (P. Callaghan, J. Playle and L. Cooper), pp. 85–95. Oxford University Press, Oxford.

Rethink (2007) *The PHC: A Physical Health Check for Mental Health Service Users*. Rethink, London.

Rethink (2008) *Rethink Policy Statement 50: Empowering People with Severe Mental Illness*. Rethink, London

Reynolds, B. (2009) Developing therapeutic one-to-one relationships In: *Psychiatric and Mental Health Nursing: the Craft of Caring* (ed. P. Barker), 2nd edn, pp. 313–20. London, Hodder Arnold.

Rice, F., Cullen, P., McKenna, H., Kelly, B., Keeney, S. and Richey, R. (2007) Clinical supervision for mental health nurses in Northern Ireland: formulating best practice guidelines. *Journal of Psychiatric and Mental Health Nursing*, **14**(5), 516–21.

Richardson, A., Tebbit, B., Brown, V. and Sitzia, J. (2006) *Assessment of Supportive and Palliative Care Needs for Adults with Cancer*. London.

Ridge, D. and Ziebland, S. (2006) 'The old me could never have done that': how people give meaning to recovery following depression. *Qualitative Health Research*, **16**(8), 1038–53.

Rigby, M. and Ashman, D. (2008) Service innovation: a virtual informal network of care to support a 'lean' therapeutic community in a new rural personality disorder service. *Psychiatric Bulletin*, **32**(2), 64–7.

Riss, J., Cloyd, J., Gates, J. and Collins, S. (2008) Benzodiazepines in epilepsy: pharmacology and pharmacokinetics. *Acta Neurologica Scandinavica*, **118**(2), 69–86.

Rivas, K. and Murray, S. (2010) EXEMPLAR: our shared experience of implementing action learning sets in an acute clinical nursing setting: approach taken and lessons learned. *Contemporary Nurse*, **35**(2), 182–7.

Robertson, J. and Collinson, C. (2011) Positive risk-taking: whose risk is it? An exploration in community outreach teams in adult mental health and learning disability services. *Health, Risk & Society*, **13**(2), 147–64.

Rollnick, S., Mason, P. and Butler, C. (1999) *Health Behaviour Change: A Guide for Practitioners*. Churchill Livingstone, Edinburgh.

Rosengren, D. B. (2009) *Building Motivational Interviewing Skills: a Practitioner Workbook*. Guilford Press, London.

Royal Pharmaceutical Society of Great Britain and Merck Sharpe and Dohme (1996) *Partnership in Medicine-taking: a Consultative Document*. Royal Pharmaceutical Society of Great Britain and Merck Sharpe and Dohme, London.

Russell, S., Daly, J., Hughes, E. and Hoog, C. (2003) Nurses and 'difficult' patients: negotiating non-compliance. In: *Journal of Advanced Nursing*, **43**(3), 281–7.

Ryan-Woolley, B. M. and Rees, J. (2005) Initializing concordance in frail elderly patients via a medicines organizer. *Annals of Pharmacotherapy*, **39**(5), 834–9.

Sackett, D., Straus, S., Richardson, W., Rosenberg, W. and Haynes, R. (2000) *Evidence-based Medicine: How to Practice and Teach EBM*. Churchill Livingstone, Edinburgh.

Sanson, B., Nachon, F., Colletier, J.-P., Froment, M.-T., Toker, L., Greenblatt, H. M., Sussman, J. L., Ashani, Y., Masson, P., Silman, I. and Weik, M. (2009) Crystallographic snapshots of nonaged and aged conjugates of soman with acetylcholinesterase, and of a ternary complex of the aged conjugate with pralidoxime. *Journal of Medicinal Chemistry*, **52**(23), 7593–603.

Schinkel, M. and Dorrer, N. (2006) *Towards Recovery Competencies in Scotland: the Views of Key Stakeholder Groups* [Online]. Available: http://www.scottishrecovery.net/Publications-Discussion-Papers/non-srn.html [accessed 21 March 2010].

Scottish Executive (2006) *The National Review of Mental Health Nursing in Scotland: Rights Relationships and Recovery*. Scottish Executive, Edinburgh.

Scottish Government (2006) *Delivering for Mental Health*. Retrieved from http://scotland.gov.uk/Publications/2006/11/30164829/0 [accessed 10 September 2011].

Scottish Government (2010) *Rights, Relationships and Recovery: Refreshed. Action Plan 2010–2011*. Scottish Government, Edinburgh.

Scottish Intercollegiate Guidelines Network (2006) *Management of Patients with Dementia*. SIGN 86. SIGN, Edinburgh.

Scottish Recovery Network (2006) *Journeys of Recovery: Stories of Hope and Recovery From Long Term Mental Health Problems*. Scottish Recovery Network, Edinburgh.

Seedhouse, D. (1998) *Ethics: The Heart of Health Care*. Wiley, Chichester.

Severinsson, E. and Sand, A. (2010) Evaluation of the clinical supervision and professional development of student nurses. *Journal of Nursing Management*, **18**(6), 669–77.

Sharples, N. (2007) Relationship, helping and communication skills In: *Foundations of Nursing Practice: Fundamentals of Nursing Practice* (eds. C. Brooker and A. Waugh), pp. 221–50. Mosby Elsevier, Edinburgh.

Shattell, M. M., McAllister, S., Hogan, B. and Thomas, S. P. (2006) 'She took the time to make sure she understood': mental health patients' experiences of being understood. *Archives of Psychiatric Nursing*, **20**(5), 234–41.

Skingsley, D., Bradley, E. J. and Nolan, P. (2006) Neuropharmacology and mental health nurse prescribers. *Journal of Clinical Nursing*, **15**(8), 989–97.

Snowden, A. (2008a) Medication management in older adults: a critique of concordance. *British Journal of Nursing*, **17**(2), 114–19.

Snowden, A. (2008b) The history of prescribing. *Nurse Prescribing*, **6**(12), 530–7.

Snowden, A. (2008c) *Prescribing and Mental Health Nursing*. Quay Books, London.

Snowden, A. (2011) Concurrent analysis: a pragmatic justification. *International Philosophy of Nursing Conference*, Dundee, UK.

Snowden, A. and Barron, D. (2011) Medicines management in mental health. *Nursing Standard*, **26**(3), 43–9.

Snowden, A. and Martin, C. R. (2010a) Mental health nurse prescribing: a difficult pill to swallow? *Journal of Psychiatric and Mental Health Nursing*, **17**(6), 543–53.

Snowden, A. and Martin, C. R. (2010b) Concurrent analysis: towards generalisable qualitative research. *Journal of Clinical Nursing*, **20**(19–20), 2868–77.

Snowden, A., White, C. A., Christie, Z., Murray, E., McGowan, C., and Scott, R. (2011) The clinical utility of the Distress Thermometer: a review. *British Journal of Nursing*, **20**(4), 220–7.

Spielmans, G. I., Berman, M. I. and Usitalo, A. N. (2011) Psychotherapy versus second-generation antidepressants in the treatment of depression: a meta-analysis. *Journal of Nervous & Mental Disease*, **199**(3), 142–9.

Starwards (2010). *Talkwell: Encouraging the Art of Conversation on Mental Health Wards*. Available: http://www.acutecareprogramme.org.uk/silo/files/star-wards-talkwell.pdf [accessed 16 September 2011].

Stenner, K., Courtenay, M. and Carey, N. (2011) Consultations between nurse prescribers and patients with diabetes in primary care: a qualitative study of patient views. *International Journal of Nursing Studies*, **48**(1), 37–46.

Stewart, A. G. (2009) What are psychiatric drugs? *British Medical Journal*. http://www.bmj.com/cgi/eletters/338/may29_1/b1963.

Stickley, T. (2002) Counselling and mental health nursing: a qualitative study. *Journal of Psychiatric and Mental Health Nursing*, **9**(3), 301–8.

Stickley, T. and Freshwater, D. (2008) Therapeutic relationships. In: *Learning About Mental Health Practice* (eds. T. Stickley and D. Freshwater), pp. 439–61. John Wiley and Sons, Chichester.

Stockwell-Morris, L. and Schulz, R. (1992) Patient compliance – an overview. *Journal of Clinical Pharmacy & Therapeutics*, **17**(5), 283–95.

Swanson, J. and Koch, L. (2010) The role of the oncology nurse navigator in distress management of adult inpatients with cancer: a retrospective study. *Oncology Nursing Forum*, **37**(1), 69–76.

Tait, D. (2007) The human lifespan and its effect on selecting nursing interventions In: *Foundations of Nursing Practice: Fundamentals of Nursing Practice* (eds. C. Brooker and A. Waugh), pp. 185–220. Mosby Elsevier, Edinburgh.

Tait, L., Ryles, D. and Sidwell, A. (2010) Strategies for engagement. In: *Promoting Recovery in Early Psychosis: A Practice Manual* (eds. P. French, J. Smith, D. Shiers, M. Reed and M. Rayne), pp. 35–44. Wiley Blackwell, Chichester.

Thompson, C. (2003) Clinical experience as evidence in evidence-based practice. *Journal of Advanced Nursing*, **43**(3), 230–7.

Thornton, T. (2006) Tacit knowledge as the unifying factor in evidence based medicine and clinical judgement. *Philosophy, Ethics, and Humanities in Medicine*, **1**(1), E2.

Trauer, T. and Sacks, T. (1998) Medication compliance: A comparison of the views of severely mentally ill patients in the community, their doctors and their case managers. *Journal of Mental Health*, **7**(6), 621–9.

Treharne, G., Lyons, A., Hale, E., Douglas, K. and Kitas, G. (2006) 'Compliance' is futile but is 'concordance' between rheumatology patients and health professionals attainable? *Rheumatology*, **45**(1), 1–5.

Trostle, J. (1988) Medical noncompliance as an ideology. *Social Science Medicine*, **27**(12), 1299–308.

Usher, K. J. and Arthur, D. (1998) Process consent: a model for enhancing informed consent in mental health nursing. *Journal of Advanced Nursing*, **27**(4), 692–7.

van Dusseldorp, L. R., van Meijel, B. K. and Derksen, J. J. (2011) Emotional intelligence of mental health nurses. *Journal of Clinical Nursing*, **20**(3/4), 555–62.

Varcarolis, E. (2006) *Manual of Psychiatric Nursing Care Plans – Diagnoses, Clinical Tools, and Psycopharmacology*, 3rd edn. Saunders Elsevier, Missouri.

Weaks, D., Johansen, R., Wilkinson, H. and McLeod, J. (2009) *There is Much More to My Practice Than Checking Up on Tablets: Developing Nursing Practice: A Counselling Approach to Delivering Post-diagnostic Dementia Support*. Edinburgh, University of Abertay, Dundee.

Weick, A. and Pope, L. (1988) Knowing what's best: a new look at self-determination. *Social Casework*, **69**, 10–16.

Weihrich, H. (1982) The Tows Matrix – a tool for situational analysis. *Long Range Planning*, **15**(2), 54–66.

Weiss, M. and Britten, N. (2003) What is concordance? *Pharmaceutical Journal*, **271**(7270), 493.

Weissman, M., Bland, R., Canino, G., Faravelli, C., Greenwald, S., Hwu, H. and Yeh, E. (1996) Cross national epidemiology of major depression and bipolar disorder. *Journal of the American Medical Association*, **276**(4), 293–9.

Wells, J., Bergin, M., Gooney, M. and Jones, A. (2009) Views on nurse prescribing: a survey of community mental health nurses in the Republic of Ireland. *Journal of Psychiatric and Mental Health Nursing*, **16**(1), 10–17.

West, H. F. and Baile, W. F. (2010) 'Tell me what you understand': the importance of checking for patient understanding. *Journal of Supportive Oncology*, **8**(5), 216–18.

Wetzel, H., Anghelescu, I., Szegedi, A., Wiesner, J., Weigmann, H., Härtter, S. and Hiemke, C. (1998) Pharmacokinetic interactions of clozapine with selective serotonin reuptake inhibitors: differential effects of fluvoxamine and paroxetine in a prospective study. *Journal of Clinical Psychopharmacology*, **18**(1), 2–9.

Wilkinson, G. R. (2005) Drug metabolism and variability among patients in drug response. *New England Journal of Medicine*, **352**(21), 2211–21.

Woodbridge, K and Fulford, K. W. M. (2004) *Whose Values? A Workbook for Values Based Practice in Mental Health Care*. Sainsbury Centre for Mental Health, London.

Worden, W. (1991) *Grief Counselling and Grief Therapy*, 2nd edn. Springer, London.

World Health Organization (1992) *The ICD-10 Classification of Mental and Behavioural Disorders. Clinical Description and Diagnostic Guidelines.* World Health Organization, Geneva.

World Health Organization (2002) *World Health Report.* World Health Organization, Geneva.

World Health Organization (2003) Adherence to long-term therapies: evidence for action. [Online] Available: http://www.who.int/chronic_conditions/adherencereport/en/ [accessed: 27 August 2011].

Young, S., Nixon, E., Hinge, D., McFadyen, J., Wright, V., Lambert, P. and Newsome, C. (2010) Action learning: a tool for the development of strategic skills for Nurse Consultants? *Journal of Nursing Management,* **18**(1), 105–10.

Zappa, Frank quotations. Available: http://www.goodreads.com/author/quotes/22302 [accessed 12 October 2011].

Zubin, J. and Spring, B. (1977) Vulnerability: a new view of schizophrenia. *Journal of Abnormal Psychology,* **86**(2), 103–26.

Index